A Progressive Traditionalist:
John M. Lyle, Architect

A Progressive Traditionalist: John M. Lyle, Architect

Glenn McArthur

Coach House Books
Toronto

Canada Council for the Arts Conseil des Arts du Canada ONTARIO ARTS COUNCIL CONSEIL DES ARTS DE L'ONTARIO Canada

Published with the generous assistance of the Canada Council for the Arts and the Ontario Arts Council. Coach House also gratefully acknowledges the support of the Government of Canada through the Book Publishing Industry Development Program.

LIBRARY AND ARCHIVES CANADA CATALOGUING IN PUBLICATION

McArthur, Glenn, 1952-
A progressive traditionalist : John M. Lyle, architect / Glenn McArthur.

Includes bibliographical references.

ISBN 978-1-55245-218-9

1. Lyle, John M. (John McIntosh), 1872-1945.
2. Architects--Canada--Biography.
I. Title.

NA749.L94M34 2009 720.92 C2009-900333-3

Front cover photograph: Union Station, Toronto
Back cover photograph: interior doors, Bank of Nova Scotia, Halifax
Endpaper: detail of doors, Bank of Nova Scotia, Halifax

Thanks to the organizations and individuals that have contributed to the publication of this book.

architectsAlliance
Fred Dalley
William Greer
Hamilton Heritage Foundation
Norris Harris
Hydro One
Kuwabara Payne McKenna Blumberg Architects
Ontario Arts Council (Writers' Reserve, 2002)
planningAlliance
George Rust-D'Eye
Stephen Otto
Anna Rehak and Patrick Loubert
Philip Somerville
Toronto Arts Council
Toronto Society of Architects
Zeidler Partnership Architects

Contents

Preface

John M. Lyle was one of the pre-eminent architects of the first half of the twentieth century in Canada. He was acknowledged by his peers as a leading architectural spokesperson, one who worked tirelessly to raise the profile of the profession through his teaching, writing, curating and lecturing. Moving to Toronto from New York City in 1905, just after the devastating Great Fire, he lived through the Wall Street crash and the Great Depression, two world wars and the rise of a radical form of architectural modernism that undermined his aesthetic principles. Through economic hardships and the lifestyle changes that resulted from them, Lyle produced a significant body of work that always expressed a highly personalized and original approach to architectural form and detail. He is perhaps best known for championing an authentic regional consciousness in building design and attempting to pave the way for a uniquely Canadian architecture.

In the preparation of this book, my research into Lyle's work led me to a variety of sources. A 1982 exhibition catalogue, *John M. Lyle: Toward a Canadian Architecture*, by Geoffrey Hunt, was indispensable, along with the collection of photographs, drawings and papers that were donated to the Archives of Ontario by the architect's daughter, Norah Harris. New material that surfaced since Hunt's publication includes several personal accounts of the work and times of the architect, including an unpublished autobiography Lyle wrote in the last year of his life, along with an extensive letter to friend and architect A. S. Mathers. These items capture the highlights of his career and his architectural achievements and give us a glimpse into Lyle's personal life. The diaries of John Jackson Beck, an architect who worked in Lyle's offices from 1923 to 1943, is also an essential resource, offering a day-by-day account of the comings and goings of his architectural practice. The Scotiabank Archive has preserved all of the work the company commissioned from Lyle, but other bank archives have not fared as well; mergers in the industry over the years have meant that much of Lyle's design work has been lost in the shuffle. The small collection of drawings in Lyle's office at 230 Bloor Street West in Toronto, a space he designed and moved into in 1920, and which was sold after his death in 1945, languished under a stairwell until it was finally rescued by conservationist Spencer Clarke. These drawings eventually found their way to the collection of the Canadian Centre for Architecture in Montreal.

In assessing and organizing Lyle's extensive body of work, I chose to focus on the critical works. His life was divided into periods that are characterized by a similar stylistic approach, while the work itself is grouped here into building types for easier critical evaluation and arranged more or less chronologically. To follow arguments across stylistic shifts, the order of building types within a chapter has occasionally been adjusted to ensure a more coherent narrative.

This publication builds upon the substantial amount of information that has surfaced since Hunt's exhibition catalogue, establishes proper dates of events and clarifies many misconceptions. There is a hope that publications of this nature will continue to build an awareness of our Canadian architectural history and heritage.

Lyle's work occasionally makes the headlines. Because of its strategic location, Union Station is regularly exposed to redevelopment plans or threatened with outright demolition, while Lyle's studio on Bloor Street West has become the centre of a development scheme that will incorporate a condominium project. The studio was a modest utilitarian structure that over the years has undergone a series of additions and renovations that leave little of Lyle's original building. The front facade will be restored to its original condition and relocated within the site as a focal point of the development; as the Lyle Café, it will feature historic plaques and decorative panels depicting the architect's contribution to the country's architecture. Acknowledging, commemorating and celebrating Lyle's life and work are the most important outcomes of this book.

The Lyle project was modelled after my experiences with previous publishing and exhibitions, but with a difference. There was to be an exhibition and publication that were meant to support each other. However, for financial and personal reasons the exhibition was held in 2007, opening at the

Opposite page: i.1 Interior stairwell of Central Presbyterian Church, Hamilton.

Introduction

ii.1 Portrait (self?) of Lyle as a young studious-looking individual, c. 1892.

John M. Lyle was born in Ireland, raised in Hamilton and educated at Yale University and the École des Beaux-Arts, Paris. At the École, Lyle learned to approach any new design problem with the plan or interior room arrangements. With this as his starting point, his design could then progress organically from the inside out. This methodology enabled Lyle to design with confidence an eclectic range of built forms that included banks, bridges, churches, commercial offices, factories, fountains, gardens, interior furniture, a jail, a library, monuments, race-track buildings, railway stations, residences, schools, a theatre and urban planning schemes. At a time when architects were becoming increasingly specialized, the sheer variety of Lyle's output was impressive.

After completing his studies, Lyle worked in New York for nine years with some of the most prestigious firms in America. In 1905, he set up shop in Toronto and through his architectural skills and a bit of good luck established a practice that grew into one of the city's largest. Through 1923, he was principally known for the élan of his Beaux-Arts classical buildings; the pinnacle of this style was Union Station in Toronto, which he designed in conjunction with architects Ross & Macdonald and Hugh G. Jones of Montreal.

Lyle was a progressive traditionalist who believed change should be a gradual process, based on historical models. In 1929, he travelled to France to report on the modern movement sweeping through Europe. While disapproving of the more radical form of Modernism, later dubbed the International Style, Lyle embraced some of its features in both form and detail. This led to an idiosyncratic shift that took him toward a regional Canadian design program for his buildings. As Canadian artists, notably the Group of Seven, turned to our indigenous landscape and forms for inspiration, Lyle too broke from the norm by turning away from classical architectural sources and toward what he called 'a rich field of inspiration lying dormant in the fauna, flora and marine life of Canada.'[1] He promoted these themes in his writings and lectures, and through the design program of his buildings – stone-carved forms of indigenous flora, fauna and native Indian imagery decorate his works of the time. These stylized motifs represented emblems of an emerging national consciousness that Lyle saw as a step toward a more authentic Canadian architecture.

This creative phase of Lyle's work ended abruptly after the Wall Street crash and the ensuing Depression, which reduced the architectural program of every building to its bare essentials. But Lyle continued to change, embracing much of the modern movement by simplifying elements, eliminating meaningless ornamentation and creating beauty through form, line and colour.

Lyle's practice was unusual for the time and reflected his architectural education, ideology and character. Described by one colleague as a 'lone wolf,'[2] he had only one partner, Herbert H. Moore, in all his years in practice, during a brief period between 1908 and 1910. Lyle, who did not believe in operating a strictly commercial practice, was jokingly accused by some of his fellow architects of running a 'philanthropic office,' implying that he continued to employ his staff even when economic conditions were not conducive.[3] Because of this, his relationship with his staff was constructive and positive, and in his forty years of practice, he had only two personal secretaries. Lyle was duly proud that draftsmen laid off due to a shortage of work never hesitated to rejoin his staff when economic conditions improved and they were called back.

Lyle also liked to run his office as an atelier. In embarking on a new project, he would start by designing the *parti*, or standard plan, and then delegate the detail work to his junior designers or associates, always ensuring that no drawing left his office without his final approval. Lyle would insist that his staff do their research and produce original work that was not directly copied from any other source. He also had his designers attend all client meetings, even if he could not be there himself. This method seemed to bring him success, for Lyle received an astounding number of commissions during his career, especially given that architects of his time considered advertising or self-promotion unbecoming, and

ii.2 This portrait of Lyle, painted shortly after his arrival in Toronto, reveals the up-and-coming architect, c. 1908.

ii.3 The architect engaging in a piece of self-mockery, c. 1926.

Lyle took great pride in never having to 'use his influence to secure any work.'[4]

Lyle was an avid sportsman throughout his life and some of his earliest childhood memories were of swimming and sailing races in the Hamilton Harbour. As a junior, he and his older brother had made names for themselves as sailors and were invited on one of the more famous boats of the day, the *White Wings*, skippered by renown Canadian yachtsman Amelius Jarvis. When he moved to Toronto, one of the first things Lyle did was to join the Royal Canadian Yacht Club and participate in competitive sailing. His passion for sports continued unabated as a spectator and fan in a number of activities, including tennis, horse racing at Woodbine Race Track and Canadian football. He eventually took up golf and, along with his wife, became quite competitive, entering major amateur tournaments in Canada, the U.S. and England.

It was not enough for Lyle to just join clubs and enjoy their facilities; he served in an executive capacity as director, president and member of the board of governors for several local organizations. He was involved in a professional capacity with, among others, the Beaux-Arts Society of New York, where he was an Honourary Member, and he was made Academician of the Royal Canadian Academy in 1926. Lyle was also a member of Ontario Architectural Association, sitting on numerous committees, and he was made a Fellow of the Royal Institute of British Architects in 1928 – only five other Ontario architects had received this honour – and the Royal Architectural Institute of Canada, two years later.[5] In 1939, he was appointed chair of the Art Gallery of Toronto (now the Art Gallery of Ontario) and served as its president from 1941 to 1945.

In 1945, Lyle recorded his life in a 100-page memoir that highlighted his successes. The bulk of the material recounts the four-year period he spent at the École des Beaux-Arts in Paris and the influence his teachers, the educational system and his fellow students had on him during those critical formative years. A nine-year period in New York, where he worked in several prestigious firms and lived a bachelor's life, also features heavily in the memoir. Surprisingly, his forty-year practice in Toronto and the many buildings he designed during that time receive less attention. The highlights of his architectural career Lyle singled out were the 1911 Royal Canadian Yacht Club Ball for the Duke and Duchess of Connaught, in Toronto, and the opening ceremonies at the Memorial Arch, Royal Military College, in Kingston, Ontario, in 1923. On both occasions, Lyle was the focal point of a large public gathering and the recipient of much adulation from his clients, friends and peers. For a man known as introspective, such public attention obviously left an indelible mark.

Lyle was a modest man with an engaging sense of humour and a love of debate and the exchange of ideas. He was very social and actively participated in a variety of public functions. In 1908, Lyle married Isabel, the daughter of George Moncrieff, a lawyer and federal Member of Parliament from Petrolia, Ontario. It was a happy and fruitful union, with Lyle describing Isabel as a 'helpmate who is a humanist.'[6] They had two daughters, Eleanor Elizabeth in 1911 and Norah Catharine in 1913.

The social circles the Lyles moved in included some of the country's leading financial, political and artistic figures. Having gained a reputation as a connoisseur of fine wine and dining after his years in Paris and New York, Lyle was also a raconteur who loved recounting his worldly adventures. One of his favourite stories was about a trip to Europe in 1937. Lyle and his wife had stopped off in Sweden on the recommendation of friend and sculptor Carl Milles and visited the famous architect Ragnar Östberg, a man Lyle greatly admired. They took Östberg to lunch on the terrace of the most fashionable hotel in Stockholm. Östberg was instantly recognized by the restaurant's patrons, with many people bowing in greeting and the Swedish king's brother, who was also lunching, rising to shake hands with him. Lyle recounted, 'Our table was the centre of all eyes and as I rose to say Goodbye to him, he learned forward and kissing me on both cheeks gave me the accolade and whispered, "Give my love to Carl Milles when you see him." Isabel enjoyed this scene as much as anyone – it was the first time I had received the accolade.'[7]

ii.4 John M. T-Square, self-portrait with Hors Concours *(*excluded from the contest *or* unrivalled*) red seal in the upper right-hand corner, revealing a sense of humour and his place within the architectural community. It is an example of Lyle's stylistic shift toward Modernism, which occurred in the 1930s.*

Chapter 1: 1872–1904

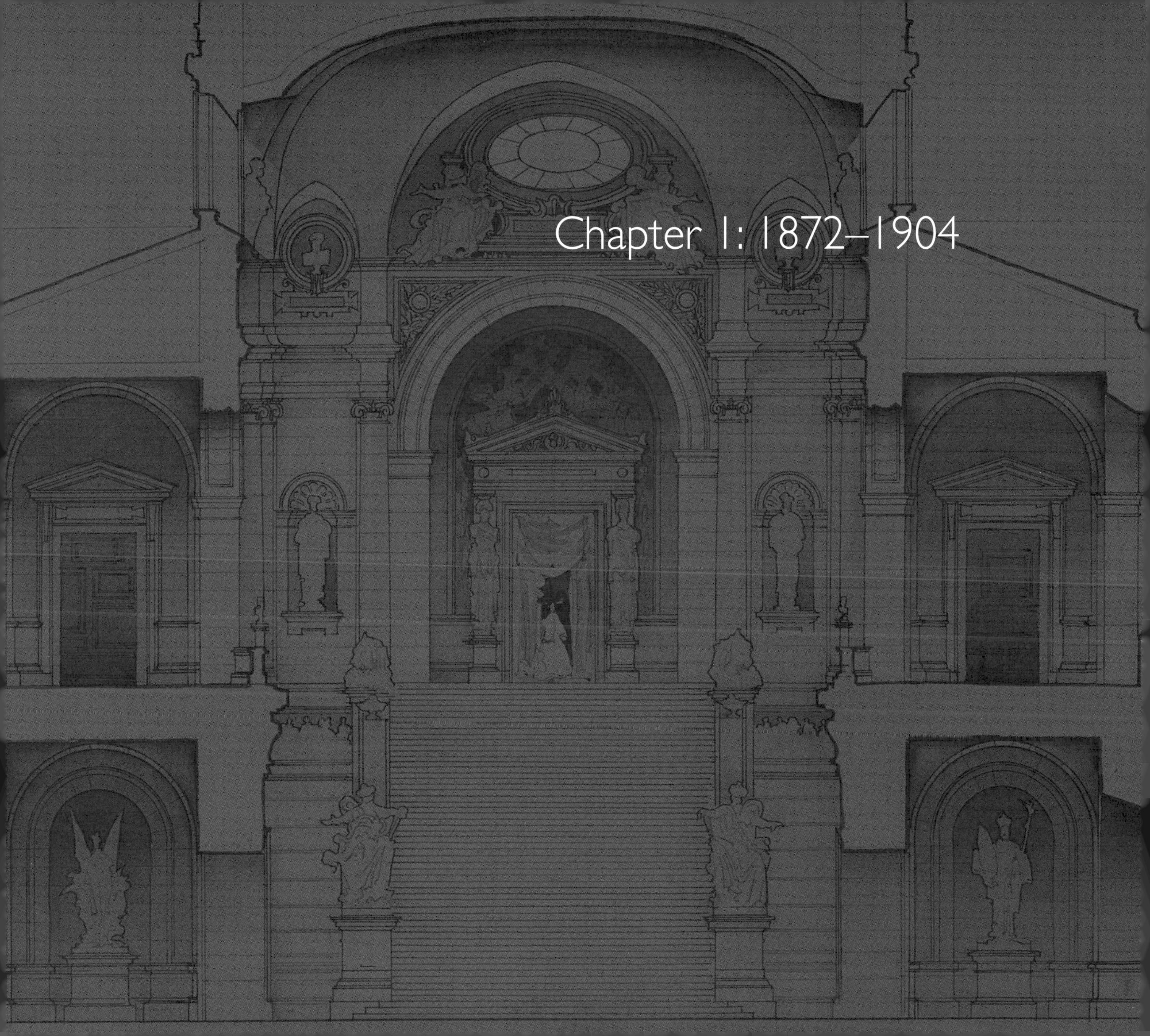

Study of Shades
Ordre Dorique
John M. Lyle
Atelier Godefroy et Freynet.
Paris Sept 22/93

Early Years

Hamilton and Beyond

The architect had the good fortune of being born into a family of intellectually engaging and progressively spirited parents in the small hamlet of Connor, County Antrim, Northern Ireland. The second son of Rev. Dr. Samuel Lyle and his wife, Elizabeth, John MacIntosh Lyle was born on November 13, 1872. His father was the pastor of the Presbyterian Church in the Irish Assembly at Connor, a position he held for ten years before emigrating to Canada in 1878 to become pastor of the Central Presbyterian Church in Hamilton, Ontario. There he served the congregation for thirty-four years, when, upon retiring, he was named Pastor Emeritus, a position he held until his death in 1919. Samuel Lyle was a man of great breadth of mind and character whose interests ranged from the sacred to the secular, and who became 'one of the most powerful influences in the development of everything that was best in the life of his community.'[1] A lover of books, he was a founder of the Hamilton Public Library, upon whose management board he served, and he formed the Browning Club, a group dedicated to reading and discussing the classics. He was also a founding member of the city's Science Association, was active on the local board of education and was instrumental in creating the Hamilton Art School. For several years he also acted as the school's president. The young John Lyle received his early training and developed his precocious artistic talents in the school's drawing classes.

John's mother, Elizabeth, was also a formidable character and, as befitted a pastor's wife, was active in issues of local social reform and philanthropy. Along with her husband, she was a leading force in the founding of a sanatorium for tuberculosis in Hamilton. Considered by a local newspaper to be 'greatly in advance of her time,' she worked alongside Lady Isabel Aberdeen, wife of the Governor General of Canada, to create the National Council of Women. She served as the organization's president from 1894 to 1897 and then again from 1912 to 1920 – the longest tenure of any president. In a local newspaper profile, Mrs. Lyle was described as a 'vigorous intellectual force and an untiring and persevering reformer.'[2]

The cultural milieu, social structure and intellectual environment of John M. Lyle's childhood was based on the Victorian traditions, customs and values of the middle classes. His family placed a premium on intellectual curiosity along with artistic and self-betterment activities. John grew up in a climate that both nurtured and encouraged achievement; he recalled his father and mother as the most ideal of parents – they gave him and his siblings the greatest gift parents could bestow upon their children: to raise them the 'hard way.' Samuel and Elizabeth strongly believed that only hard work and a sound education would lead to success in life.

Following in their parents' footsteps, the children were all successful in their chosen careers. The eldest, William Gordon, after graduating from Central School and Collegiate Institute, went on to Cornell University and then pursued a medical education at Columbia University's College of Physicians and Surgeons. Graduating in 1892, he became a pathologist and was appointed director of the Harriman Research Laboratory at Roosevelt Hospital in New York City. Brother Henry Hamilton, who was born two years after John, also studied medicine at Cornell and Columbia, graduating in 1900. A distinguished surgeon, he worked at several hospitals in New York City. Another brother was Norman Wood, who became a lawyer with practices in Hamilton and Ottawa. His wife was the first woman hired as chief librarian of the Hamilton Public Library, in 1926, keeping the Lyle name linked to the institution the family had helped found. The Reverend and Mrs. Lyle's only daughter, Mary Elizabeth, was born in 1878, and married the son of a Toronto preacher, to become Mrs. Alex Warden. The couple split their time between Toronto and Hamilton. James Cameron, the youngest of the Lyle children, died in a swimming accident in the Hamilton Bay in 1893.

John, like the rest of his family, received his formal education at the Central School and Collegiate Institute, graduating in 1888. Informally, though, his more important study was at the Hamilton Art School with head instructor John Ireland, an English-trained artist. The school, founded in 1886 and opened for classes the following year, offered courses in a

Opposite page: 1.1 A study of light and shade cast on a Doric column. A student exercise from the atelier préparatoire class Lyle attended before gaining entrance into the École.

variety of media to full- and part-time students. John took full advantage of the program, attending both evening and Saturday classes, and receiving many drawing awards.

How Lyle made the transition from art to architecture is a mystery. There were only a few architects in the city that he would have had any direct contact with. One such designer was Frank Freeman, whom Lyle knew before he relocated his practice to New York City. Hamilton, however, was home to several architectural gems. It possessed fine churches, residences and commercial buildings designed by some of the country's leading architects, including St. Paul's Presbyterian Church (1854) by William Thomas and Dundurn Castle (1835) by Robert Wetherell. Whether inspired by external influences or an instinctive calling, Lyle was determined to pursue his architectural education in the best institutions he could, which meant travelling a long way from family and home.

In the latter half of the nineteenth century, to acquire the necessary education, most aspiring architects in Canada had to apprentice with an established firm. This practical experience gave them the tools they needed to begin practicing, and any additional knowledge they might require would simply percolate down to them from their firm's principal partners. Other educational avenues for architects were limited, as university architectural programs had not yet evolved. It was not until the end of the century that things had begun to change: in 1890, the University of Toronto started offering a limited program through the School of Applied Art and Engineering, and in 1896, Montreal's McGill University became the first Canadian university to offer a full architectural program. Modelled on the École des Beaux-Arts in Paris, its program was similar to that of some American schools.

In the United States, the opportunities to study architecture at a university were much greater. By 1891, there were four-year courses at Cornell, Illinois, Philadelphia and Columbia universities and the Massachusetts Institute of Technology in Boston. Following the Beaux-Arts model, these schools provided students with a thorough technical training in rendering, painting and sculpture, with an emphasis on isometric and perspective drawing. The teaching projects strove to nurture the means and most importantly the method of preparing plans, perspectives and working drawings. Instruction was offered in plane geometry, stone cutting, the nature and strength of materials, and the principles of engineering and construction.

It is not surprising, then, that Lyle would look first toward the United States for education. His initial attempt at this was, however, plagued by bad luck. In 1891, he was accepted into Cornell, a favourite school among aspiring Canadian students. The drawing skills Lyle had developed at the Hamilton Art School were so advanced that he was given two years' credit and placed in the third year in that subject. He attended the first semester at Cornell, but a bout of jaundice meant he failed the fall examinations and had to return to Hamilton to convalesce.

Still, he was undeterred from his dreams to study architecture at the famous École des Beaux-Arts in Paris, which according to Lyle and others was the 'greatest school of art and architecture.'[3] In 1945, he recalled that 'my father agreed that I should spend a year or more at the Yale School of Art, which school had been highly recommended to him by several American professors. As I was too young to go to Paris, I spent about a year and a half at Yale, to great advantage and with much pleasure. This term was followed by a year in the office of an old Hamiltonian architect, Frank Freeman, who practiced architecture in New York City. By this time it was thought that I was old enough to go to Paris, so in the early summer of 1892 I sailed on the steamship "Vancouver" of the old Allan line.'[4]

The École des Beaux-Arts in Paris, founded in 1671 by French statesman Jean-Baptiste Colbert, offered students the opportunity to study in studios under some of the country's most prominent artists and architects. The school offered separately run divisions for architecture, painting, sculpture and engraving, each with its own faculty and curriculum. At the heart of the educational process were the studios, or ateliers. There were three official studios devoted to architecture, and eight or nine semi-official ones scattered throughout

Top left: 1.2 A watercolour by Lyle possibly depicting his bucolic Hamilton childhood.

Top right: 1.3 Head with turban, an early drawing exercise from the atelier.

Bottom left: 1.4 One of a series of Paris bridges Lyle painted.

Bottom right: 1.5 Windmill, Holland, 1894, painted during the summer break Lyle toured Europe on a sketching expedition.

1.6 A dusk scene of a Paris bridge, tugboat and barge that Lyle exhibited at the Architectural Eighteen Club, Toronto, in 1905.

the Latin Quarter. Each studio was named after the professor, or *patron,* who supervised it. During Lyle's time, the most famous were the ateliers Lalox, Redon and Blondel. The ateliers were self-governed but run by a *massier*, or chief student. The *patron* would visit perhaps twice a week to critique the students' work.

In the 1890s, the first step for most aspiring architectural students, or *aspirants,* was the *préparation atelier*, which trained them for the entrance exams into the École. Once a student had passed the exams, he could enter the school as a second-class student. Becoming a first-class student was the next step and, upon successfully completing all the prerequisite credits, the student received a diploma. Only French-born students could compete for the most prestigious award the École offered – the *Grand Prix*. Students progressed through the program at their own pace and went as high as they could or wanted to. The École was a democratic institution; there were no tuition fees, anybody could attend and acceptance was based solely on the students' ability to pass the entrance exams.

In 1892, to prepare himself for the École's entrance examination, Lyle enrolled in the *atelier préparatoire* classes taught by Jules Godefroy and Jacques Freynet. The student spent about two years as an *aspirant*, although for most North Americans like Lyle that time was often a little shorter since most had already studied at architectural schools in the U.S.

The *atelier préparatoire* courses in architectural design and theory focused largely on classical forms, composition, clarity of plan and rendering. Drawing was the basis for architectural communication, and every student was expected to be able to render in an elegant style. This skill was acknowledged and admired by many architects and educators such as Percy Nobbs, an English-trained professor at McGill University who noted in 1904 that 'the French draftsman is something on an altogether different level from our rough English work and I can only envy him his clever fingers.'[5] As key as drawing skills were, however, they were never considered as important as the conception and development of the design.

The drawings Lyle produced during his classes with Godefroy and Freynet, such as *Study of Shades – Orde Dorique*, were admirable studies in tonal contrast and the interaction of light and shadow on surface texture. Lyle was becoming an excellent draftsman and constantly drew outside of the atelier, producing several watercolours of Paris scenes, which he exhibited at the Architectural Eighteen Club in Toronto in 1905. During the summer break in 1895, he had toured the scenic countrysides of Belgium and Holland, describing one location as 'a little fishing village near Amsterdam where there is plenty of sea and plenty of sketching.'[6]

Entrance into the École involved a five-part examination. The first and most important section consisted of successfully resolving an architectural problem. The problem given to Lyle was to design a museum in a French provincial town. He needed to complete rendered plans, sections and watercolour elevations in an eight-hour session. The other parts of the exam included freehand drawing from a cast, modelling in clay, and written and oral tests in mathematics and history.

Lyle's training had prepared him well for the entrance exam. When the results were published, he wrote home, proudly declaring that 'there were 440 students who tried the entrance examinations, which were both written and oral. I passed No. 19 and was the youngest English-speaking student at the École.'[7] This was quite an achievement. In Lyle's year, only fifty-three other students successfully completed the exams. His former Hamilton Art School teacher, John Ireland, boasted in the *Canadian Architect and Builder* published the following year: '[In the] competition for scholarship at the École des Beaux Arts, in Paris whereat hundreds of the best students from all parts of the world competed, Mr. John Lyle, a late student of this school, took the third place in the art subjects, and fifth place in modeling in clay, and gained his admission to what is considered the most advanced art academy known.'[8]

In fact, Lyle and J. Omer Marchand of Montreal were the first Canadian students admitted into the architectural program, entering the École des Beaux-Arts on August 1, 1894. In Paris, the two quickly became friends and, preparing for the exams together, grilled each other over what Lyle considered his most difficult area, 'the dreaded subject of Descriptive Geometry.'[9]

After admission a student could enroll in the studio of his choice. Lyle chose the 'free' studio of Paul Blondel, a private studio separate from the three official studios of the École. His next hurdle was to undergo his introduction as one of the *nouveaux*, or first years, to the *anciens*, or seniors, by the *patron*. (The *nouveaux* were subservient to the *anciens*, responsible for the menial tasks around the studio, filling the stove with coal or building wooden frames for the *anciens*' exhibition drawings and, most importantly, providing sweets for the afternoon tea.) On occasion, this introduction could prove a traumatic experience for more sensitive individuals. Lyle wrote home:

> My patron Paul Blondel, was a distinguished looking man – he was a Government architect for the Louvre Museum and Tuilleries, also for the law courts. I met our *patron* outside the *atelier* and he escorted me in, where about forty men of different ages were busily engaged over drawing boards. 'I wish to present a new comrade, Monsieur Lyle,' he said, that was all, and he left me and proceeded on his round of criticisms. I was surrounded by several of the *anciens*, one of whom said, 'and where do you come from little one?' I replied, 'Je suis du Canada.' He responded, 'Ah, c'est très bien mon garçon, vous êtes presque Français.' I was then smartly slapped on the back and shaken by the hand.[10]

The first known portrait of Lyle is a watercolour, presumably by a fellow student, completed during his stay in Paris. It shows the young man in profile with his head slightly bowed, apparently in deep thought. His hair is brownish black with slight thinning on the temples, and his facial features delicate, with a moustache he no doubt grew to appear more dapper and mature. He would keep this feature throughout his life. In the portrait he is smartly dressed with jacket, starched collar and red bow tie, and tucked behind his ear is a pencil – the primary tool of his intended trade. A photograph from the same time shows Lyle in an atelier, sitting facing the camera with watercolour brush dipped in a bowl, ready to work on the drawing on his desk. Here Lyle is fashionably dressed in a striped shirt collar and tie with suspenders. He looks meticulously groomed and dressed in comparison to the other students in the photograph. His workstation is littered with tissue drawings and references, but the drawing itself is clean and uncluttered, and by his side, neatly organized, are his brushes and drawing material. This image reveals someone who is self-possessed and conscious of his physical appearance and in a financial position that he can afford to be as well turned out as his *patron*, who appears in the background. The image also illustrates Lyle's method of designing, where numerous sources of information are laid out in front of him to assist in the decision-making process. He is a well-organized individual with his tools and resources neatly arranged before him, revealing someone who is focused, motivated and serious about his work and himself.

The architectural Beaux-Arts program sought to instill a particular approach to any design problem, or *parti*, through a system of monthly design competitions called *concours d'émulation*. The competition format was a reasonable replication of the conditions students would later encounter as practicing architects in their dealings with clients and contractors. There were two kinds of competitions: the sketch, or *esquisse*, and the rendered projects, or *projets rendus*, which were given on an alternating monthly basis. The *concours esquisse* was a single drawing that the student had twelve hours to complete; the *projets rendus* consisted of three drawings to be submitted after two months. For each competition, the *patron* would set a hypothetical problem for the students, who were to be *en loge*, or restricted to their cubicles. The object, according to Marchand, was 'to develop the artistic sense of the pupils and to train them in grasping in as short a time as possible the spirit of a program and of a *plan parti* (standard plan).'[11]

Left: 1.7 A student group photograph with Lyle second row from the top, second from the right.

Above: 1.8 Lyle (foreground) with sleeves pulled up, working on a project in the atelier, c. 1895.

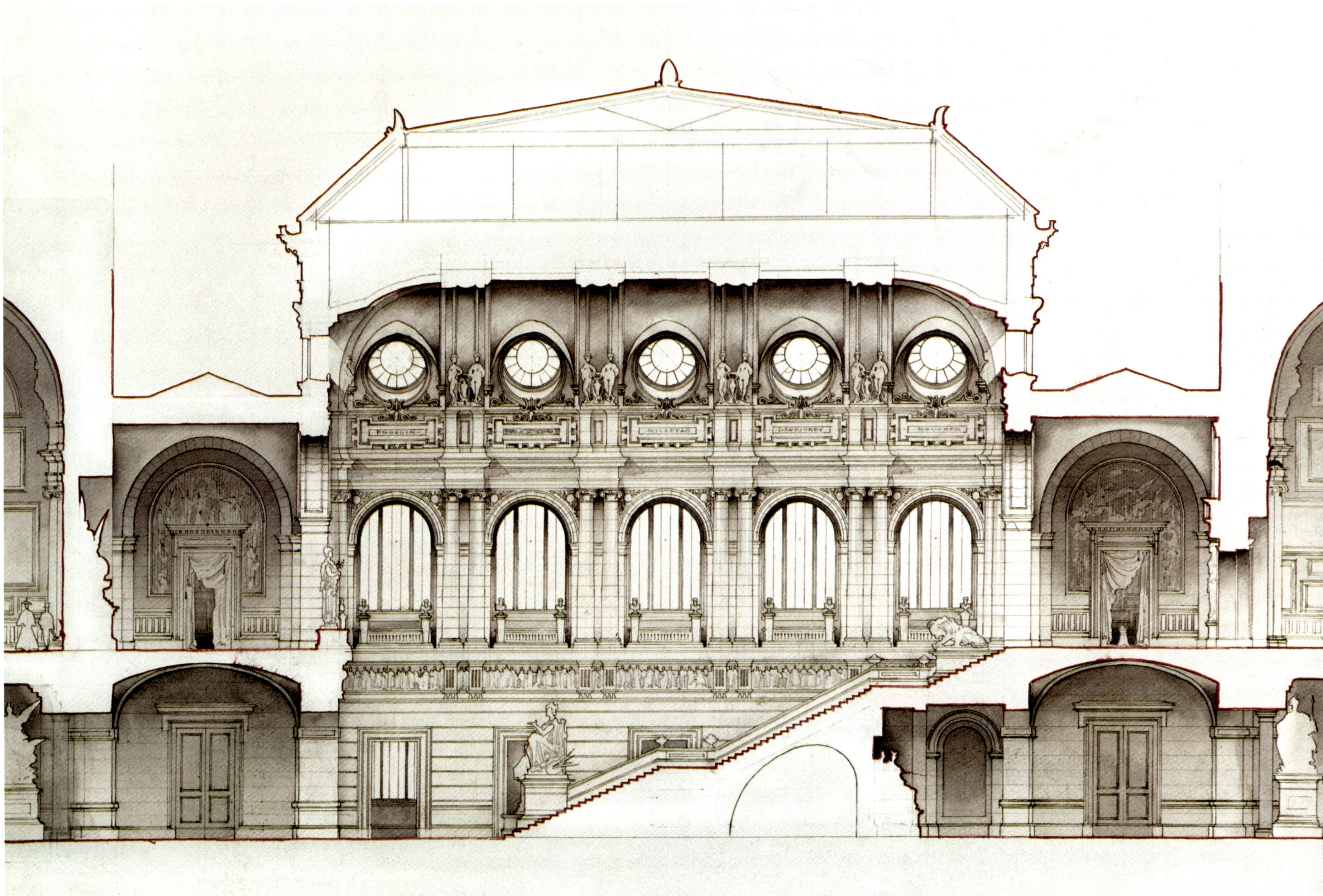

Series of student projects signed 'J. M. Lyle, Elève de M. Blondel, 1894.'

Opposite page: 1.9. Stairhall for a Palace of Fine Arts that included horizontal and transverse sections.

Top: 1.10. Two elevations of a plan for a palace bedroom.

Left: 1.11. The ceiling detail for a palace bedroom.

This trained the student to focus on problem-solving, and the problems were not trivial. If the task given by the *patron* called for a museum or an athenaeum, the plan would have to be worked on the width, with the paper horizontal; if the plan required several dispositions on the axis, such as is required in a large institution, the plan would have been worked on the length, with the paper vertical. As Marchand observed, 'with this as a starting point we commence by grouping the plan, studying it in detail and scaling the sizes of the different rooms required, and then a clear tracing of it is made, bringing out the most important motives of construction, till the last study presents a satisfactory arrangement and harmonious whole, after which we pass on to the facade which sometimes is of minor importance.'[12]

For the *projets rendus*, the student's proposal, or sketch, would consist of a plan, elevation and section, done in pencil then rendered with a wash, and shadow details. These drawings were usually distinct, with some finer details worked out, all elements clearly indicated and all drawn correctly. These *esquisses* were kept on file for reference. The student then had two months to work out the design in greater detail. If the finished *projet rendu* did not match the original *esquisse*, the entire project would be disqualified.

In Lyle's correspondence home, he described the frantic pace and the types of projects he was working on: 'Wednesday I went up *en loge* for my next project which I shall have to have finished in two months. At the same time we have to render a project for the professor of the history of architecture, which will take us fifteen days, so I shall be very busy for the next two months. For our project this time we have to study the difference in two styles of vaulting.'[13]

Within the atelier, the students could progress to first class by accumulating points, which were issued by the *patron* on the merits of the students' competition entries. They needed credits in a construction *concours*, as well as mathematics, perspective and several architectural compositions. The most challenging of these was the construction *concours*, which could take three months to complete. It required about a dozen drawings, showing how a projected building would be put together, with attention to the detailing of the stone, iron and woodworking, along with the mathematical calculation that would ensure the building could stand.[14]

Students were also given design projects to learn how to handle the interaction of architectural elements, such as the effects of combining various materials, colour, texture and details. These design problems were studies in composition, elevation and applying decorative ornament to give a structure character and personality. Students received a thorough training in elemental architectural forms, how they originated through the necessities of construction and how they had developed throughout history. The point was not to copy directly from the past but to be inspired by it and adapt the forms freely, thereby developing a personal expression and vocabulary. Research into other architects' work was encouraged at different stages of the design problem – at the beginning when only the general scheme was being developed, then later, when the student reached the stage of working on the details.

Lyle was admitted to the second class on August 1, 1894, and during his two years at the École he was awarded one mention each in both *dessin ornemental* and *exercices d'histoire de l'architecture*, two in *éléments analytiques* and three for *projets rendus*.

The school's diploma was awarded to students who had obtained all the required mentions and then had successfully completed a thesis of their choosing. The projects had to include all the practical details of construction and all the corresponding mathematics calculated, and finally the whole thesis had to be supported by an oral defence. Most North American students didn't bother to pursue the diploma because it meant little back home, but it was a requirement for those who wished to practice architecture in France.

A consequence of life in the atelier and the critical and co-operative process, which was essential to the learning experience, was the tremendous bond that developed among the students – not only with each other but also with their

Opposite page: 1.12 A project for a provincial town hall, elevation for Caisse d'Epargne de Lyon, 1894.

CAISSE D'EPARGNE DE LYON

patrons. Canadian architect William S. Maxwell, who attended the École a few years after Lyle, wrote about this connection: 'The warmest ties of affection bind these men to those teachers and *patron*.'[15] The co-operative spirit of the atelier meant that the second-year students would assist the first whenever possible. They would be interested in the others' projects and critique them, help with the finishing touches to the completed drawings and with mounting them for presentation.

But it wasn't only hard work that defined the atelier; Lyle reported home about some of the students' pranks and practical jokes. Once they turned the studio into an aviary, complete with flying doves and dive-bombing parrots; next they brought in snakes that were allowed to roam freely. This prank ceased abruptly when, during a life-model drawing class, a snake slithered up the back of the model's chair – the room was soon filled with piercing shrieks as the model ran naked through the atelier, hurling obscenities at the students.

Outside the atelier, the never-ending drama that was unfolding in the streets of Paris made a big impression on the young Lyle. The public display of emotion and passion about the nation's political, military and intellectual heroes was something he had never witnessed before and it moved him. He joined revelling Parisians during several spontaneous street celebrations, such as the festivities that ensued after the signing of the French-Russian Alliance of 1895, and the return from exile of the great French journalist Henri Rochefort, with shouts of '*Vive la Sociale!*' And along with the other Parisians, Lyle watched in sombre silence, from a perch high up in the limbs of the old oak trees lining the Champs Elysées, the funeral proceedings for political figures such as Patrice de Mac-Mahon and President Carnot, and for the most famous dignitary of them all, France's great scientist, Louis Pasteur.[16]

Generally, though, Lyle's studies kept him from enjoying a social life outside the atelier. However, he always stayed in touch with family and friends back home, arranging whenever possible to meet them on their visits to Europe. He also spent time with those friends from home already living in Paris; the Canadian painter William Blair Bruce and his wife, the Swedish sculptor Caroline Benedicks Bruce, often had Lyle over for dinner.

Like other North Americans, Lyle did not complete his diploma, but reflected on the benefits of the previous four years, writing that he was 'so thankful that I have had the advantage of being able to study at the École, which has so entirely changed my architectural ideas.'[17] The ideas and methods instilled in him would be the foundation for his architectural practice. Many years later, in 1922, he gave a speech at the Toronto Architectural Club entitled 'American Architecture,' later published in *The American Architect – The Architectural Review* and, in an abbreviated form, in the *New York Times*. Here he praised the virtues of current American architecture, singling out its scholarship, solidity and simplicity, restraint, execution and the handling of monumental work – the very principles that were the basis of his education at the École.

One of the most important aspects of Lyle's education was that he learned how to study and solve a design problem from the inside out, as well as that the exterior massing of a building should reflect the interior plan. He also learned that a building was to be readable from the exterior, that the circulation of people in and through the interior spaces was of primary importance, and that these spaces should provide for social rituals. At the École it was considered essential that the creator's personal touch should be reflected in the selection of building material and the worldliness of the finished work. To achieve these ends, Lyle and his colleagues were taught that a scholarly study of similarly built forms was essential, not just via printed publications, but also through actually seeking out the known examples and examining them first-hand. Further, buildings should be solidly and simply constructed, and they should be timeless, with attributes of the eternal. The École emphasized honest construction over trickery or fads.

There were other principles: a building should be well-composed and proportional in its massing, and only the appropriate amount and placement of decoration should be used. Buildings should also be constructed as safely as possible, using the most suitable materials and the best workmen available, and designs should be executed in the most expedient manner within the limitations of the client, site, materials and budget. At the École, the focus was on providing projects on which the students could hone their designing skills. Perhaps most significantly for Lyle, there was a particular emphasis on large monumental work, and the students learned how to confidently handle the grandest of public buildings. Other important architectural concepts the École promoted and Lyle embraced were the comradeship between student and *patron* and the necessity for honest critical discussion among peers. Lyle tried to promote these aspects of the profession during his career, through his writing, teaching and relationship with his students, staff and fellow architects.

In early 1896, Lyle had received an offer from Howard Hadden, a recent graduate of the architectural program at Columbia University whom he had befriended while working for Freeman in 1891, to open an office in New York in a partnership. Hadden, who was well-connected both socially and financially, thought he could generate enough 'small stuff' to keep them going while they tried their luck entering open competitions. Lyle's response to this offer, the merits of which he debated in a letter to his mother, reveals much about his temperament and personality, and the cautious, methodical approach he took to his architectural career:

> In one way it would be perhaps a good thing for me, as in a good architectural firm it is almost necessary that one should do the designing and the other should look after the superintending and the business end of the concern. Then I should probably learn as much doing a house for myself as by designing one for an architect in his office. At the same time I feel that a more conservative course is the wiser one. My schooling here has been an excellent one but at the same time I need at least a year or two of experience in a good office before commencing on my own hook. For a badly built house in the commencement of my career would not tend to improve my reputation. As I am young yet, one of the youngest of the Americans in the school (the youngest, in fact) I think it would be wise to wait a little.[18]

Through corresponding with Freeman, Lyle knew the economic conditions in North America were not promising, but he still stood a better chance of finding work there than anywhere else. In the late summer of 1896, Lyle said adieu to his beloved Paris and set sail for what he described as 'the Mecca of all aspiring young architects, New York.'[19]

New York

North America was not the same place Lyle had left in 1892. The 1880s had been characterized by such economic excess that the stock market crash of 1893 was virtually inevitable. Several factors precipitated the crash and the resulting depression, the worst of the nineteenth century. The most actively traded and widely held industrial stock on the New York Exchange was National Cordage. When the company's top executive was caught diluting the stock's value, its share price collapsed by one-seventh, causing massive losses on the exchange. Railway expansion of the last decade had been overly optimistic and the debt load for most of these firms had doubled. The companies were not making money from their freight handling and carriage fees but from savvy manipulation, takeovers, threats of parallel lines and other market techniques. The overbuilding contributed to rate wars between the major companies, with several railways going into receivership. Finally, there was the silver-mining industry. When India, the world's second-largest consumer of the metal, unexpectedly closed its mints, the price of American silver dropped by almost half, causing many of the mines to close and the industry to collapse. The three-year depression that followed resulted in over 500 banks failing across the country, the stock market losing 35 percent of its value, nearly 1,500 companies going bankrupt and

1.13 The Court of Honor at the World's Columbian Exposition, Chicago, in 1893.

approximately 30 percent of the United States' railway system becoming financially insolvent.

Despite the alarming economic situation, one major event in 1893 would change the course of architecture in the United States: the World's Columbian Exposition in Chicago. Acting as chief architect of the event, Daniel Burnham set a new course for American architecture by selecting East Coast firms to design the fair's principal buildings. Located around the Court of Honor, these structures all utilized the same neoclassical architectural style and features, with a uniform cornice height, arcades and colour scheme. The men selected to design the buildings were the first generation of American Beaux-Arts–trained architects. They included the New York firms of Richard M. Hunt, George B. Post, and McKim, Mead & White, and from Boston, Peabody & Stearns. With the exception of Charles B. Atwood's Palace of Fine Arts, local Chicago architects such as William Le Baron Jenney and Louis Sullivan had been relegated to the design of less prominent buildings. The huge success and publicity generated from this event endorsed and popularized Beaux-Arts architects and the classical style at the expense of the Chicago firms, making it the standard style for public architecture well into the next century.

One of the first things Lyle did on his arrival in the U.S. was to join the newly established Beaux-Arts Society of New York, which had received its charter in 1894. Through the society's many functions, Lyle made a number of valuable professional connections and lifelong friendships. The members included the second generation of Beaux-Arts–trained architects, such as John M. Carrère, Thomas Hastings, Whitney Warren, John Galen Howard, along with the newly graduated Benjamin W. Morris, Donn Barber and Howard Greenley. The Beaux-Arts Society was mandated to educate and promote the ideals and teachings of the École. In the spirit of the free educational program offered by the school in Paris, the Society established ateliers around the country with a local practicing architect who acted as the *patron* and taught aspiring students who could not afford to study abroad. Following the *esquisse* principle, the New York offices set the problem and the local *patron* assisted students in solving it on their own time before critiquing it. The drawings were sent to New York to be exhibited and judged by a panel of architects who awarded medals to the most successful plans and published the results in *Architecture* magazine. The Society met frequently, usually in French restaurants in New York, and Lyle was appointed to the dinner committee. His task was to arrange and reserve tables at the most fashionable restaurants. If the evening's food and drink were a success, he would receive much praise, but if the event turned out to be a disaster, he would have to endure teasing from his fellow members.

Due to the economic uncertainty in New York upon Lyle's arrival, he had great difficulty finding work. As he noted: 'I was told by my American friends that all one had to do in New York was announce that you were a Beaux-Arts man and you were welcomed with open arms. It turned out to be quite different…'[20] Resourcefully, he proposed to John Galen Howard of Howard & Cauldwell, an up-and-coming firm, that he would work for them for free as a draftsman if they would allow him to leave whenever he found another job. In only three weeks he found a paying job through one of his Beaux-Arts connections, in the offices of Raymond Almirall. Almirall had completed his studies in Paris and had moved back to New York, where he established a small practice focusing on residential work, mostly in Brooklyn. But Lyle did not remain with Almirall for long. When the economy picked up, Howard & Cauldwell lured him back to their offices with a paying job.

Howard was a rising star in the New York architectural community. He had studied at the Massachusetts Institute of Technology and the École des Beaux-Arts in Paris, and worked in the offices of Henry Hobson Richardson in Boston and the New York firm of McKim, Mead & White, before launching his practice in partnership with engineer Samuel M. Cauldwell in 1893. Howard was greatly admired by all the younger architects, and it is not hard to understand Lyle's attraction to him. He was a tall, very blond and charismatic individual who inspired and motivated his staff. Lyle 'was an early victim of

1.14, 1.15 Lyle's drawing skills were fully utilized by Howard & Cauldwell, architects, for a number of competition entries, including a Newark High School, New Jersey (top), and an armoury in Providence, Rhode Island (bottom).

his great charm and often used to walk home with him up Fifth Avenue when the office closed.' He looked up to Howard for his 'inspiring personality'[21] and was so drawn to Howard's personal and professional qualities that he referred to him as 'the master.'[22]

Some of Lyle's duties in the office were to take Howard's preliminary elevation designs for a given project and render them as a perspective drawing for clients or competitions. These drawings were in pen and wash, often three-dimensional, highlighting the building in its site, with people, horse and buggies or automobiles mingling in the foreground to provide scale and a sense of urban vitality. During Lyle's tenure, the Howard & Cauldwell office was responsible for the Renaissance, 1897–98, and the Essex, 1896–98, both hotels in New York City, as well as several townhouses, including the house for arts philanthropist A. D. Julliard in 1896. In 1897, through an open competition, the firm won a high school project in Newark, New Jersey. Lyle quickly rose within the organization from draftsman to senior architect.

Another significant architectural event in 1893, along with the World's Columbian Exposition, was the Tarsney Act, passed by the U.S. Congress – a reform measure to improve the quality of federal buildings and forestall the appointment of architects based solely on political patronage. The bill, which the American Institute of Architects had lobbied for heavily and was widely supported by the profession, opened up federal commissions to independent architects through competitions. Following this model, other organizations also began to select their architects through competitions. Determined that the choice be based solely upon the architects' abilities to design within the stated budget, oversight boards imposed conditions and restrictions on the size, colouring, material and views of the submissions. If the plans were not up to presentational standard, or they were poorly rendered, firms would be at a huge disadvantage, so the choice of a draftsman to prepare the drawings was crucial. This put Lyle, with his rendering abilities, in a prestigious position and in high demand. But it also put new pressures on architectural draftsmen who had to inhabit two worlds – both architecture and art. The success of the perspective drawing depended mostly on their artistic imagination and technical skills in capturing the buildings' texture, colour, site, scale, detail and, above all, beauty. The architectural component of the rendering meant the drawing looked and could be built as the designer intended.

During Lyle's tenure with Howard & Cauldwell, he produced all the perspective drawings for the company; the firm entered many major competitions, including the international open competition for the University of California in 1898, where it placed fourth. The two most important competitions Lyle was directly involved with were those for the New York Public Library, in 1897, and the New York Yacht Club a year later. These two buildings would become landmarks of the Beaux-Arts style in New York.

The New York Public Library competition was arranged in two stages. The first was an open competition, and then a select few from that round were pitted against more established firms. In May 1897, the competition received eighty-eight entries, twelve of which were selected and awarded a premium of $400 each. A second elimination followed, and the six surviving firms included Howard & Cauldwell. The executive committee then invited six established firms to join in with the surviving up-and-comers for the final competition in August. These firms included McKim Mead & White, George B. Post, Carrère & Hastings, Cyrus Eidlitz, Ernest Flagg, Charles C. Haight, and Peabody & Stearns.

Lyle's unpublished memoir captures some of the excitement and energy of this time:

> The day before the drawings were to be handed in Carrère & Hastings and some of the staff came to visit 23rd Street to see what we had done. Then the next night we were down to Carrère & Hastings office, which was then near the foot of Broadway. They were in a bad *charette* and were late with some of their drawings. The drafting room was crowded. John M. [Carrère]...was lying full out

Top: 1.16 Carrère & Hastings, New York Public Library winning entry, front elevation.

Middle: 1.17 Howard & Cauldwell, New York Public Library, competition drawing, front elevation.

Bottom: 1.18 Howard & Cauldwell, New York Public Library, competition perspective drawing.

1.19, 1.20 Warren & Wetmore, winning design for the New York Yacht Club clubhouse (top), and Howard & Cauldwell, losing entry (bottom).

> on his stomach, blackening the walls of the ground floor plan. There was the atmosphere of an *atelier en charette*, with clouds of smoke and much banter. But the great shock to me was the magnificent rendering of the facades by Charles Aldrich. My rendering had not been pushed so far. So I felt that the judges would be impressed by Chester's [Charles] drawings.[23]

Unfortunately for his firm, Lyle was right – the Howard & Cauldwell entry lost by one vote to Carrère & Hastings' plan. The jury agreed with Lyle's assessment: Carrère & Hastings' plans 'presented a consistent, skillful and artistic solution of the structural problem,' and were 'direct and dignified in treatment.' The jury called the Howard & Cauldwell entry 'decidedly inferior' in both 'the unity and character of exterior design and in the details of the interior arrangement.'[24]

In 1898, the New York Yacht Club held a competition for a new clubhouse on West 44th Street, a site donated by Wall Street financier J. Pierpont Morgan, the club's commodore. Seven architectural firms prepared plans, including Howard & Cauldwell and Warren & Wetmore, the eventual winners. Lyle prepared the drawings for the competition. The site was in the middle of a city block, sandwiched between two buildings, so the drawing was rendered as a full frontal perspective. In an attempt to define the building's function, it was laden with the appropriate symbolic ornamentation. There was a fence of capstans and chains, entranceway tridents and a feature that both Howard & Cauldwell and Warren & Wetmore's designs had in common – a low-window sitting room on the second floor that was based on the projecting oriel windows of sailing ships. Lyle was surprised by this, since 'neither of us had the other's drawings and the strange coincidence is no doubt due to the French method of studying a new problem.'[25]

Lyle's drawing and painterly skills were becoming highly marketable. After working for Howard & Cauldwell for about three years, he spent a brief period in the offices of Warren & Wetmore before he was lured away to work with Carrère & Hastings. John M. Carrère, the chief architect in charge of the Pan-American Exposition in Buffalo, approached Lyle and confided in him that 'he was having some trouble about the colour cartoons that were being made for the exteriors...and suggested that I should take over this job and see what could be done with it.' Lyle noted that there were about fifteen or twenty draftsmen making colour charts of the exteriors of the buildings and that it 'was a difficult and rather complicated job, because none of the drafting force had ever had much experience in dealing with colour.'[26] Lyle was hired to assist with the colouring of the architectural models and the eventual application to the buildings.

The fabled Chicago World's Columbian Exposition of 1893, called the White City, was the standard all fairs were compared to. Its major architectural theme was uniformity; it permeated all aspects of the buildings' design, from architectural style and detail to material and colour. But the Buffalo Exposition was meant to create an experience for its visitors unparalleled by any other fair. To distinguish itself with a landmark feature, and taking its cue from the exposition's flamboyant combination of Latin and Spanish influences, Buffalo decided to introduce colour as its major theme. Colour was to be used throughout the structures to create a Rainbow City.

The board of directors for Buffalo's exposition selected eight prominent architects for the design and planning of all the buildings and grounds for the proposed fair – Carrère & Hastings, Howard & Cauldwell, and Peabody & Stearns from New York, and three local firms, including George Carey. Reflecting the prominence to which his firm had risen in the architectural community, John M. Carrère was selected chairman. At one of their preliminary meetings, the board adopted the rough general plan sketched out by R. S. Peabody, which used the natural beauty of Delaware Park. The plan was on an inverted 'T' with the vertical element forming the court and major buildings. To maintain a classical unity throughout, all of the central court's buildings were to be designed in a Renaissance style. The outer buildings and midway had few restrictions imposed upon them. A network of canals terminated at the apex of the exposition, which was John Galen Howard's Electric Tower.

Progressing from the entrance at the Triumphal Bridge to the Electric Tower, the colour scheme gradually moved from bright primary tones associated with primitive conditions to a pastel palette, representing the more advanced cultures. This colour experiment had never been attempted, so a small army of creative architects and designers was hired to work on it, among them Charles Yardley Turner, the president of the National Society of Mural Painters, who was the director of colour.

During the fall and winter of 1900, Turner devised the colour scheme and a large corps of young architects working in his New York studio applied it to scale models of the proposed buildings. Each building's palette had to express its function, distinguish it from its neighbours and at the same time avoid clashing with them. Lyle, with his artistic abilities and colour sensibilities, was particularly well-suited for this work. He would later be known for being as meticulous over the interior detail colour schemes of his projects as over the design of their elevations, often spending weeks on painters' scaffolds to ensure the right colours and effects were being achieved. Lyle spent six months in Buffalo working at the exposition for this 'rather complicated job.'[27]

The exposition gave Lyle the opportunity to actually design a structure and have it built – for the first time in his career. He entered a competition offered by Carrère & Hastings for the design of the two main bandstands that were prominently located between the Triumphal Bridge and the first grouping of buildings along the main esplanade. Although half a dozen other designers entered the competition, Lyle's plan was, according to the papers, 'the only one considered by the chief architect.'[28] The design was an Art Nouveau–inspired work, his only known use of that style, featuring a form Lyle jokingly but aptly described as an 'umbrella-butterfly.'[29] It consisted of a ribbed dome with four cusped arches supported by flower-laden posts at the angles, with each giving rise to a flagpole. A harp, symbolic of music, crowned the structure.

1.21, 1.22 In 1901, Lyle won a limited competition to design two bandstands at Buffalo's Pan Exhibition that became the focus of nightly concerts.

The base was carefully designed to complement the lines of the arches and the dome, while a balustrade kept the crowds at a distance from the musicians. In contrast to the intense reds and browns of the neighbouring buildings, the colours were muted, with shades of a grey green on the exterior and soft pastel lavender inside. The two bandstands were hailed by a local Buffalo newspaper as the 'most conspicuous of the minor buildings on the grounds. They will also be the most graceful.'[30] Lyle later claimed it was sheer luck that 'enabled him to hit on the umbrella idea.'[31]

After the opening of the exposition, Lyle returned to New York, where his reputation as a designer and renderer had grown so much that he could afford to work independently. He was becoming extremely confident in his skills and abilities, and when one of the leading architects in the country, Daniel Burnham, asked him to join his firm in Chicago, Lyle, flattered by the proposal but not wishing to leave New York, responded with a salary demand so high he never heard back.[32] And when the two principals of the firm of Bright & Bacon decided to go their separate ways in 1903, James Bright, the remaining partner, proposed that Lyle take up the vacant position. Lyle, not wishing to tie himself down in a relationship that might not work out, offered to spend time working with Bright to see how they got on together. After a couple of months, he suggested to Bright that he 'should find someone else.'[33]

Lyle's years of Beaux-Arts training, with its emphasis on drawing skills, coupled with his various summer sketching trips throughout Europe, meant his formidable technical skills and artistic 'clever fingers' were in great demand. He did not enter any competition on his own at this time but acted as designer and draftsman in partnership with many senior architects. In conjunction with George Carey, the Buffalo architect he had met while working at the Pan-American Exposition, he entered two competitions – the Soldiers' and Sailors' Monument, Philadelphia, in 1902, where he placed fifth, and Freeman's Hospital, Washington, D.C.[34] He also worked on submissions for Brooklyn City Hall, the Washington, D.C., City Hall and the San Francisco Customs House.

A particularly important competition was one for West Point Military Academy, which he entered in conjunction with Charles Haight. This presented a challenge because the academy had to be Gothic in character. This was Lyle's second attempt at a Gothic program and while no drawings survive to show how well he handled it, his commitment and seriousness are evident: 'The terrain was very hilly and covered a large territory, which I used to tramp over for days at a time, because the planning and the designing of the individual buildings were linked up with the placing of these buildings in a practical and comprehensive scheme.'[35]

Haight was so pleased with their efforts that he showed them off to friends and notables, among them art critic Royal Cortissoz and New York City socialite Fredrick Vanderbilt. Haight offered Lyle a partnership if they were successful with their entry, and Lyle, in his exuberance, had the legal papers drawn up for a temporary agreement. But their design did not even place in the competition and the project was awarded to the well-known firm of Cram, Goodhue & Ferguson, specialists in the Gothic style.

Lyle was so much in demand that he was in the enviable position of being able to pick and choose his projects and command top dollar. And while he could not always expect the offer of a partnership, he could certainly ask for a bonus if the project won a competition, and once asked for $5,000 – a huge sum in those days. But perhaps the highest tribute to his skills was when Harold Van Buren Magonigle, considered one of the finest line draftsmen in the U.S. and later author of several books on architectural rendering, turned to him for help on a drawing for the President McKinley Memorial to be erected in Canton, Ohio. Magonigle's monotone wash drawing was due to be shipped to the competition the next day but it had not turned out well. With little time left and in complete despair, Magonigle called upon Lyle's services. Lyle recalled arriving at the studio, taking a look at Magonigle's attempt and concluding that 'it was terrible!' Lyle took off his coat, rolled up his sleeves and 'asked for a large bucket of clean water and several sponges of different sizes. The drawing was on

Watchman [Whatman] paper… I decided to sponge the whole drawing over and get it in such a state that the general tone would be lighter, so that it could be re-rendered. Working all that day and well into the night, I rendered it again… I had to lay out flat on the drawing board… [T]he drawing was finished about noon the next day, packed and shipped for judgment.'[36] Reminded of his student days in Paris with the *atelier en charette*, frantically putting on the final touches before submission, Lyle found the experience exciting and fun and he was equally delighted when the submission won the competition.

This was a period of growth for Lyle, both professionally and personally. The architectural milieu in New York was highly stimulating, with some of the finest Beaux-Arts buildings and skyscrapers being constructed in the city. Lyle had a direct and personal connection to some; others he would have studied and avidly discussed among friends and colleagues. His social milieu was also developing, revolving around student friendships formed in Paris, his Beaux-Arts Society activities, as well as his working connections. And he was fortunate to have his younger brother, Henry, who was working at the New York City Hospital, living with him in a midtown West Side apartment. Starting to move within wealthier circles, Lyle often spent his weekends outside the city as an invited guest at friends' summer houses.

However, successful as Lyle was socially and artistically, as a draftsman and renderer he was growing impatient. He wasn't content to rise through the ranks of another architectural office, or to find a compatible senior architect to partner with. Lyle wanted to start his own practice, but making a go of it as an architect in New York City without a direct connection to a wealthy patron or influential circles was a difficult task. He had been back to Canada several times to see family and friends in Hamilton and was keeping an eye on Toronto as a possible site for relocation. But although he visited the city, he 'was not impressed that there was a field for an unknown man.' He returned to New York 'with many ideas simmering in the back of my head,' and waited for the right opportunity to present itself.[37]

In April 1904, an article in the New York papers caught his eye – a new Union Station was being contemplated in Toronto by the Canadian Pacific and the Grand Trunk Railway companies. This was a commission Lyle could hope to win. When, a few days later, a devastating fire struck Toronto, the confluence of events was too much to ignore. While fires are terrible tragedies for most people, they represent opportunity for ambitious architects, and so Lyle decided 'to make a trip to Toronto and look the field over.'[38] He had no professional connections and few social ones in Toronto, with the exception of his sister. But the desire to pursue the dream of his own practice led Lyle to abandon his profitable New York career and move to Toronto in January 1905. There, 'I rented a room at No. 14 Leader Lane and hung up my shingle.'[39]

Chapter 2: 1905–1914

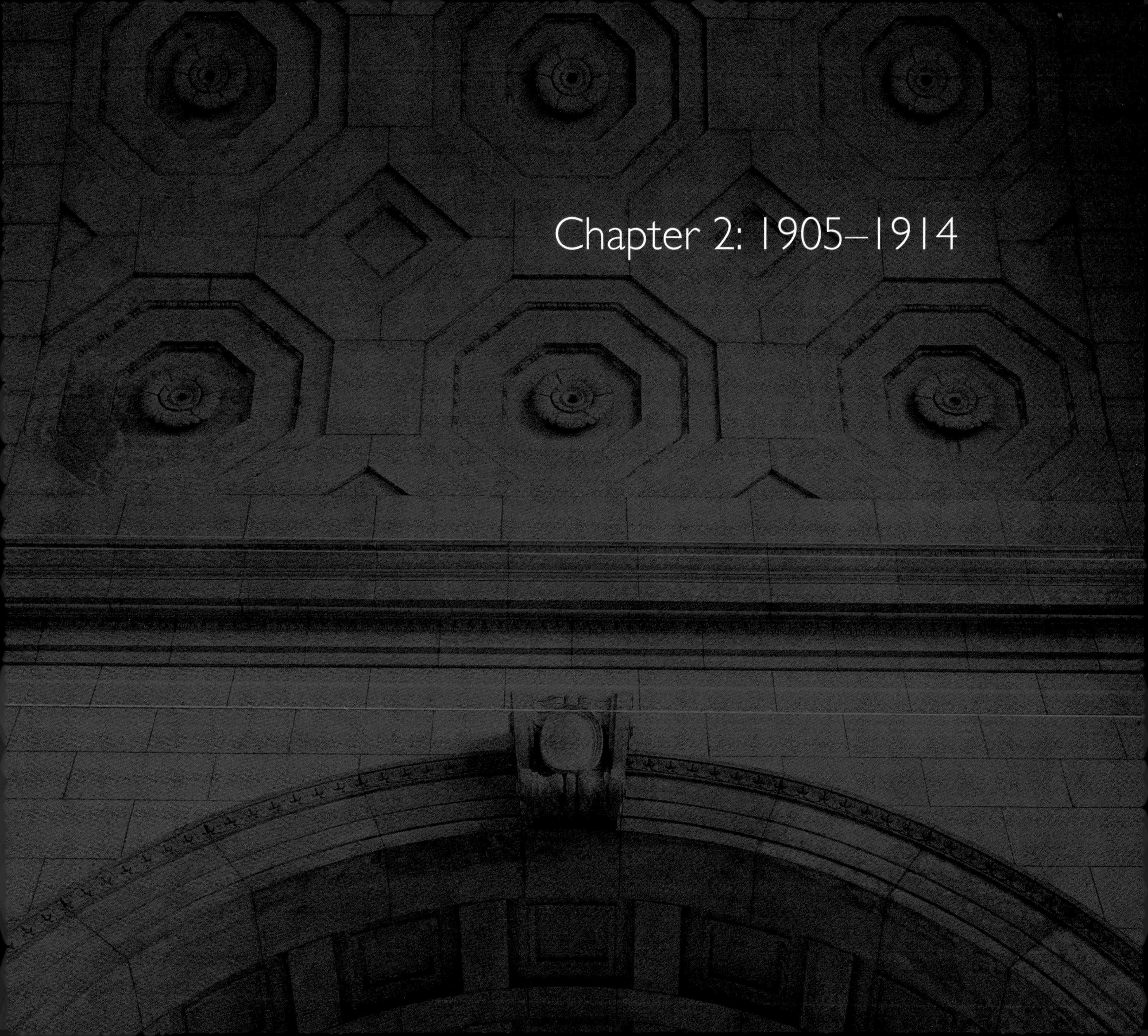

WINDSOR · SAULT ST. MARIE · SUDBURY

A Pinnacle of Beaux-Arts Classicism

Putting Down Roots

Lyle's family connections through his father gave the young architect a leg up into circles of potential clients to boost his new architectural career in Canada, but he still had to prove himself worthy of their trust and deliver the goods on time and on budget. Lyle quickly made three important connections – the Hendrie family of Hamilton, J. L. Englehart of Petrolia and the Mulock family of Toronto.

The Hendries, old friends and influential businessmen with commercial interests in and around Hamilton, were also prominent thoroughbred horse racers, a world that included the province's wealthiest people. One family member, John Hendrie, a commissioner with the Hydro-Electric Power Commission, had a hand in Lyle's appointment to design a series of eleven power stations for the corporation, and recommended him as architect for the Provincial Penitentiary for Ontario in Guelph, in 1909. Through connections of his wife, Isabel, whom he met two years after his arrival in the city, Lyle befriended J. L. Englehart, one of the founders of Imperial Oil and the Temiskaming and Northern Ontario Railway, and both companies hired on the young architect. And the early connection with the Mulock family in Toronto produced the high-profile work of the Royal Alexandra Theatre, which helped to create a network of personal and business connections leading to commissions that were instrumental in establishing Lyle's reputation. These networks and connections were invaluable to Lyle because he believed that self-promotion was undignified for a professional man and that commissions would come to him based on his reputation as an architect and on the strength of his personality.

With Toronto now his permanent home, Lyle quickly immersed himself in the architectural and cultural communities. Within weeks of being in the city he had staked out creative territory that would become lifetime involvements and was in part the foundation for his rapid rise in the architectural ranks of the country. Lyle also joined several social, artistic and athletic clubs that would integrate him into the community and provide a network of friends, and he was instrumental in offering a new and exciting option for aspiring architects by helping to establish a Beaux-Arts Club and an atelier, where he acted as the *patron*, modelled after the one he belonged to in New York. Shortly upon arriving in Toronto he wrote to a local newspaper lending support to an exhibition of new urban projects proposed for New York City. Lyle encouraged readers to see the show because of its implications for potential urban development in Toronto. Thus began Lyle's advocacy and work for the beautification of the city through urban planning – he would become one of its leading promoters and critics.

When Lyle arrived in 1905, Toronto was a thriving community of 250,000 people, most of whom, like the young architect, were from the same cultural and religious stock – British and Presbyterian. Toronto was the economic and political hub for the province and rivalled Montreal as the country's financial centre. It was also a city recovering from its worst disaster since 1849. The Great Fire of 1904 had started in the early evening of April 19 at the premises of E. & S. Currie, a neckwear company on the north side of Wellington Street between Yonge and Bay. By the time the fire was brought under control the following morning, it had swept through fourteen acres of the downtown core consisting mostly of four- to five-storey buildings constructed in the mid to late nineteenth century and used for storage, distribution or light manufacturing. Approximately 122 buildings were destroyed, including eighty-six large commercial structures. A number of smaller railway warehouses and storage sheds along the tracks to the south of Front Street and running along the Esplanade were also burnt down. With a fire of such magnitude, it was miraculous that there was no loss of life.

Lyle's new digs were close to the affected area, which at this point was still a smouldering ruin, just east of Yonge Street on Leader Lane. Several other architects, including one of the country's leading firms, Darling & Pearson, were also located in this section of town. Although Lyle had moved to the city to take advantage of the possibilities brought on by the fire, he did not actually design any structures in the devastated area

Opposite page: 2.1 Interior detail of Toronto's Union Station Great Hall.

Top: 2.2 Toronto's great fire of 1904, Bay Street looking south from Wellington Street.

Bottom: 2.3 Yonge Street, one street east of the fire on Bay, one year later.

until Union Station in 1913. But it wasn't long before his talents and skills were called upon. One of the first to find Lyle's training, experience and classical Beaux-Arts sensibilities attractive were the country's banks.

Banks: Lucrative Clients

Lyle's working relationship with the Canadian banking establishment continued to sustain him throughout his career. He was involved in the design of alterations, renovations, extensions and new structures, including designs for fixtures, furniture and counters, of both head offices and branches, for approximately ninety buildings. The bulk of these bank designs, forty branches in all, were done in the years before World War I. The companies he worked for included the Canadian Bank of Commerce, the Bank of Nova Scotia, the Bank of Toronto, the Bank of Ottawa, the Metropolitan Bank and the Sterling Bank. His best and most lucrative client was the Dominion Bank who, over an eighteen-year span, commissioned him to design twelve branches.

Lyle's first opportunity to design a bank, in 1906, was a branch building built on a modest scale for the newly chartered Sterling Bank in Port Dalhousie, Ontario. He went on to design banks right across the country, from Halifax, N.S., to Nelson, B.C., but most were situated in Toronto. One of the unique features of the Canadian banking system was the freedom given to institutions to establish branches, a right granted to them in the 1871 statutes of the Bank Act. This act encouraged the development of large, centrally located chartered banks with a network of smaller local branches reaching into every financially viable small town or community. At the time of Confederation, eighteen banks had been granted charters for Ontario and Quebec, five for Nova Scotia and four for New Brunswick. By the turn of the twentieth century, there were thirty-four chartered banks and nearly 1,000 branch banks, an increase attributed to both 'the banking system and the rapid growth of the country.'[1]

Bank architecture in Canada at the time of Lyle's arrival had moved away from the flamboyant, picturesque styles of the last century to the refined, ordered elegance of the Beaux-Arts classicism. This was largely due to the New York firm of McKim, Mead & White, whose 1901 design for the renovation and extension of the Bank of Montreal's head office on Place d'Armes, in Montreal, exerted an enormous influence over bank architecture in the country. Lyle's ease and familiarity with the style was a great asset.

The bank institutions realized that a consistent style was important for their corporate images, and although they were not dogmatic about it, they did strive to maintain certain features. Most banks were based on classical designs – free interpretations of various historic Greek, Roman, Italian and French sources. For example, the Bank of Montreal's style was based on their home office, which used a simplified Greek form consisting of a Doric portico with a column entrance and pediment, and the Canadian Bank of Commerce's smaller branch buildings were designed in the classic style, with typical column and pediment facades. When designing for the Dominion Bank, Lyle utilized the classical design vocabulary and standardized the physical exterior characteristics by using, 'when possible the same deep red brick and limestone trimmings… and simplified wall surfaces with decorative motifs largely confined to the main entrance and on the lintels of the windows.'[2]

The approach most architects took, regardless of which bank they were designing for, was summed up by Darling & Pearson, the preferred firm for the Canadian Bank of Commerce. They had two objectives in mind: first, to utilize every available inch of floor space in the 'most advantageous arrangements,' and second, to impress the clientele with the 'character and security of the bank.'[3] There were two different types of models for bank branches: the single- and two-storeyed. The single-storey building was more flexible, could work for both interior or corner sites and was generally used in less urban communities as it could also accommodate small storefront shops that could be rented out. When the expansion of the bank's business demanded increased floor space, the separating partition wall would be demolished, and the counterplan extended. More urban centres could utilize

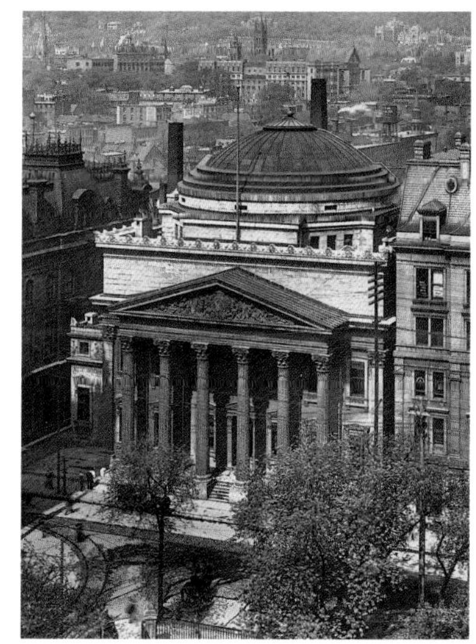

2.4, 2.5 Exterior and interior views of the McKim, Mead & White renovation to the Bank of Montreal's head office in Montreal.

2.12, 2.13 The Royal Alexandra Theatre in the heart of Toronto's King Street theatre district was modelled after Carrère & Hastings' residential design for R. H. Townsend in Washington, D.C. (top).

Opposite page: 2.14 The crowds gather just before showtime at the Royal Alexandra Theatre.

Yonge Street. Lyle had worked for the firm in New York, but had no current relationship with them in Toronto. It is not known how, but Lyle somehow outmanoeuvred Carèrre & Hastings for the Royal Alexandra job.

In his memoirs, Lyle claims that winning the commission was due to a bit of good luck and being at the right place at the right time. However it is likely that Lyle, having met the young millionaire Cawthra Mulock, the driving force behind the project, convinced him on the strength of his experience and personality that he was the right architect for the job. Or perhaps Mulock wished to avoid criticism for choosing an American architect over a local one; such criticism had been levelled against other buildings and owners. A decade earlier, the local architecture press protested when Cleveland architect S. R. Badgley was used to design Massey Hall. Lyle – out of a sense of guilt, or by ironic fate – did pay homage to Carrère & Hastings by modelling the Royal Alexandra exterior after their 1896 residential design for R. H. Townsend in Washington, D.C. These buildings share many design features, including material usage, fenestration pattern and the same French Renaissance vocabulary. This was not the last time Lyle was to be pitted against Carrère & Hastings for an important commission in Toronto, but it was a competition Lyle won and could savour.

Cawthra Mulock, son of Sir William Mulock, the Postmaster General of Canada, had three partners for the theatre project, including local businessmen Robert Smith, Jim Caffery and Lawrence Solman, who was to become the theatre's manager. The financiers were correct in determining that the timing was right for this speculative adventure in Toronto. At the turn of the twentieth century, the city's cultural life was vibrant enough to support many theatres and music halls. The Princess Theatre accommodated touring productions from London and New York, the Grand Opera usually presented Irish musicals, while the Toronto Opera House and Massey Hall featured primarily classical music. New cultural facilities for the city were needed, and Mulock's organization was the first to react by building the elegant and opulent Royal Alexandra, followed a year later by the smaller and less impressive Gaiety Theatre on Queen Street. Mulock was granted a patent to use the word *Royal* in honour of Queen Alexandra, consort of King Edward VII. The location his group chose was the former playing fields of Upper Canada College, across the street from the Lieutenant Governor's residence and St. Andrew's Presbyterian Church, just west of the city's commercial district.

Lyle convinced Mulock and his partners to travel to New York to study the latest architectural developments. Not only did they study the older theatres they would have already been familiar with, but they also met with theatre producers, including the up-and-coming Schubert brothers, to gain their perspectives. The newly constructed Lyceum Theatre, built in 1903 on 45th Street, in the heart of New York's theatre district, caught Lyle's attention. It featured several innovative ideas, including an auditorium that was wider and shallower than normal and a cantilevered balcony. These features permitted an unobstructed view of the stage from all vantage points. Lyle, whose main concern was to maximize the theatrical experience for the audiences and performers, modelled his plan for the Royal Alexandra on the Lyceum, 'as it brought a large percentage of the audience in close touch with the stage, both visually and orally,' making for an intimate connection between audience and performer.[6] Another priority for Lyle was better accommodation for performers, both in the size and number of dressing rooms, as well as accessories.

Lyle's design program for the Royal Alexandra is composed of three areas: the administration offices, the auditorium and the space for the performers, which includes the stage and dressing rooms. The symmetrically arranged ground-floor plan has its entrance on King Street. The box office, manager's room, men's smoking room, cloakroom and lavatory, and gallery entrance are on the right. The left side is a near mirror image, with the owner's room, ladies' waiting room, cloakroom and lavatory, and gallery exit. The main staircase foyer leads to the auditorium, which is comprised of main-floor seating with two balconies and gallery, with a seating capacity of 1,525.

Dirty Dancing
THE CLASSIC STORY ON STAGE
ROYAL ALEXANDRA THEATRE
JERSEY BOYS

Right: 2.15 Cantilevered and steep pitched balconies give the theatre an intimate feeling.

Opposite page: 2.16 Local Toronto artist Frederick Challener painted the decorative panel of Aphrodite discovering Adonis in the centre of the proscenium arch.

Opposite page: 2.17 First-floor stairwell with exotic fumed oak and Circassian walnut wood wall panelling leads to the upper balconies.

The balcony and gallery have separate staircases accessed from both sides of the foyer. Four box seats are arranged on either side of the stage, two on the main floor and two on the balcony level, and all are subdivided, creating eight separate boxes. The balcony patrons are also given a spacious foyer and tea room. To ensure unimpeded sightlines for the upper-gallery patrons, the floor is at a vertigo-inducing angle of fifty-five degrees. The stage, whose size was designed to accommodate touring shows supplied by the Schubert theatrical circuit, has twenty-eight movable sections, including one with a trap door. The dressing rooms are arranged in four tiers behind the stage and a fireproof wall. They have their own lavatories and wash-basins – rare conveniences for performers of the era.

Other concerns that influenced the design program of the theatre were around fireproofing and temperature regulation. Fireproofing was a priority: Toronto's worst fire had wiped out much of the downtown core just two years earlier, and a year before that, fire had gutted the Toronto Opera House. But even more devastating, a fire at the Iroquois Theatre in Chicago killed over 600 people in 1903. The shock that followed spurred amendments to most North American cities' fire codes for all theatres and public buildings. The Royal Alexandra was the first fireproof theatre in Canada, and its use of materials and fire exits exceeded all Toronto fire codes. Reviewing the building, the architectural magazine *Construction* noted that the Royal Alexandra was 'as thoroughly fireproof in every particular as modern invention will permit' and was 'constructed in accordance with the most stringent building regulations of the largest cities in America.'[7] Some of these unique fireproofing measures included an asbestos curtain that could seal off the stage area from the auditorium and a water spray system that was fed from a rooftop water tank large enough to extinguish any conflagration. In case of a fire or other emergency, the number and placement of fire escapes were such that even with a full house, the theatre 'could be emptied in two-and-a-half minutes.'[8] *Construction* reassured its readers that 'such a disaster as occurred at the Iroquois Theatre in Chicago, could not take place in this building.'[9]

The Royal Alexandra was also the first air-conditioned building in Canada. Its innovative ventilation system used fans located in the basement that drew air from large, ice-filled tanks in the summer and from two cast-iron boilers in the winter, forcing air into the auditorium through vents under the seats, while exhaust vents kept air circulating in the ceiling. This system kept the building at an even temperature of sixty-five degrees Fahrenheit, even during the dog days of summer. Air-cooling systems were a rarity in North America, with only Carnegie Hall and a few other New York buildings sporting similar schemes. Lyle patterned his design after one used at the Gaiety Theatre in London, England.

The Royal Alexandra Theatre is designed in the late French Renaissance or Louis XVI style, although more loosely interpreted on the interior. The facade, like the interior, is also divided into three sections. The ground-floor masonry is heavily channelled with a large glass marquee over the entrance (since replaced). The second-storey windows are recessed behind balustrades, framed between Ionic pilasters and dressed with festoons, cartouches and consoles. A mansard roof with three-bonnet dormers sits atop a dentillated cornice, and the theatre's name is inscribed on the parapet.

In addition to the building's elevation, Lyle custom-designed all of its interior details, including its fixtures, hardware, furniture and plasterwork. The theatre's interior was lavishly decorated, suiting its regal name, with the most expensive and exotic materials ever used in a public building in Toronto. These included Verde antique marble for the entrance walls, panels worked in fumed oak and Circassian walnut, and wall coverings of silk. Lyle attended to every detail in the theatre, including the colour scheme – he 'lived on the scaffolds for weeks on end and no colours could be put on without my sanction.'[10] There is a bold but sophisticated use of colour throughout the building, with the scheme of yellow and old gold for the auditorium, 'presenting a rich, cheerful and cozy appearance,' dusty rose and French grey for more intimate spaces, while the coffered plaster ceilings are in blues, reds and golds.[11]

THEATRE
CAPACITY
1497

Lyle had made many contacts during his tenure in New York and did not hesitate to bring in foreign talent when appropriate. During construction, one of the stage rooms was temporarily converted into a sculpture studio for Losty and Newman of New York City. Considered by Lyle 'the greatest architectural modelers in America,' they were responsible for all of the interior plasterwork mouldings of garlands and cartouches in both the auditorium and administrative areas.[12] The curtain was originally designed to open in the centre and to be let down from either side to close. Its lambrequin of embroidered cloth of gold in heavy relief was made by specialists Arnold & Constable, also of New York.

But Lyle did not confine himself to importing craftsmen. In fact, it was on the Royal Alexandra that he began his pattern of utilizing the best of local talent, as he did when he commissioned Toronto artist Frederick S. Challener to paint the decorative panel in the centre of the proscenium arch. The panel that overlooks the theatrical activity below is of Aphrodite discovering Adonis in a well-painted bright and vivid swirling Baroque style.

The success of what was essentially a speculative enterprise can be measured by its longevity. Since its opening on August 26, 1907, with a production of Mark Swann's *Top o' the World*, the theatre has been home to countless touring shows from England and the U.S., with some of the most distinguished names in theatre history gracing its stage. The theatre is now the centrepiece of Toronto's thriving entertainment district, which includes Arthur Erickson's Roy Thomson Hall, built in 1982, Peter Smith's Princess of Wales Theatre, constructed in 1993, and Jack Diamond's Four Seasons Centre for the Performing Arts, completed in 2006.

Churches: The Father, Son and Holy Smoke

The Reverend Samuel Lyle had financed his son's education at Cornell, Yale and the École des Beaux-Arts in Paris. He also continued to support John's architectural aspirations with a loan that helped him set up and run his first office in Toronto. As if that were not enough for this supportive father, Samuel Lyle was unexpectedly presented with another opportunity to help his son advance his career when his parish church, the Central Presbyterian in Hamilton, caught fire and was totally gutted in the summer of 1906. The Reverend convinced the congregation to purchase a new and larger site for the reconstruction of their church and to hire his son as the architect.

At the turn of the twentieth century, Canadian religious architecture still maintained the characteristics of the revival styles that had prevailed during the Victorian era. English Canada was dominated by the Gothic Revival style, with classical forms used occasionally, while in Quebec the styles were interchangeable depending on religious traditions and geographic location. In the United States, church design was also divided into two camps. The most influential and respected ecclesiastical architect in the United States was Ralph Adams Cram (1863–1942) of the firm Cram, Goodhue & Ferguson, the leading exponent of Gothic Revival. When constructing a church, Cram advised prospective architects to 'build in stone or brick; plan with rigid simplicity; design both the interior and the exterior with reserve, formality and self-control; have the mass simple, the composition equally so; imitate no form or detail of larger structures, but work for the dignity and the reverence that are theirs. Above all, let the spirit be that of the unchanging Church, the form alone that of the present day.'[13]

On the classical side were those architects who had trained at the École in Paris. Some of the best examples of their ecclesiastical approach include McKim, Mead & White's Congregational Church in Naugatuck, Connecticut, 1901–03, and Carrère & Hastings' First Church of Christ Scientist in New York City, 1904. Not surprisingly, Lyle's first ecclesiastical commission features a revival style similar to that of his New York colleagues, in what he described as 'Free Georgian.'[14] But Lyle was no slavish revivalist – he adjusted the historic forms and details to his contemporary needs. Central Presbyterian Church in Hamilton is constructed out of red brick with stone dressings, a minimally adorned projecting frontispiece with a portico entrance, surmounted by a

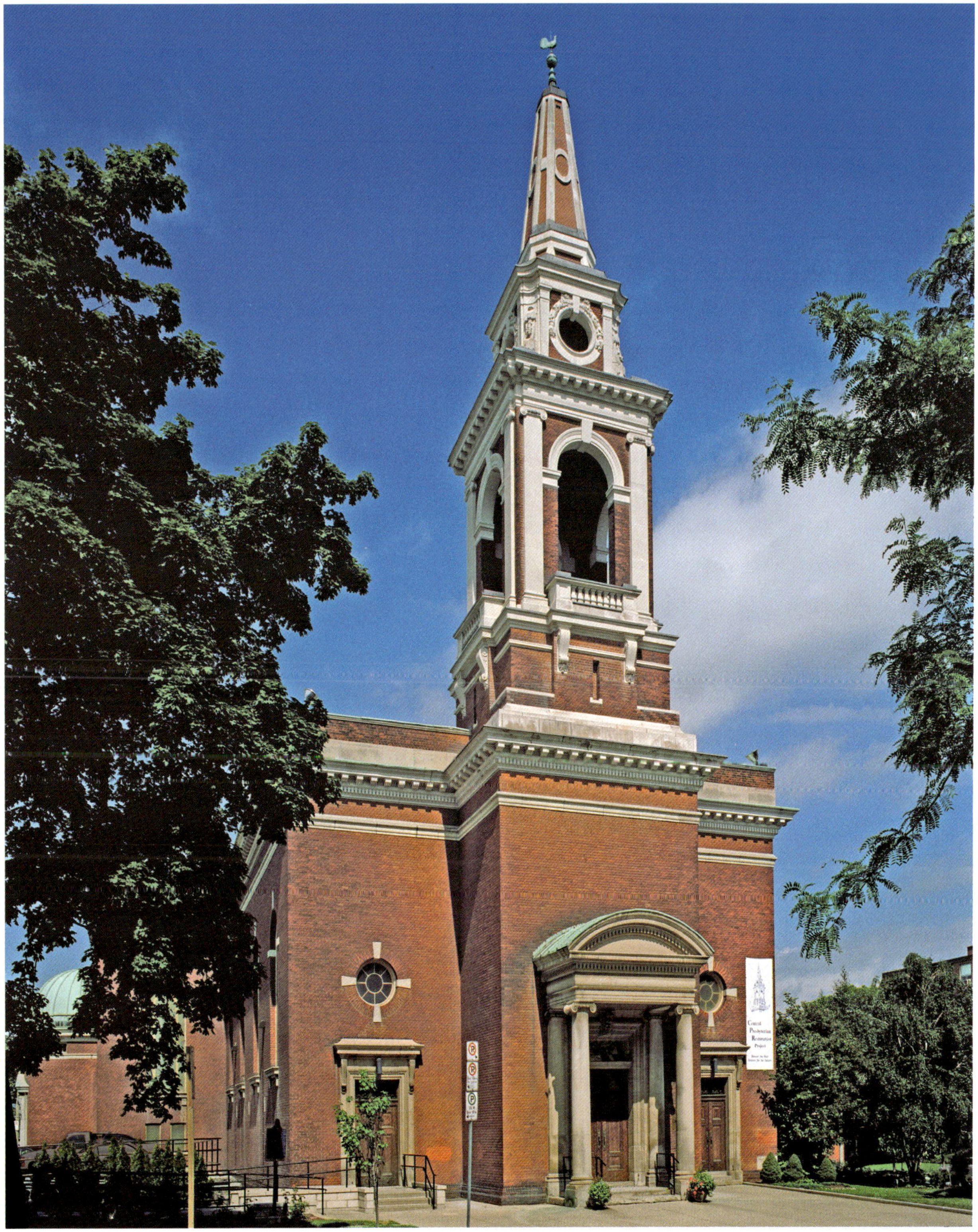

2.18, 2.19 Lyle modelled the Central Presbyterian Church in Hamilton (right) after McKim, Mead & White's Congregational Church in Naugatuck, Connecticut (above).

Above: 2.20 Wood-carved detail over the main interior door: Nec Tamen Consvmebatvr, *'Nevertheless, it is not consumed.'*

Right: 2.21 Interior of Central Presbyterian Church.

three-staged tower. The flanking bays both have additional entrances with bull's-eye window motifs above. Originally, the church had a dentillated cornice and open balustrade. This has been replaced with a simple brick parapet that conceals an unusual and contemporary feature of the building – its flat roof.

The well-preserved records of the construction of the church are the first and best example of correspondence between Lyle and the parties involved with the project and reveal much about the young architect. His businesslike manner and thoroughness is evident, he praises workers and contractors when the job has been good, and he is quick to point out and correct inaccurate or shoddy construction. A stickler for detail, Lyle ensured that clients received the quality of material and workmanship they had paid for and were entitled to, and that the schedule was strictly adhered to. If not, he made sure the offending parties faced financial consequences. The budget for the church's construction was significant – approximately $170,000 – and Lyle was keen to have the funds judiciously allocated so the church would serve as a lasting legacy for both himself and his father. In this regard he helped the building committee allocate the funds and encouraged them to spend money where it would show most, taking special care with the details. There was, for example, a $10,000 expense for an organ by the famous makers Casavant of Quebec, who Lyle designed special cabinets for. His original pew design was reconsidered and adjusted as a cost-cutting measure, but he was unwilling to compromise when it came to the quality of the stained glass. Contemporary American glass was more opalescent and considerably cheaper, but to Lyle 'it was out of spirit of the architectural period in which the church was designed,' and he rejected it in favour of the more expensive but appropriate antique English treatment.[15]

It was fortuitous that Lyle devoted so much energy and care to this work, as it turned out to be his representative ecclesiastical piece. The only other church commission Lyle produced was a more modest effort for the Presbyterian Church in Cheltenham, Ontario, in 1907.

Institutional: Revival and Penal Reform

Another of Lyle's 'Free Georgian' building designs was Pickering College in Newmarket, Ontario, of 1906. Originally located in the village of Pickering, the 1878 school that had served the Quaker community was destroyed by fire in 1905. The rival community of Newmarket petitioned the school's board to persuade it to relocate to their town, and sweetened the offer with financial inducements including free electricity and 'an all-night telephone service.'[16]

The building committee asked several architects to submit plans for the rebuilding project. They clearly approved of Lyle's original proposal, but it was a much grander structure than the one they ended up with. Lyle's plan was based on classical forms, with a large projecting frontispiece, end pavilions, a continuous open stonework parapet and a large central dome. Due to monetary restrictions, however, the design program was cut drastically, and many of Lyle's proposed elements were simplified or eliminated completely – including the dome. As a result, Lyle changed his stylistic approach, choosing a simple Georgian Revival. The school's elevation consists of the main administrative offices, located behind a projecting Corinthian, four-column portico with the classrooms arranged flanking in the wings. When the end pavilions from the original design were eliminated, Lyle enlivened the building's exterior red-brick facade with windows featuring white-brick accents for the keystones and caps. The portico windows were more elaborately embellished and capped with pediments. Strong horizontal banding counterbalances the window treatment with the use of a white-brick stringcourse on the ground floor, the first floor and the roofline cornice.

The 1909 Provincial Penitentiary for Ontario in Guelph was an important early commission for Lyle, not only for its prestige and financial rewards, but also because it represented a new type of prison being built in the country. William John Hanna, the Provincial Secretary and Registrar General whose responsibilities included the province's penal institutions, hired the architect to design the new prison, on the recommendation of Lyle's old family friend and commissioner of the province's

Hydro-Electric Power Commission, John Hendrie. Contemplating a major change in the type of prison to be built, Lyle was sent to inspect a number of different jails as well as industrial prison farms throughout the U.S. and to report his 'findings, together with a suggestion as to the type of prison that should be adopted.'[17] Lyle toured various institutions including Mansfield and Bridgewater in New York State, and Elmira and Cleveland in Ohio. The recommendations in his report called for an industrial prison farm facility with an elaborate program of about twenty buildings to house the institution's administration areas, prisoner cells, recreation, dining hall and medical treatment facilities, along with a number of outbuildings for the planned industrial and farm production.

The Guelph facility denoted a marked shift from the nineteenth-century penal concept of reform through religious penitence. The established Canadian incarceration practice had been based on the Auburn Prison in New York State, where prisoners were confined to common workrooms during the day and windowless cells for the night. Since 1834, starting with the Kingston Penitentiary in Ontario, the well-established plan in use in both federal and provincial jails consisted of an administration building housing offices and inmate services, in front of a cellblock containing cells of the Auburn type. The latter consisted of two rows of cells with back-to-back walls, separated by surveillance corridors located on the outside walls. In the new system, criminals were to be reformed through work – both in order to repay society, and to learn a trade or skill that would help integrate them back into the community. Another reason for the appeal for penal change was economic. At the time of Lyle's commission, the government was in charge of ten different health and penal institutions with an inmate population of over 9,000 people. A new government policy mandated that all goods consumed by public institutions in the province should be, if at all possible, produced at the Guelph facility and therefore cut the expenses of maintaining these institutions.

The working relationship between Lyle and Hanna was problematic from the onset and filled with tensions. Hanna was not the type of client who allowed the architect much freedom or engaged in discussion regarding design decisions. On several occasions he overturned Lyle's recommendations, which eventually led to an unworkable situation and his withdrawal from the project. The most critical issue they disagreed on was the architect's fee, which is usually calculated as a percentage of the building's cost, in this case five percent. However, the material usage and labour costs to construct the prison were for the most part to be supplied by the inmates themselves and therefore the building's actual cost was difficult to determine. In a letter to Hanna, Lyle optimistically proposed that he 'would leave the question of the total cost of the buildings, the amount on which my final Commission would be based – in the hands of the Government – trusting to their fairness in the adjustment of this final commission.'[18] This naiveté on Lyle's part meant the issue of appropriate compensation for his design dragged on for years and was played out in the media with numerous newspapers reporting on the events. The situation was not resolved until 1918 when the *Toronto Star* reported that Lyle was awarded a $49,000 fee based on an estimate of prison labour, which was calculated to be $175,000 over a five-year period, along with the material cost that was also factored in. This made the prison the largest facility owned and operated by the provincial government, with an overall price tag calculated at $1,200,000 – approximately the same construction expense as Toronto's Union Station and the Bloor-Danforth Viaduct.

Lyle and Hanna's relationship was equally contentious when it came to a number of the prison's design features, especially cell size and heating systems. Lyle's decisions were generally based on his research of similarly styled buildings. When he proposed a particular feature, it was a choice that was well thought through; however, Hanna, who had very strong opinions, often intervened and overturned the architect's recommendations. For example, Lyle had proposed a forced-air heating system for each cell, but Hanna changed the specifications to steam radiators placed in the corridors that he thought would be sufficient. He based his opinion on the assumption

Opposite page: 2.22 The front facade and main-entrance portico, Pickering College, Newmarket, Ontario.

2.23 Lyle proposed a new type of industrial prison farm facility for the Provincial Penitentiary for Ontario, Guelph.

Opposite page: 2.24 Interior corridor of the jail.

2
FIRE

2.25 The Toronto Stock Exchange on Bay Street in Toronto was the first project in Canada that Lyle won in an open competition.

that the interior doors would be left open because the 'prisoners are not at all the same desperate class that is to be found say in the Penitentiary at Kingston or in other prisons where men are serving long-term sentences and have, therefore, the motive always impelling them to break away.'[19] Lyle argued that, given the winter climate conditions and the proposed location of the cells on the outside walls, Hanna's proposal was not a suitable arrangement, but he was ignored. Time eventually proved him right when years later the authorities were compelled to correct the situation.

Having designed the temporary structures for the prison construction workers, as well as the permanent buildings, Lyle found the working relationship with Hanna untenable. Hanna had continued to question many of his design decisions and, over the objections of Lyle, he 'chose to use provincial staff for key design jobs, including the organization of the grounds, the design of a bridge (demolished) and the plans for houses, barns and stables.'[20] After 1915, Hanna had shifted much of the design responsibilities and construction supervision to James Govan, a former employee of Lyle's who had left the firm and established a working relationship with the provincial department after successfully designing the Whitby Psychiatric Hospital a few years earlier. According to historian Julie Harris, 'from that point onwards, the design of the Guelph Reformatory buildings was clearly in the hands of provincial staff and the planning of the grounds was shared by reformatory managers and staff of the Ontario Agricultural College at Guelph.'[21]

Because of this stormy relationship, the buildings do not have the stamp of Lyle's usual meticulous standards of design and use of material. Nevertheless they do show the architect's abilities in resolving a varied and complex plan. The building's plan was arranged with a clear axis. As in previous Canadian prisons, the administration building is located strategically in front of the cellblock, connected to it by means of a corridor that passes through the five-storey guard tower. The cellblock and dormitories are on an 'E'-shaped plan and the cellblock consists of three floors, each with thirteen individual cells and a corridor. The major break from prison convention in this jail was that the cells were aligned in a single row and, even more unusually, that they were located on the outside wall, allowing inmates direct access to light and air. At right angles to the cellblock are five wings for the dormitories. Three storeys in height, each dormitory could accommodate up to twenty-five inmates. A corridor connects these areas to the dining hall and kitchen facilities that are at a right angle to the dormitories, creating an enclosed exercise area. Access to the various shops and work areas was also from the dormitory wings. On the exterior, a prominent cornice tied the buildings together. The three-storey administration building and the five-storey guard tower rising behind it countered this horizontal massing. All were made of locally quarried materials, principally limestone. In keeping with the serious and sober purpose of the building, there are few decorative highlights, with the exception of the administration building whose main entrance is accentuated by voussoirs, a keystone of the Scales of Justice and a stone carving of the provincial coat-of-arms on the parapet wall.

The administration building was the first to be ready for use but it took several years for the facility to move into full operational mode. No sooner had it done so, however, then it was abruptly switched from an industrial prison farm to a military hospital to accommodate the casualties of World War I. It remained a hospital until November 8, 1920, and when it was reopened in 1921 it had changed its name and became known as the Ontario Reformatory. The building has gone through many additions over the years and served its original purpose until the turn of the millennium, when its use as a jail was finally abandoned. Its future status remains undecided.

Competitions and Competitors

The board of the Toronto Stock Exchange, wishing to keep up with other North American financial exchanges such as Montreal and New York, whose new buildings were designed by American architect George B. Post, held an open competition to replace its aging facility. This was Lyle's first successful attempt at an architectural competition in Canada.

Top left: 2.26 Competition entry for the Department and Court Buildings, Ottawa.

Bottom left: 2.27 Three views of Lyle's neo-classical competition entry for Government House, Toronto.

Bottom right: 2.28 Unexecuted proposal for a hotel project in Toronto.

Above: 2.29 Competition entry for the Memorial Tower, Halifax.

2.30 Unexecuted proposal for International Petroleum Company, Toronto.

Opposite page: 2.31 A Masonic temple proposal originally planned for Bloor Street and Spadina Avenue, Toronto.

Many architects resented open competitions because there was little value placed on their efforts and no compensation for the time, expense and intellectual and creative work that went into preparing a proposal. The firms or individuals that entered competitions therefore were usually young and up-and-coming, hoping to land a high-profile job that would launch their careers. More established architects would occasionally participate as assessors in competitions but would often encourage juniors within their offices to submit proposals. For the organizations running the competition, the objectives were twofold: to be able to choose from a wide selection a design that best matched their visual, aesthetic and financial needs, and to gain publicity from the event.

Lyle's thoughts on competitions were that as 'they are now conducted in Canada, they are very unsatisfactory.'[22] He felt that the adjudicators insisted on too many drawings, especially basement and roof plans that, while having no bearing on the submission's *parti*, meant extra work for the architect. Another concern was the wording of the programs. Lyle thought the instructions were so specific that they precluded any variation or creative interpretation, 'thereby defeating one of the primary objects of the competition.'[23] In the period journals, opinions were equally divided on the pros and cons of competitions. An editorial in *Canadian Architect and Builder* summarized it best: 'In every competition there can be but one man made happy, all the others being more or less convinced that injustice has been done them, and, so long as human nature remains imperfect, competitions, in whatever line they may be, can never bring unmixed joy to all competitors. It has been argued that select competition is but a trifle better than direct selection, and that limited local competition savors of trades unionism. This, it is said, ensures mediocrity will be the order of the day, and that paid competition tends toward creating an aristocracy in the profession. This result scarcely follows. There are competitions and competitors.'[24]

Lyle had been hardened to the process by his years in New York and the many competitions he had entered there and 'always bore in mind the experience of Carrère & Hastings, who were in thirty competitions before winning one.'[25] But Lyle's experience was little better than that of Carrère & Hastings. Although he won the very first competition he entered, for a pair of bandshells at the Buffalo exposition in 1901, it would be ten years before he won another – for the Toronto Stock Exchange. Undeterred, Lyle entered most of the major competitions in pre-war Canada and his success rate was on par with other prominent architects.

In 1911, the Toronto Stock Exchange purchased the site for their new building from Sir Henry Pellatt, who undoubtedly funnelled the money into financing the ongoing construction of his residence, Casa Loma. Local architect F. S. Baker was the architectural assessor on the competition and Lyle's proposal, calling for a modest structure on Bay Street, in the heart of the city's financial district, was the winner. Shortly after the competition, however, a building adjoining the site became available, and the Exchange's Board of Directors quickly purchased it. Not wishing to have another design competition nor having the budget to tear down and rebuild on this site too, the executive board simply decided to tear off the facade of the adjoining building and alter Lyle's winning design, extending it across the face of the two structures. As Lyle remarked, 'It was a tough job, as it meant a new facade across the whole frontage and behind a marriage with the old Fisher Bldg. on the left. I tried my best to persuade the Directors of the Exchange to take down the old Fisher Bldg., but without success.'[26] The new facade doubled in size and ran across the complete frontage. This marriage presented several design challenges for Lyle; the original plan had to be radically adjusted to accommodate the new conditions and the different floor levels had to be tied together. On the exterior, to create a unified frontage, a larger parapet was required to mask the upper storeys of the Fisher Building. This was an important commission for Lyle, and one in which he continued to provide his services for alterations and renovations until the building was eventually replaced with George and Moorhouse with Samuel Maw's 1936–37 Stock Exchange building.

MASONIC · TEMPLE

Other prominent competitions Lyle entered were the federal government's Department of Justice buildings, Ottawa, in 1907, in which he placed sixth, and the Department of Public Works of Ontario for the proposed new Government House, Toronto, in 1909. This latter competition had some unexpected results. Although George W. King and George W. Gouinlock were the top winners, with Lyle's plans coming in third, the competition's assessor, Francis R. Heakes, Ontario's chief architect, decided to put a stop to the competition. Setting aside all the entries under the pretext they were too expensive, he proceeded to redesign the structure himself, using parts of King's elevations combined with Lyle's floor plan, and dressed in a chateaux style complete with spiked turrets. Ironically, by the time the project was completed, it ended up costing the provincial taxpayers over $1 million – almost five times the sum allotted the competition entries.

In terms of competitions, 1910 was a very unsuccessful year for Lyle. He placed second in the competition for a Carnegie Library in Hamilton, third for the Royal Architectural Institute of Canada's Memorial Tower in Halifax and fourth for Knox College at the University of Toronto. Two other pre-war competitions Lyle entered were for the Canadian government's Department and Court buildings on Wellington Street, Ottawa, in 1913, and a year later for the Masonic Temple near Bloor and Spadina in Toronto. Lyle did not even place in the first competition and placed second behind H. P. Knowles of New York in the latter. However, he did not lose out on much, because both projects were halted with the outbreak of World War I.

Although competitions were a necessary fact of life for most architects, their preferred way of working was through proposals. Commissioning architects to prepare a set of plans for a project ensured that even if the project didn't proceed, at least the architect would receive remuneration for his time and talents as well as a set of beautifully rendered perspective drawings for his portfolio. One of Lyle's first such proposals in the city was for the Caven Memorial Library for Knox College at the University of Toronto in 1905. Although a local newspaper reported that the college's building committee had accepted Lyle's plans, nothing came of the project, perhaps because the college's location at the head of Spadina Circle was ill-suited for expansion.

Lyle had by this time built a fair number of projects and a variety of building types. His first attempts at high-rise structures were his proposals for the International Petroleum Company and a hotel building for Lawrence Solman, one of the partners and manager of the Royal Alexandra Theatre in Toronto. In both proposals Lyle shows a competent handling and thorough understanding of the then-current approach to tall buildings, an approach that had been advanced by American architect Louis Sullivan in 1896 and had since become established practice. In an article entitled 'The Tall Office Building Artistically Considered,' Sullivan had given the high-rise an 'inherent' tripartite form, with lower levels consisting of entrance, showrooms and mezzanine offices, middle levels of repetitive office floors and a top that contained the mechanical rooms. This approach to high-rise design was widely used in New York and Chicago and for Toronto's few skyscrapers.

Homogeneous Units

If there was a weakness in the École des Beaux-Arts curriculum, it was that by placing so much emphasis on the design of monumental public buildings there was little time left over for domestic residential projects – the grand formal styles used for public buildings were not always appropriate for the intimate setting of the domestic home. Montreal architect William S. Maxwell noted this deficiency, saying the French work was 'not up to the standard which we demand, and the French admit that the English and American work is superior.' He identified the problem as being not only the result of their educational system, but of lifestyle: 'our superiority is due to the place which the home occupies in the life of the Anglo-Saxon. Our pleasures and social life in reality revolve around the home. The great number of houses put up in later years has evolved a standard of excellence – which we strive to maintain.

Frenchmen who have lived in this country are enthusiastic over our small houses and their many conveniences. That the graduate of the École can do good domestic work is proven in American practice.'[27]

In Canada, residential buildings were dominated by both British and American stylistic influences. The prevailing attitudes toward domestic architecture in the U.S. was summarized in 'Artistic Conditions: Traditions and Tendencies of Styles' in the periodical *Architectural Record*. It described the stylistic residential environment, which retained many of the elements of nineteenth-century eclecticism: 'As architects strive for a more modern and personal style they should choose a historical model, either romantic or formal based on its associations and appropriateness.'[28] Architects were free to choose between 'historic styles, combinations of elements of different styles, fresh compositions with elements of one style, or the production of a literal historic example.'[29] The range of sources that were acceptable for American architects to work in included the Renaissance, Italian, English, Colonial and, to a lesser degree, French and, in warmer southern regions, Spanish. The Tudor style as seen through the eyes of contemporary English architects Edwin Lutyens and Charles F. A. Voysey were also deemed suitable.

The dominant British influence was the Arts and Crafts Movement, a product of the late Victorian Era. More of an ideology than a stylistic movement, its principal exponents were William Morris and Phillip Webb, who actively promoted and worked toward a closer alliance between architect and craft. The movement's principles were loosely based on architectural writer John Ruskin's musings on 'truth' in design and the use of materials, advocated in his various publications, including *The Stones of Venice*, from 1851. Ruskin posited that a building's design must be suitable for the purpose for which it was intended, and its decorative program was to use handcrafted objects. This combination of traditional craftsmanship that paid homage to historic processes and materials, along with the old British domestic building forms, came to be known as the English Domestic Revival. The three leading architects of this style in Canada were the prolific Eden Smith in Toronto, the academic Percy Nobbs, who in 1903 became the head of McGill University School of Architecture in Montreal, and on the west coast, the consummate designer Samuel Maclure.

When developing a residential plan, there were certain elementary axioms most architects followed – primarily the relationship of aspect to prospect, and simplicity to economy. Aspect, the amount of natural light each room receives for every season, based on the room's orientation, could be calculated using a device designed by Robert Kerr called the aspect compass. While studying the problem of aspect, the 'thoughtful architect will be fully alive to the advantages and possibilities of prospect,' the placement and orientation of rooms to take full advantage of the available light.[30] In a period article on house design, Grant Helliwell considered that the most important rule for architects to follow was that of simplicity. It was considered 'an unerring test of excellence' because it was reasoned that a 'plan may be simple without being good, but it is not too much to assert that no plan can be good without being simple.'[31]

Lyle's approach to residential design was not radically different from his contemporaries' and showed a competent knowledge and handling of the vocabulary. He liked to use a romantic style based on old French sources, which was similar to the Tudor style, in being half-timbered and stucco-based, but using a more compact massing with a quieter silhouette, bellcast roofs punctuated with attic dormers and large chimney stacks. Lyle's designs for a Stucco House (not constructed) that was shown at the Ontario Association of Architects' 1910 exhibition in Toronto illustrates a sensitive handling of the Arts and Crafts aesthetic and pays homage to Voysey's work. For the more formal styles, Lyle, like his American counterparts, looked to Colonial or French Louis XVI sources for inspiration.

Where Lyle distinguished himself from his Canadian contemporaries was in the care with which he approached the residential plan. As could be expected from one with Beaux-Arts

Top: 2.32 William Hendrie residence, Aberdeen Avenue, Hamilton.

Above: 2.33 George L. Robinson residence, Beaumont Road, Toronto.

Right: *2.34 Unexecuted design for a Stucco House.*

Below: *2.35 Samuel Lyle residence, Glenfern Avenue, Hamilton.*

training, his first concern was with the 'plan and the practical working side of the home, the second with the aesthetic and decorative side, and the third with the floor coverings, window hangings and furniture.'[32] In developing a plan, Lyle would carefully study the relationships of the different rooms and floors to each other. He considered the essential elements of a successful plan to be 'simplicity and ease of circulation,' and was always mindful of the proper orientation of rooms to take full advantage of sun exposure and views. In devising circulation patterns for his ground-floor plans, he tried to include generously proportioned front hallways that were strategically placed to ensure easy access to the kitchen, dining and living rooms. His dining rooms were usually self-contained to ensure intimacy and privacy for the ceremony of eating; they adjoined the kitchen or pantry for ease of setting and clearing the table, and were orientated to an eastern or southern exposure to get the morning sun. His living rooms' focal point was always the fireplace; Lyle wrote, 'great care should be given to the placing and design of this feature, as it is actually the hearth of the home.'[33] Generally Lyle strove for a grand, bright and spacious interior effect. This meant larger and fewer rooms with correspondingly bigger windows, and more glass area per room, as well as doing away with smaller dens, libraries or sun porches. Lyle kept his roofline simple so as not to have the second-storey bedrooms' interiors cut up by gables or sloping rooflines that would create odd interior wall spaces and make the placement of bedroom furniture more difficult.

Working toward making the house a 'homogeneous unit,' Lyle would try, when budget permitted, to model his work after that of Scottish eighteenth-century architectural firm the Adam Brothers. He admired the firm's all-encompassing approach to designing a client's house that included every detail of the interior furnishings. Lyle would consult with his clients and develop colour schemes for each room, select

furniture and on occasion design the principal pieces. For these tasks, he thought it was essential for the architect to have 'a knowledge of historical styles...together with a sense of scale and appropriateness.'[34]

Lyle designed several romantic-styled houses based on French themes. The vernacular rural French architecture was so deeply engrained in him that during a trip to France in 1929, he wrote that he could have 'studied with profit the great variety in the simple farmhouses that lined the roadway. It is an architecture that has for us in Canada a great appeal, as it is northern, as it is simple, and as it is linked to Canada through ties of French Quebec.'[35] An example of this style was Lyle's first job in the country, a residence for his old family friend, the prominent industrialist William Hendrie, on Aberdeen Avenue, Hamilton, in 1905. The style of the building was based on picturesque themes of 'French farm house sources, together with a romantic simplicity.'[36] Another Hamilton residence based on these themes was for his parents on Glenfern Avenue in 1908. Here Lyle designed a large, red-brick two-storey-plus-attic house, a short walking distance from his father's Central Presbyterian Church. The prominent feature of the house is the street facade, whose projecting two-storey bay terminates at the attic, surmounted by a symbolic round pinnacle at the apex of the gable end. The plan was very simple, with generously proportioned interior rooms consisting of kitchen, dining and living rooms on the ground floor, and bedrooms on the second and attic storey.

Both in terms of its size and location, the John M. Lyle residence that the young architect designed and built for himself on Avondale Road, Toronto, in 1908 was an extremely ambitious and optimistic undertaking. The house is a good illustration of how Lyle's Beaux-Arts training influenced his design. The lot was in Rosedale, one of the most fashionable and expensive neighbourhoods in the city, and situated on a downward-sloping, tree-filled ravine, which presented many design challenges. The drops in elevation of the site, from the back lot line to the street, dictated the plan; because the kitchen had to be easily accessed from the rear service lane, its placement drove the design program. Locating the kitchen at the back, or south side, of the building on the ground floor meant the only available option for the principal entrance into the house was through the rather unusual feature of a side basement doorway served by a pathway from the street. In other respects the plan is compact and meticulously arranged, with the ground floor consisting of three separate modules, each with its own function. These were composed of the kitchen, including two stairways and a pantry, the dining room and a rectangular living room that, if divided in half, would produce two squares. These small, square modules, when viewed as a whole, construct a building with an almost square footprint.

Left: 2.36 Col. J. B. MacLean residence, Wells Hill Road, Toronto.

Top: 2.37 J. Coulson residence, Rosedale Road, Toronto.

Above: 2.38 Sir William Mulock, sunroom, Jarvis Street, Toronto.

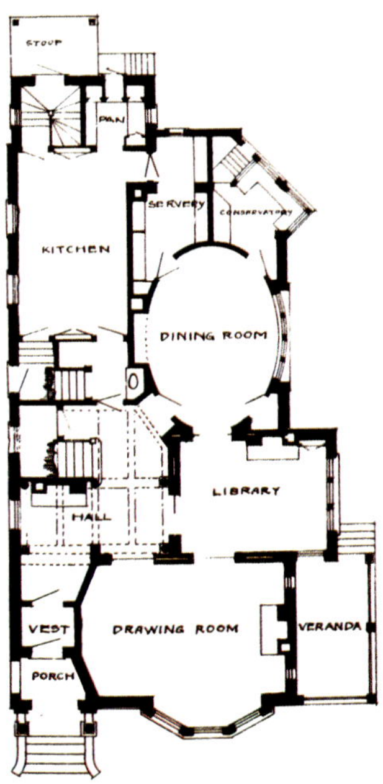

2.39, 2.40 George W. Gouinlock residence, Walmer Road, Toronto, and first-floor plan.

Lyle preferred simple room forms, usually squares and rectangles, and avoided intrusions into the wall surfaces such as columns, stairways or large chimneys, or even bay windows or niches. But to allow as much available light as possible into the principal interior rooms of his own residence, which was north-facing, he introduced a pair of symmetrically placed two-storey semi-octagonal bay windows. The style of the house, in Lyle's preferred simplified French-inspired Tudor, was dictated by the plan and the picturesque site. The street facade is dominated by the pair of half-timbered stucco bays and the steep, bellcast roofline with two tall, picturesque chimneystacks.

The uniqueness of Lyle's approach is more clearly illustrated when his Avondale plans are compared to that of fellow architect George W. Gouinlock's residence on Walmer Road in Toronto, constructed the same year. Gouinlock was born and educated in Paris, Ontario, and received his architectural training as an apprentice to various firms in Hamilton and Winnipeg. Returning to Ontario, he practiced independently until he was hired as the principal architect for the Canadian National Exhibition, and designed many of its buildings. Gouinlock's plan for his own residence was comparable to what was being produced by other, like-trained architects. Both designs were similar in their use of a romantic style for the exterior, but Gouinlock's residence had a very busy plan with many small and odd-shaped rooms. He seems to have been more concerned with the picturesque exterior massing created by these rooms than with an economical or efficient interior, a fact that becomes more obvious when his design is compared to Lyle's simple, compact, modular arrangement.

Lyle's other romantically styled houses of this period include the George L. Robinson residence on Beaumont Road in Toronto of 1909, and the Hugh Stevens residence on St. Clair Avenue East in Toronto, circa 1909. Most of his formal designs of this period, however, were Georgian, such as the Toronto residences for Col. J. B. MacLean and J. Coulson, with one notable exception. This was not a full residence but an addition of a conservatory and sunroom on the residence of Sir William Mulock on Jarvis Street, Toronto, in 1909. These rooms were added to the south side of the house, which was originally designed in 1888 by William G. Storm, with extensive alterations added over the years. The conservatory surrounded the sunroom on three sides, so that even in the dead of winter, greenery and blooms could be seen from its windows. The sunroom was illuminated by means of a skylight in the deep barrel-vault ceiling that was embellished with bull's-eye-motif windows and elaborate plasterwork surrounds. Prominently featured below these items was the fireplace mantel, by which Lyle indicated that this was to be the new hearth and social gathering place for the family. A pair of French doors led to the conservatory. The style Lyle chose was based on a free interpretation of the late French Renaissance, and its unifying reed-design motif, which consisted of a fan pattern, was echoed in the room's furniture, marble floor and plasterwork. This was Lyle's only project of this period that had a sufficient budget to permit him to design the furniture as well and complete the 'homogeneous unit' he strove for.

Monument: Grand Heights

A royal visit by the newly appointed Governor General of Canada, the Duke of Connaught, to Toronto in 1911 gave Lyle the opportunity for what he considered one of his 'outstanding achievements.'[37] The highlight of the royal visit to the city was to be a massive ball at the Armouries on University Avenue, hosted by the Royal Canadian Yacht Club (an organization Lyle belonged to and for whose Toronto Island clubhouse he was to design an addition the following year). The Armouries was the only building in the city large enough to accommodate the expected crowds, but its atmosphere was not exactly festive. Lyle was entrusted with the responsibility of converting the building's austere and utilitarian interior into something befitting royal patronage. The event required a dining room, reception area, dance floor, dressing booths, serving accommodations, washrooms and a temporary heating system, all to be delivered on a limited budget and in eight days.

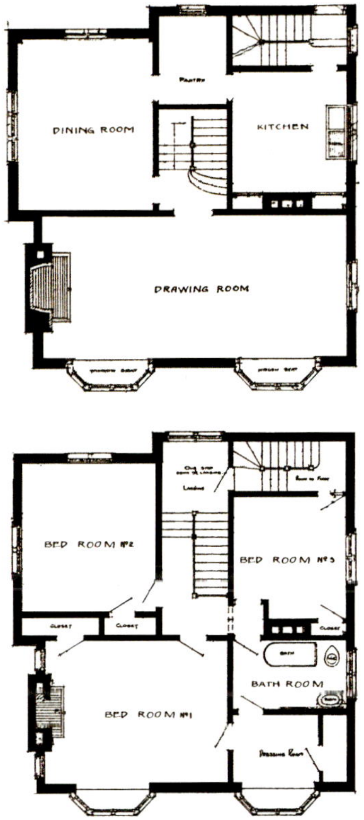

2.41, 2.42 John M. Lyle residence, Avondale Road, Toronto, and first- and second-floor plans.

Lyle approached this challenge as he would any purely architectural problem – by starting with the plan. He systematically divided the hall into three sections, consisting of the reception area in the middle, and the dance floor and dining rooms on either end of the building. The reception area was more formal, so he kept the full ceiling height of fifty feet and used fabric in the royal colours. For the dance floor, a lighting system with draped fabric gave a festive mood, and to give more intimacy to the dining areas he used large marquee tents, with the walls banked in smilax (a climbing plant) and a model of a large harvest moon suspended from the ceiling. All around the building Lyle gathered, pulled and draped yards of fabric over the ceiling trusses and barren walls in the Yacht Club colours of blue and gold.

Meeting the challenging deadline by coordinating all the materials and resources and using an army of people all working toward a common goal must have been an exciting experience for Lyle – not unlike the excitement of his student days at the École with an *atelier en charette*. To top it all off, his efforts did not go unnoticed or unappreciated; during the ball the Duchess sought him out and requested a grand tour of the building. She was so overwhelmed by the beauty of the space that she commented that she had 'never in my life seen anything like this. It reminds me of Russia, the vast scale and grand heights.'[38]

A Head, a Heart and a Pulse to Toronto

Lyle's interest in urban planning and beautifying Toronto was made evident within weeks of his arrival in the city. In winter 1905, he wrote to a local newspaper, commenting on the quality of the drawings of proposed changes to the squares and bridge terminals of New York City by the architect Henry Hornbostel at the galleries of the Ontario Society of Artists. Lyle expressed his views by writing, '[T]hat Toronto is destined to become a city of worldwide importance is conceded on all sides, and now that there are so many projected public improvements the time seems indicated for great efforts to be made to draw up a scheme for the present and future beautifying of the city.'[39]

Undoubtedly moved by Lyle's enthusiasm for urban planning, Sir John Willison, editor of the *Toronto News*, asked him to write a series of articles on civic improvement for his newspaper. The issues and possibilities of urban planning that Lyle and other architects were reacting to were sparked by the events at the 1893 World's Columbian Exposition. This exhibition was primarily known for its impressive buildings, but the site plan by landscape architect Frederick Law Olmsted was to exert as much influence as the architecture. The beautifully conceived grounds created public awareness of the possibilities for urban planning and landscape design to combat the chaotic sprawl that was plaguing most North American centres. Olmsted was one of the first to enunciate the principles of the City Beautiful Movement, which evolved out of the desire to make urban centres cleaner and healthier places to live and work through a sense of order in both architecture and landscape. The movement had an 'enormous impact on American and Canadian urban planning for the next generation.'[40]

Under Olmsted's influence, many American cities began to beautify their own communities. In 1901, Washington, D.C., engaged Daniel Burnham, Charles McKim and Frederick Olmsted, Jr., to study its park system, and in New York, Julius Harder proposed an urban scheme in 1905. Working independently, Burnham was also involved in preparing plans for San Francisco, Cleveland and later Chicago, with designs that included diagonal roadways cutting through the usual urban grid pattern, as well as civic squares and parkways.

In Toronto, whose population had doubled between 1900 and 1912, concerned planning advocates attempted to guide and control the nature of development and to beautify the city. Spearheaded by architects, businessmen, lawyers and politicians, three groups worked to achieve these goals: the Guild of Civic Art (later the Civic Guild), the Ontario Association of Architects and the Toronto Architectural Eighteen Club. These organizations hosted lectures and wrote articles promoting the themes – being put forward in various American cities – of urban planning, land-use segregation and a reworking of the city's grid pattern with diagonal avenues.

At the 1906 Ontario Association of Architects convention, William A. Langton, a member of the Civic Guild and editor of *Canadian Architect and Builder,* recommended the development of a radial road system similar to those proposed for Washington and Chicago. His report was well-received within the architectural community, but Mayor Emerson Coatsworth was less enthusiastic, commenting that as far politicians and ratepayers were concerned, the impending sewage system held a higher priority. Bloodied but not beaten by the lack of political support for its scheme, the Civic Guild continued to refine its plan. In 1907, the guild received a small grant from the city to hire British architect Sir Aston Webb, who had worked on the Mall approach to Buckingham Palace, and an accompanying draftsman to help with its quest.

Despite the raised expectations about the infusion of such a high-profile architect into the project, little was accomplished, and the Civic Guild's revised report of 1908 contained minimal changes. A year later, however, having received further research from members of the planning committee who had visited a few American cities, including Washington, Philadelphia and Baltimore, the guild finally produced an impressive brochure outlining its hopes and aspirations for Toronto. Arguing that Civic Improvement and City Planning were the remedies for the evils of congestion, the guild noted that 'thirty-nine American cities are now adopting, to a greater or lesser degree, a systematic plan for future development.' It bolstered its case by pointing out that the other cities' proposals were similar to the guild's, in that they all called for 'wide continuous business thoroughfares, parks, parkways, playgrounds, aquatic sports, pure water, sanitary sewage disposal, rapid transit, clean streets, underground wires, curtailment of sign and noise nuisances, building laws for structural, sanitary and fire safety and tenement laws to restrict the congestion of population.'[41]

Following continuous lobbying by the Civic Guild, the mayor and city council created a new body in 1909 to 'prepare a comprehensive plan for the improvement of the City,' and so the Civic Improvement Committee was born. It had many

Top: 2.43 Plan for improvements to Toronto, supplement to Canadian Architect and Builder, *February 1906.*

Bottom: 2.44 Plan showing the changes proposed by the Civic Improvement Committee, 1911.

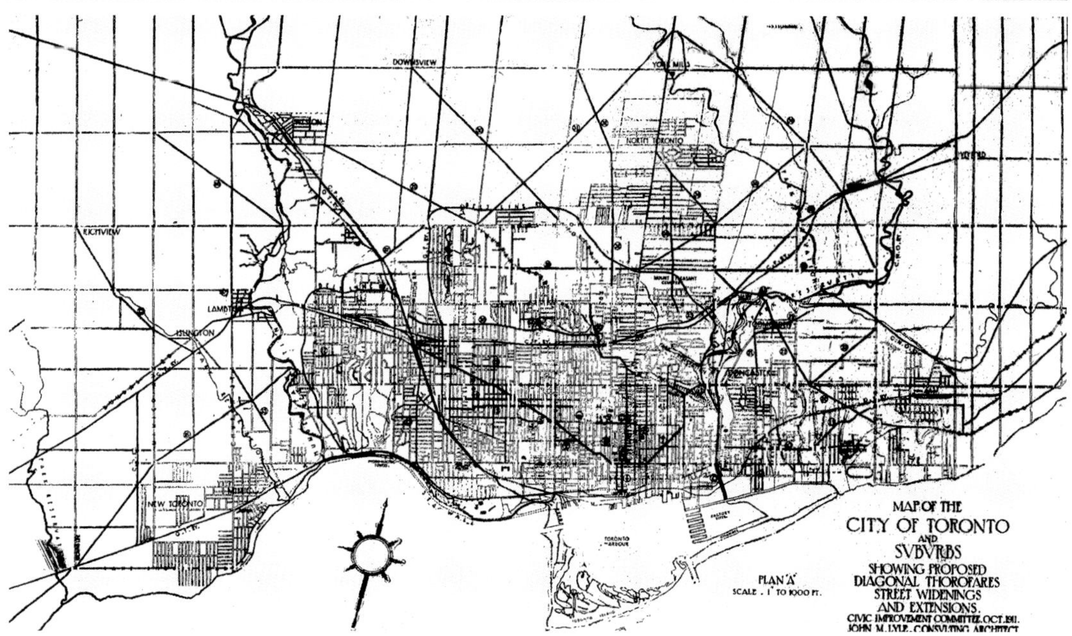

of the same members as the Civic Guild, but arranged itself into four sub-committees that included Lyle and fellow architect Edmund Burke.[42] Lyle was also appointed as their consulting architect and was 'given a room in the tower of the City Hall, in which to prepare our drawings.'[43] This appointment was a mixed blessing for Lyle, as it put him in a potentially compromising position. As a member of the committee as well as its architect, he might have found himself in situations where he would have to sit in judgment of his own work. To resolve the issue, Lyle resigned as committee member and was rehired as the Civic Improvement Committee's architect for a salary of $1,000 per year, plus a stipend of $25 per week for a draftsman.

In 1911, the Civic Improvement Committee presented its findings to the City Council with over forty recommendations. These included many of the same elements as earlier proposals, along with a design for the Bloor-Danforth Viaduct, although not the one finally approved by electors in 1913. The most interesting recommendation, and the one that created the most excitement, was a majestic boulevard called Federal Avenue, to be situated between Bay and York streets, beginning at Union Station, which would serve as a portal into the city, and terminating at an imposing Civic Centre to be located where Nathan Phillips Square now stands. In the plan, grand Beaux-Arts classical buildings lined both sides of the boulevard, a Toronto equivalent to Chicago's White City. It also called for public gardens behind the proposed legislative buildings and a military parade ground next to the then-existing armouries on University Avenue. In Lyle's words, if followed, the plan would 'give a splendid setting for our public buildings; give open spaces and plaza for public demonstrations; eliminate slum conditions now existing in St. Johns Ward; relieve the downtown congestion; give a fine new business street to the city – in short, a head, a heart, and a pulse to Toronto.'[44]

The Federal Avenue scheme was the largest proposal by the Civic Improvement Committee, the majority of recommendations being more modest and practical, including street widening at several major intersections, some of which were implemented. One large project Toronto's politicians could not ignore, however, was the proposal for a Bloor-Danforth Viaduct. There had been, for some time, a grassroots movement of local east-end business interests and commuters to connect Bloor Street and Danforth Avenue, which were separated by the Rosedale Ravine and the Don Valley. By 1910, the newspapers were heavily promoting a scheme to join these streets with a viaduct, while the city's engineering department pushed for a steel bridge that would span from Sherbourne Street in the west to Broadview Street in the east, in one continuous straight line. This scheme would have transversed over and ignored the natural beauty of the Rosedale Ravine and the Don Valley, and cut through the existing residential community.

The Civic Guild opposed the plan and prepared an alternative proposal, which consisted of Lyle's plans. These plans called for a continuance of Bloor Street eastward, along a land-filled terrace section overlooking the Rosedale Ravine, as well as two bridges. One bridge would start at the head of Parliament Street, span the ravine and continue through to Castle Frank Crescent. The other would cross the Don Valley and connect into Danforth Avenue. Lyle presented these plans to City Council at a meeting heavily attended by the supporters of the straight-bridge proposal. As Lyle noted, 'It was quite evident that the proponents of the straight viaduct down the centre of the ravine would ask for an early vote and an adoption of their plan.'[45] After listening to the arguments in favour of the straight viaduct, however, the mayor allowed Lyle to explain his scheme to council and show his drawings. Convinced by Lyle's arguments, the mayor decreed that there should be further study of the problem, appointing a committee to examine the proposed schemes and report to City Hall in a year. This Special Committee included local politicians as well as architects Edmund Burke and Lyle, as a result of which, Lyle spent 'the whole of one autumn and winter tramping through the different areas affected along the Rosedale Ravine.'[46]

The following year, at a special meeting, thirteen different plans were submitted and each proponent was given fifteen

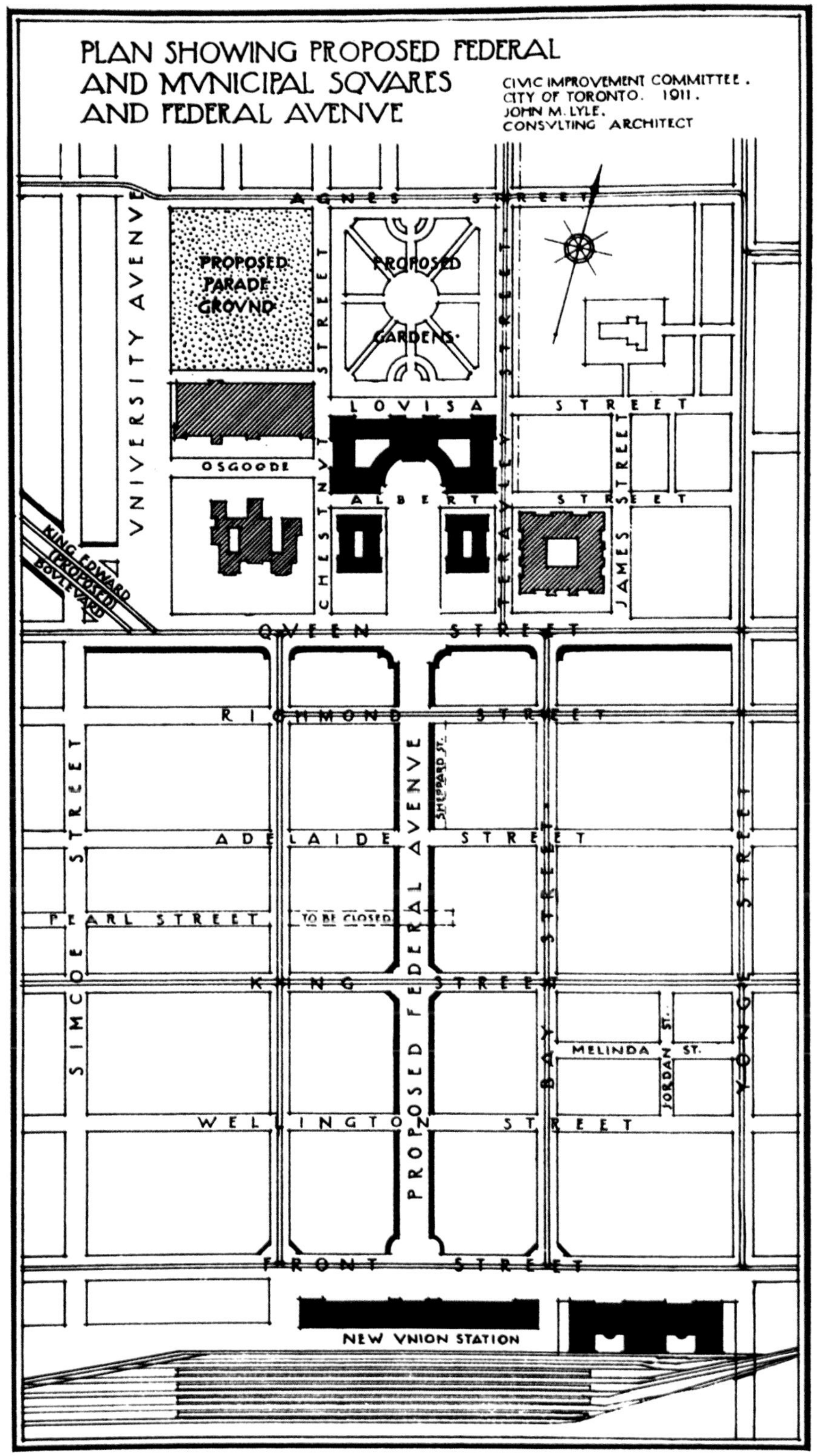

2.45 Civic Improvement Committee, Plan Showing Proposed Federal and Municipal Squares and Federal Avenue, Toronto, 1911.

minutes to present his scheme. After he presented, Lyle 'sat down and prepared to hear a lot of objections. To my astonishment Billy McLean [editor of the *Toronto World* newspaper] got up and said that Mr. Lyle had given nine reasons why he considered his scheme the best route to be adopted and that while he himself had always been in favour of the straight viaduct, he would withdraw this support and stand behind Mr. Lyle's scheme. I cannot remember what else happened at the luncheon, but from our point of view it was a great success.'[47]

Although he determined the layout of the roads, terraces and bridges for the viaduct, and along with two other firms, produced a design for the Bloor-Danforth Viaduct bridge, Lyle was not selected as the bridge's architect. The reasons may have been political, as the design responsibilities were given to Edmund Burke, who worked with the City Engineer's office as an architectural consultant for bridges. Construction began in 1915, progressed rapidly and was completed by 1917. Lyle was extremely pleased with his planning scheme and the completed project, with one exception. His original plans had called for terraced and landscaped areas along the north of Bloor Street from Sherbourne to Parliament, overlooking the ravine. These areas, suitable for bandstands and public promenades, similar to Dufferin Terrace in Quebec City, were not, to his regret, included.

Lyle's only other opportunity for an urban planning scheme was an unexecuted proposed town plan in 1911 for Iroquois Falls, one of the emerging communities developing along a new line of the Temiskaming and Northern Ontario Railway.

Few of the grand schemes proposed for North American cities by various Civic Improvement Guilds came to fruition. In Canada, major schemes proposed for Montreal, Ottawa and

2.46 Don Valley, looking north from around Gerrard Street toward Castle Frank, Toronto, c. 1910.

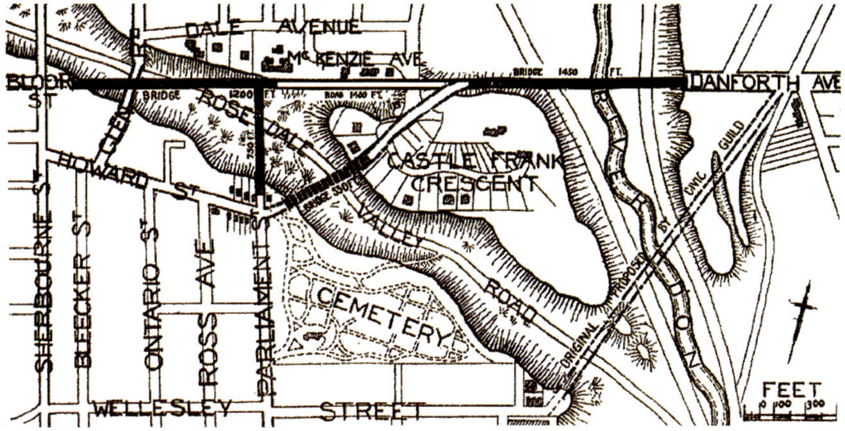

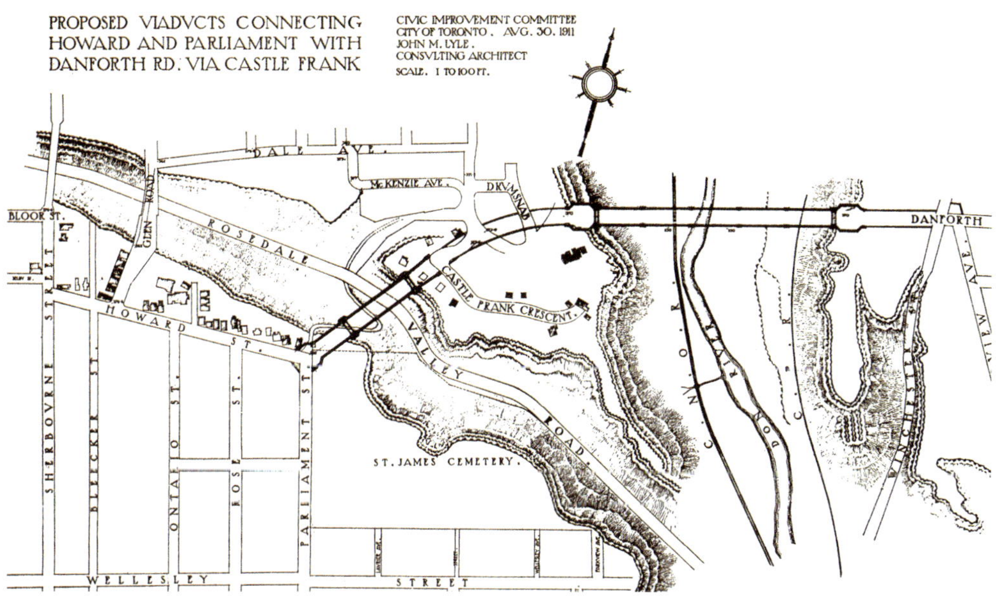

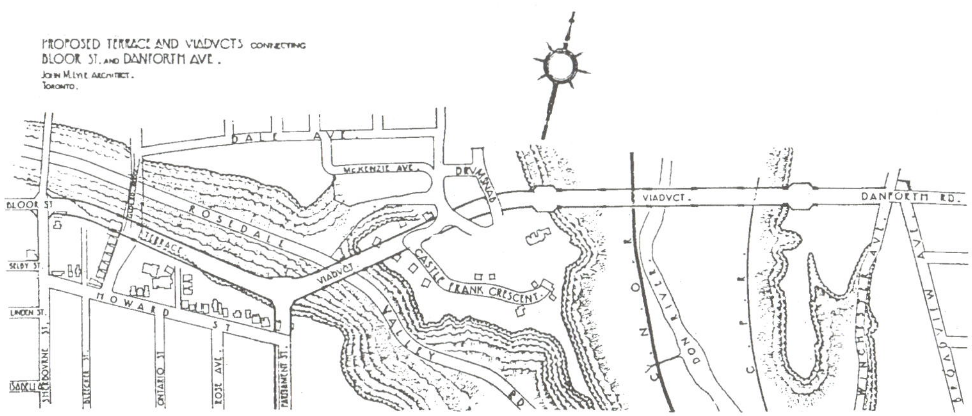

2.47, 2.48, 2.49 Various proposals for the location of the Bloor-Danforth Viaduct, Toronto, including the city's engineering department design (top), Lyle's Civic Guild proposal (middle) and his revised plan (bottom).

2.50, 2.51, 2.52 Three design proposals for the Bloor-Danforth Viaduct: John M. Lyle (top); Hedrick & Cochrane, consulting engineers, Kansas, Missouri (middle); and L. G. Mouchel & Partners, Ltd., London, England.

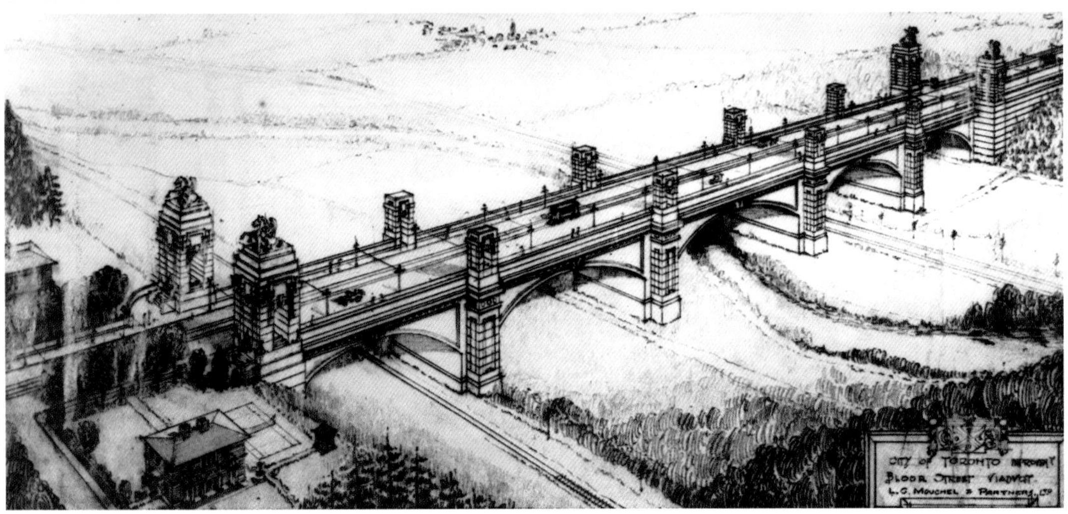

Calgary met similar fates; beside the prohibitive cost, most communities realized that city planning was something more than a paper Beaux-Arts project – it was a process not of instant creation, but of slow, gradual development. In Toronto, as elsewhere, despite all the work that had gone into the various proposals, the City actually did very little. Considering that the gains obviously did not offset the costs, that most elected officials were not motivated by the proposed changes and that taxes for large public work projects had to be decided by public referenda, these results were not surprising. But Lyle was not discouraged from future participation with political and architectural bodies, although they did not receive his full attention as they did during this period in his career. In the mid-twenties Lyle was involved with similar schemes for the city, and his writing on civic beautification made him an ideal candidate for election as a member to the American Civic Association in recognition for promoting architectural improvement in Toronto.

Railway Stations: A Modest Legacy

In Ontario, a number of emerging enterprises were deemed worthy of financial and political support by the provincial government, including a hydroelectric power network and the expansion of railway lines into the north to serve burgeoning communities and to foster economic possibilities.

In 1906, the Ontario Legislature passed the Power Commission Act and created the Hydro-Electric Power Commission, mandated to supply municipal utilities with electricity generated by private companies already operating at Niagara Falls. The first chairman was Adam Beck, minister without portfolio in the provincial government of Sir James P. Whitney, while John Hendrie, one of Lyle's old family friends from Hamilton, was a commissioner. In 1909, the Hydro-Electric Power Commission hired Lyle to design eleven step-up and interswitching transformer stations in Dundas, Guelph, Kitchener, London, Niagara Falls, Preston, St. Marys, St. Thomas, Stratford, Toronto and Woodstock. These buildings, utilitarian structures of one or two storeys and constructed of red brick with accentuated keystone and quoins, varied in size and architectural detail, and some are still in use today.

Another provincial initiative was the creation of the Temiskaming and Northern Ontario Railway, with a mandate to open up the north and link some of the remote communities that extended from North Bay, located on the shores of Lake Nipissing, to James Bay. The railway also had an economic incentive when gold, silver and other minerals were discovered in these regions. In 1909, to serve the mining communities that were sprouting up, Lyle was commissioned to design railway stations in the towns of Cobalt, Cochrane and Matheson.

The railway companies had developed four different categories of stations, based upon their location and traffic volume. Beginning with the first-class stations, which consisted of large, custom-designed buildings for the most important cities, they decreased in both size and significance, ending with the lowly fourth-class station. Architecturally, these structures generally belonged to one of two types – one had a 'complication of surfaces and forms, the other saw a movement to massive solidity.'[48] All three stations designed by Lyle at Cobalt, Cochrane and Matheson were of the second class, and belonged to the movement toward 'massive solidity.' In their use of more permanent materials, they also represented a clear endorsement of the towns' financial futures. The stations were designed as long, asymmetrical structures with a second-storey brick tower and swooping rooflines that emphasize the horizontal. Towers were becoming a standard feature of train stations of this period, as they not only served a functional purpose as lookouts for traffic and places for administrative and telegraphic operations, and functioned as picturesque elements for breaking up the horizontal massing of the buildings, but they also served as local landmarks.

One reason for Lyle's relocation to Toronto from New York was the possibility of being commissioned to design the new Union Station, and again he was to find himself in the fortuitous position of being the recipient of a commission that had already been awarded to his former employer Carrère &

2.53 The completed viaduct, Toronto, c. 1917.

2.54 Lyle designed three similarly styled railway stations for the northern Ontario towns of Cobalt, Cochrane and Matheson.

Hastings. The outcome of this situation, as in the case of the Royal Alexandra Theatre, was not planned or orchestrated but occurred purely by circumstance and serendipity.

In Toronto, the competitive, independent and uncooperative nature of the various railway companies had given rise to numerous stations, each serving its own interests and needs. The city's first station was a frame shed built around 1853 by the Northern Railway on Front Street between Bay and York streets. Five years later the Grand Trunk Railway (GTR) built the first Union Station, a wooden structure on the west side of York and Station streets, while the Great Western Railway constructed its own station in 1866 on the Esplanade, east of Yonge Street, from designs by William G. Storm. These buildings slowly fell out of use for passenger service, when the second Union Station, by E. P. Hannaford, the British-trained chief engineer of the Grand Trunk, was constructed in 1871, on the same site as the original. A seven-storey addition in 1893, designed by Strickland & Symons, ensured that Union Station remained the centre of passenger-train service to the city.

Passenger traffic at the old Union Station was significant, with 100,000 people and nearly 200 trains moving through each day. This was comparable to the traffic in large American cities such as Washington and Chicago. However, the city's needs were unique – it was reported that the 'average number of pieces of baggage per passenger is greater in Toronto than in any other large centre on this continent.'[49]

Toronto's new Union Station, 1913–27, was born out of the Great Fire of 1904 that swept through the core of the city. The disaster removed many of the temporary warehouse sheds that had sprung up on what was then Lorne Street, between Bay and York, south of Front Street to the Esplanade, presenting an opportunity for the railway companies to redevelop the area. The GTR proposed to expropriate the lands south of Front Street, between Yonge and York, and replace their aging Union Station with a grand, monumental structure. Making use of the financial subsidies and tax incentives offered by all levels of government to railway companies, the GTR negotiated a sweetheart deal with the city, allowing the railway access to the land for all time to come, with the stipulation that it was to be used for a passenger station.

The economic boom arising from the opening up of the western prairies, as well as the financial and population expansion of local economies, created a mood of confidence during the first decade of the twentieth century that led to the construction of new railway stations all over North America. Large stations were built in Boston, Omaha, New York and Washington, D.C., each outdoing the other in scale and grandeur. Some of the leading architectural firms in the United States, including Daniel Burnham, McKim, Mead & White, and Warren & Wetmore, were behind these projects. In Canada as well, plans for new structures in Ottawa, Winnipeg and Vancouver were being drafted by Ross & MacFarlane, Warren & Wetmore, and Barott, Blackader & Webster respectively.

Around the time of the Great Fire of 1904, several local architects, including Darling & Pearson, Edward J. Lennox and Alfred Chapman, had had their names attached to the design of the new Union Station. A year later, however, the GTR turned to the New York offices of Carrère & Hastings and commissioned them for plans. To handle the local affairs,

Middle top: 2.55 Pennsylvania Station, New York, McKim, Mead & White.

Middle left: 2.56 Canadian Pacific Railroad Station, Winnipeg, Edward and W. S. Maxwell.

Middle right: 2.57 Union Station, Washington, D.C., Daniel Burnham.

Bottom left: 2.58 Canadian Pacific Railway Station, Vancouver, Barott, Blackader & Webster.

Bottom right: 2.59 Union Station, Ottawa, Ross & MacFarlane.

Above: 2.60 North Toronto CPR Station, Yonge Street, Toronto, Darling & Pearson.

Opposite page: *2.61 Union Station at dusk.*

Carrère & Hastings hired other firms connected with the two railways, Ross & MacFarlane and W. S. Painter of Montreal and, as the Toronto associate, F. S. Baker.

In 1906, the two main competing railways – the GTR and the CPR – formed a joint company, the Toronto Terminals Railway Company, to oversee the design and maintenance of the station, which, in Carrère & Hastings' design, consisted of a five-storey structure stretching from Bay to York streets. These plans contained one feature that became a contentious issue – the position of the trains' access into the station. For the trains to have a street-level entry into the building, the original plans called for the closing of Yonge, Bay and York streets, to be replaced with a single bridge east of Bay Street. Disapproving of this idea, the City studied the issue, recommending in its report an elevated viaduct that would carry the trains into the station and leave the streets to continue unimpeded toward the waterfront. The ensuing squabbles and legal battles delayed the project for years. The lack of progress so frustrated the CPR that it built a new station for itself on Yonge Street below Summerhill Avenue in 1912, putting the Union Station project into doubt.

Eventually, however, facing the pressure of legally binding contracts, the parties resumed their efforts. At this point, several new players entered the scene, and a new team of architects and engineers were selected to design the station. Montreal's Ross and his new partner Robert H. Macdonald, and Hugh G. Jones, were appointed architects. In order to have a local representative, John M. Lyle was hired as their associate, along with a team of engineers from the two railway companies. According to Lyle's memoirs, '[W]e all worked harmoniously together and after many preliminary sketches we finally decided on the type of building and plan of the building erected... The architects and engineers visited all the important stations in the United States, each man making notes, taking measurements and making comments on the different buildings visited. We went to Boston, Baltimore, New York and Omaha. Each architect and engineer forwarded to Montreal his notes and comments, which were all co-ordinated and bound in compact form to present to the officials. It was the most thorough job and the information contained in this booklet was invaluable.'[50]

The design of the station was completed in spring 1914, but the start of World War I delayed the beginning of construction until fall 1915. The building permit was applied for after construction had begun, and it was granted in December 1916. Shortages of material, as well as labour strikes, meant it was not until 1920 that the first wing – the station office – was completed and occupied. The collapse of the Grand Trunk Railroad, the eventual formation of the Canadian National Railway between 1919 and 1923, and the City's insistence that all approaches and viaducts be completed before the building could be opened meant that the station did not receive its first passengers until 1927. The station was officially opened by the Prince of Wales (later Edward VIII), the Duke of Windsor and Prince George, with two prime ministers – Stanley Baldwin and Mackenzie King – and local politicians attending, on August 6, 1927. The ceremonies included the usual ribbon cuttings and music, and then the royal party was escorted first to the CPR's and then to the CN's ticket booth, to be the first ticket buyers.

According to architectural historian Harold Kalman, 'the scale and grandeur of Toronto's Union Station were unprecedented in this country.'[51] The front facade of the building, which extends 230 metres, was designed on an 'E' shape with a projecting frontispiece and end pavilions consisting of a massive colonnade of eighteen Greek Doric columns. Its projecting portico consisted of four columns made of Indiana limestone. The station's stately elegance is achieved through the repetition of key features and the subtle manipulation of masses. A prominent cornice and entablature counterbalances the building's verticality, which is created by the columns, pilasters, end pavilions and central porch projections. The entrance porticos lead into the dominant interior feature of the building – the Great Hall. The hall is eighty metres long and twenty-seven metres high, with a herringbone-patterned floor whose mauve-toned, pink Tennessee marble corresponds to the

CANADIAN PACIFIC RAILWAY
UNION STATION
ERECTED BY THE TORONTO TERMINALS RAILWAY COMPANY
ANNO DOMINI
GRAND TRUNK RAILWAY

Right: 2.62 Union Station Great Hall.

Opposite page: 2.63 Reflected light from surrounding buildings breaks through the front facade's colonnade onto the exit ramp area.

Arrivals
Arrivées

2.64, 2.65 Lyle's perspective drawings of the exterior facade and the interior of Union Station.

square-coffered Guastavino tile ceiling. Lyle would have seen this system in Montreal on the 1901–05 head-office addition to the Bank of Montreal, designed by McKim, Mead & White. The Great Hall is encircled with a carved frieze of the names of the principal cities served by the railways, making the room the central hub of the country, the thoroughfare that links the nation. Natural light illuminates the space through arched, four-storey-high glassed corridors on both ends. According to architectural writer Trevor Boddy, the Great Hall 'remains, save for that of [New York's] Grand Central Station, the most heroic Beaux-arts station space in North America.'[52]

The original perspective drawings of 1913–14 reveal interesting details that were unfortunately changed by the time the building was finally completed. On the exterior, the most notable is the roofline of the central block, which was reduced in overall height, and the gable ends and dentillated cornice, which were replaced by a hip roof, similar to the pavilion ends, and a more simplified cornice. The sculpted figurative groupings over the two entrance porticos, depicting the railroad builders, were eliminated, reducing the extent to which they projected forward. In some respects the changes were for the better. The bays connecting the central block to the end pavilions were given more interest by recessing them slightly and creating pilasters between windows. This maintains the column rhythm from the central block and, with the added surface depth, creates an interesting interplay of light and shadow. In the interior, the Great Hall was designed with a flat coffered ceiling, modelled after early basilica church designs. This was changed to a segmental barrel vault eliminating the potential problem of dark corners, making for a gentler transition from wall to ceiling and helping create a more balanced light and sound environment. The wall pilasters were eliminated and the frieze moved down below the cornice, which changed the emphasis, making the space less vertical and cavernous, and more horizontal and intimate.

The architect's design of the interior took into consideration Toronto passengers' excessive baggage requirements, with a plan based on the complete separation of incoming and outgoing traffic. The geographic conditions of the site helped in this decision. Entering passengers use the main floor, on the same grade as the exterior sidewalk. Once inside the building, gently sloping ramps aid in the movement of luggage-bound traffic to the boarding areas. Exiting passengers can either use the side exits that lead to the grade-level streets or the front basement exit that leads back to the street by ramps. According to the chief engineer of the project, the plan's most outstanding feature was 'its elasticity, which allowed huge volumes of traffic to be handled easily, this due in part to the decision by the design team to separate the flow of traffic by having separate areas for incoming and outgoing passengers.'[53] The interior architectural spaces are well-suited to the building's traffic patterns. Where passenger movement is slow, such as at ticket offices or waiting rooms, the spaces are well-lit and grand in scale; where the movement is swift, as upon the entering and exiting of trains, the spaces are low and small. On the exterior, the building is set back from the street, creating a plaza that not only facilitates movement in and out of the structure but also gives it an air of public grandeur. Summarizing the aims of the Union Station architects, Lyle maintained that their idea was to 'avoid everything fussy and useless' while at the same time striving 'to have the finest station in Canada and the best equipped.'[54]

Lyle's attempt to infuse the city with a head, a heart and a pulse, as reflected in his proposed Federal Avenue plan, did

2.66 Lyle's proposed scheme for a grand avenue with Beaux-Arts buildings was only partially realized with Union Station (foreground) and the Federal Custom and Excise Building (distant) on Front Street, Toronto.

have a modest legacy. Although his plan was not implemented as such, his vision of a grand avenue of classically ordered buildings forming a visually coherent streetscape with Union Station as its focus was eventually realized. The federal government, who owned the site on Front Street between Yonge and Bay, had long been encouraged to participate with a large public building that would conform to Lyle's proposed scheme. It responded with the Federal Custom and Excise Building, originally selecting the site in 1911, but it was not designed and constructed until 1929–35. The building's plans adhere to the gentle curve of Front Street and reflect the grand Beaux-Arts design of Union Station. Dominating the streetscape, these impressive buildings represent a high-water mark for Beaux-Arts and City Beautiful aesthetics in the country and hint at what might have been, if Lyle's urban plans had been fully realized.

Ontario Association of Architects and the Architectural Eighteen Club

At the time of Lyle's arrival in 1905, the architectural community of Toronto was a house divided. Two organizations purported to represent the needs and aspirations of the local architects – the Ontario Association of Architects and the Architectural Eighteen Club. The OAA had been formed in 1889 to promote, regulate, and deal with issues relating to the practice of architecture in the province, with forty-one members from within Toronto and another twenty-one from other regions. Trying to regulate a body of individualistically minded architects and have them come to consensus over issues that would restrict their entrenched methods of practice proved, however, extremely difficult. In 1899, when the Architectural League of America was formed in the United States, it asked the OAA to join in its membership. When the OAA declined the offer, a splinter group, the principal figures of which were Eden Smith and Edmund Burke, calling themselves the Architectural Eighteen Club, sent local architect J. P. Haynes as its representative to the first ALA convention. The club often acted in opposition to the OAA and agitated for reform in the areas of education, exhibitions and legislation. After 1906, it changed its name to the Toronto Society of Architects, and then eventually folded back into the parent organization in 1912. Upon arriving in Toronto, Lyle had quickly associated himself with this group. He participated in all of its exhibitions and served as vice-president in 1907. Later that year, he was also appointed the organization's spokesperson, chiefly responsible for communicating directly with the ALA.

One of the Architectural Eighteen Club's attempted joint ventures with the ALA was a series of annual group shows that began in 1901. The ambitious size and scope of the first couple of shows reflected the organizations' faith in the future of the partnership. Over half of the works were by local club associates, but the ALA's contribution was impressive and included exhibits by most of the prominent New York firms. Lyle also participated in these events, showing in the 1905 exhibition a number of his European watercolour sketches, student drawings and New York competition entries. Two years later, he also contributed works to the ALA exhibition in Washington, D.C.

These shows continued until 1910, when an incident of hurt national pride put an end to the idyllic relationship between the club and the ALA. The story began with the Bank of Toronto's limited competition for a new head office, which was won by Carrère & Hastings, over local architects Sproatt & Rolph, George Gouinlock and Lyle. The *Toronto Star* published an interview with the winning firm's associate architect, Eustace Bird, who was Canadian-born but had trained in Carrère & Hastings' New York office. He claimed to have designed the bank building by himself, saying only that the plans 'were examined and approved by Carrère & Hastings.'[55] To that bit of self-aggrandizement, he also added his thoughts on the state of architecture in Canada, describing his land of birth as a 'new country' in which 'architecture is necessarily undeveloped. As in any other branch of Art it is necessary for us in Canada to rely on established principles, which have been perfected in New York or Europe.' As if that weren't bad enough, he added a supercilious defence for the choice of the New York firm, saying, 'Carrère &

Hastings are conceded to be the leading architects of North America, and surely Toronto wants the best buildings that can be secured.'[56]

This hit a raw nerve with the Canadian architectural community. The editor of *Construction* magazine was quick to respond with a blistering, if somewhat defensive, editorial that called the *Star*'s interview 'An insidious attack upon Canadian Architects.' The editorial attacked Bird and the firm he represented for 'casting aspersions upon the architectural profession of Canada and belittling our appreciation of the aesthetic in architecture.' Rising to the defence of the three Canadian entries, the editorial described Sproatt & Rolph, Gouinlock and Lyle as being all 'excellently trained' and having 'to their credit many structures that have established them as architects of no mean ability.' The three architects' work had never before received such unstinting praise. Sproatt & Rolph's recently erected Library of Victoria College was 'the most beautiful gothic structure in Canada.' Gouinlock's newly constructed buildings in Toronto's Exhibition Park were 'the finest permanent exhibition buildings in the world.' Lyle merited two mentions: his Royal Alexandra Theatre was called 'one of the most beautiful appointed theatres on the continent' and his newly constructed Provincial Penitentiary for Ontario was 'the largest and most completely equipped institution of its kind in Canada.'[57]

In a letter to the editor published in the subsequent issue of *Construction*, Carrère & Hastings defended themselves and Eustace Bird. They claimed that Bird had been misquoted and that the editor of *Construction* was misinterpreting his statements. They also cleared up the question of who actually designed the Bank of Toronto: 'The designs were made by us in our office in New York in collaboration with Mr. Bird, and developed into working drawings by Mr. Bird in our office in Toronto. This same statement applies to all our Canadian work. Mr. Bird is not our representative in Canada, as you state, but our full associate.'[58]

However, the locals were not to be appeased, and the incident brought out into the open the architectural community's rising resentment against the use of American architects in Canada. Editorials in *Construction* continued to condemn the practice of hiring foreign architects for prize Canadian jobs, and during the Toronto Society of Architects' annual dinner in 1911, the members adopted a hardline resolution stating that 'there should be no American architects employed on Canadian buildings.'[59] The TSA's 1912 exhibition catalogue continued the nationalistic theme with a front cover that proclaimed the contents as being 'All Canadian.' The publication's preface stated that it 'is composed of the work of Canadian architects exclusively. We are convinced that Canadian problems in Architecture can be dealt with by those who are themselves Canadians, familiar with the National and local requirements of their Country, having their Country's interests at heart, and imbued with their Country's spirit. This Exhibition will prove that our architectural problems are being fairly faced, intelligently studied and worthily solved.'[60]

The cross-border venture between the architectural associations foundered on the rocks of nationalism and, left to its own devices, the TSA lost its momentum and ended its group shows in 1912. But this last show was not to go unnoticed; it included forty-six architects from across Canada, University of Toronto architectural students, as well as representatives from the allied arts such as mural painters, sculptors and makers of

2.67, 2.68, 2.69, 2.70 Bank of Toronto competition entries: John M. Lyle, (top), George Gouinlock (middle), Sproatt & Rolph (bottom) and Carrère & Hastings' winning design as constructed (left).

stained glass, wrought iron and other decorative works. Most of the pieces displayed were photographs or drawings of existing buildings and some perspective drawings. Lyle's contribution consisted of eighteen pieces, the largest number exhibited, featuring the most diverse range of built forms and rendering media. It was an extraordinary collection, featuring photographs of finished residential projects, competition drawings, building details, a design for a Jacobean-styled piano, line drawings for the town plan of Iroquois Falls, as well as the Terrace Scheme for the Bloor-Danforth Viaduct along with a design for a bridge to be located between Parliament Street and Castle Frank Crescent. There could be no doubt as to the diversity of Lyle's skills and interests.

During its twelve-year existence, one of the principal concerns of the Eighteen Club and the TSA was the debate over whether architecture was an art or a profession, where practices would be regulated by legislation. The club's members, among whom Lyle figured prominently, 'were the most articulate Canadian spokesmen of the 'architecture as an art' faction.'[62] Lyle's paper 'Architecture and Its Relation to Art,' first given in 1910 at the OAA's annual meeting and subsequently published in various trade periodicals including *Construction* and *Contract Record* in Canada and *New York Architect* in the U.S., took a firm stand on the issue. Claiming 'architecture is a fine art – the greatest of all, a combination of many arts,' Lyle described his vocation using the ethereal words of his Beaux-Arts atelier *patron*, Paul Blondel: 'Architecture is a jealous mistress, who yielded her favors but rarely, and then only after the most earnest and persistent endeavors on the part of her devotees – the architect.' Suggesting numerous ways in which, both individually and collectively, architects could use education and promotion to create a healthier architectural environment in the country, he concludes by reinforcing his position that 'architecture is a fine art.'[63] When Lyle constructed a building in 1920 to house his practice, he always referred to it as a studio rather than an office, indicating that he continued to perceive architecture as an art.

The debate continued to divide the architectural community, even after the club rejoined the OAA in 1912. In fact, despite many attempts to address the issue of registration, it wasn't until 1931 that a bill was finally passed allowing the OAA to establish a Registration Board to monitor and set standards, examine candidates for admission and oversee disciplinary issues. The OAA was not the only governing body experiencing this problem. The architectural profession in the U.K. had been similarly divided over the issues, and Britain did not pass its own Architects Registration Act until that same year.

Atelier Lyle

Throughout his career, Lyle took very seriously the job of educating the next generation of architects and giving a higher profile to the field of architecture and the allied arts. In Toronto he had quickly become involved with and initiated several educational ventures that advanced the cause of the profession.

The educational options available to aspiring students had not improved since his graduation from high school almost fifteen years earlier. The number of students enrolled in full-time architectural programs in the country was small, with McGill University reporting an enrolment of fifteen students, an improvement over previous years, while the University of Toronto also struggled with its program. Only the OAA and the Toronto Architectural Eighteen Club had more success with their joint program, which provided its part-time students with classes in mathematics and studio. This program, started in 1902, had an enrolment of about sixty.

Lyle was to offer a new and exciting educational option for aspiring architects when, within weeks of arriving in Toronto, he established a Beaux-Arts Club and atelier, modelled after the one in New York. Its members consisted of the young draftsmen who were working in the offices of other city architects. The club's objective was the 'development of art ability and the love of art and incidentally a feeling of companionship among the younger men.'[64]

The organization met weekly downtown and followed the same system of monthly design competitions, or *concours d'émulation*, that were provided by the New York Beaux-Arts

Society. In 1907, the atelier, whose membership was by now at about forty students, moved to the corner of Yonge and Yorkville, a more convenient location for its patron.

Since most Canadian architects had grown up under a system of apprenticeship, the atelier system, as reported in *Construction*, did 'not meet with the approval of many members of the profession in Canada.'[65] Lyle, however, was convinced that giving students a greater diversity of subject matter would improve their skill and broaden their knowledge, as well as ground them 'in the ethics of their calling by bringing about a feeling of fraternalism, which should in after years reflect the honour and dignity of the profession.'[66]

In 1911, the University of Toronto Architectural Club was formed with a mandate to 'encourage a closer study of architecture and its allied arts, to bring the professional body into more intimate relation with the Department, and to foster the '*atelier* spirit' among its members.'[67] Lyle was elected honorary president of the club in 1913, a position that was rotated annually, and became the *patron* of the university's atelier the following year. With only a handful of members in its first year, the club quickly expanded. In 1915 it included thirty-three students along with practicing architects Lyle and Henry Sproatt, and professors C. H. C. Wright and A. W. McConnell. Its functions and programming included lectures and tours. Members went on field trips to examine buildings such as James Govan's Insane Asylum in Whitby, followed by discussions with the architect. Lyle, 'the staunchest friend of the Architectural Club, gave a confidential talk on the New Union Station.'[68] Other lecturers included the up-and-coming artist A. Y. Jackson, who spoke on the sister art of painting, and City of Toronto architect William Pierce, who enlightened the students on new techniques of skyscraper construction.

This was an extremely busy period for Lyle. He spent three or four afternoons a week setting programs and acting in the capacity of *patron* for the University of Toronto, as well as giving lectures and night classes, coupled with running his own atelier – all while attending to his private practice.

Lyle's pre-war work with the fledgling Architectural Department at the University of Toronto came at a critical period in its history. He devoted much time and energy to developing the essential programs required to instill in students the proper methodology, ethics and artistic rendering skills, and he did it with little to no financial remuneration.

Although most of Lyle's educational activity came to a halt during the war years, he resumed his involvement with the university after the war with lecturing and teaching sessions in 1920 and 1923. He continued to be actively involved through judging student work and reviewing it on occasion in the *Journal of the* RAIC, as well as instituting a policy of hiring two graduates a year to work in his office.

2.71, 2.72 University of Toronto, Architectural Department (left), 1914 (Lyle is seated in the first row, fifth from right), and the Architectural Club, 1915 (above), including Lyle (seated middle) and the few students who did not go off to war with the first wave of combatants.

Chapter 3: 1915–1923

THE BANK OF NOVA SCOTIA
THE BANK OF NOVA SCOTIA

Golden Moment

The War Years

Members of the architectural profession, like other Canadians, were quick to respond to the patriotic call of 'For King and Country.' The staffs of entire offices joined the forces, and nearly 85 percent of the country's architects, designers and draftsmen enlisted. Large firms like Ross & Macdonald of Montreal, where Lyle had worked while designing Union Station, dropped from a staff of thirty members to only seven, with most of their employees going overseas with the first contingent. From 1914 to 1918, almost all construction in Canada that was not directly related to the war effort came to a virtual standstill. In Toronto, where construction starts had peaked in 1912, when over $27.5 million worth of building permits were issued, construction by 1916 had declined to only $6.5 million. What construction was being done was primarily for the building of new factories or the expansion of firms manufacturing goods for the war. In Toronto, though, the Bloor-Danforth Viaduct and Union Station construction continued throughout the war, showing the high priority of these projects.

Like everyone else's, Lyle's workload during the war dropped drastically. With a pre-war staff of twelve, and anticipating further growth, he had, in 1913, bought a lot at 230 Bloor Street West and designed for it a large, two-storey studio. But with his staff gone during the war years, Lyle was forced to suspend plans for his new studio, close down his Leader Lane office and work out of his residence on Avondale Road. (Shortly after the war, Lyle revisited his studio plans, but the final result was a smaller version of the original.)

During the war, Lyle, who was too old for active duty, worked alongside Sir Glenholme Falconbridge and W. R. Johnston, the executive of the Toronto chapter of the Secours National, a non-governmental agency that, like the Red Cross, provided relief for the civilian population in Europe. While there are no records kept of its wartime efforts in Toronto, most of its activities revolved around fundraising benefits such as art exhibitions at the Grange House, or musicals and dramatic events, for which, on occasion, Lyle was enlisted as a performer. He was also involved in less frivolous tasks. In 1915 he was awarded the Secours National's Silver Medal for civilian relief work, and at the conclusion of hostilities in 1919, a special committee of the French government that recognized foreigners who had contributed to the relief effort presented Lyle with the Reconnaissance Française medal for his involvement in residential building projects in France and Belgium. Drawings for these houses were featured at an exhibition held at the Garden of the Tuileries in Paris and were reported on by the Toronto *Globe*, which noted that 'among the houses shown which it is proposed to erect in the regions that have suffered from the invasion…[are] one…given by Mr. Rochereau de la Sabliere and one by Mr. John Lyle of the *Secours National*.'[1] It is not known whether Lyle provided the designs for the houses, or the financial support, or both.

Despite the war, Lyle had continued to focus on issues facing the architectural profession, and in 1916 he addressed these in an article in *Construction* entitled 'Status of the Canadian Architect.' Looking at issues such as payment for services and the architect's position within the community, Lyle considered Canadian architects 'decidedly the worst off.'[2] He complained that private firms were missing out on large and important commissions because so many clients, including governments and corporations, had their own architectural departments and suggested that architectural bodies needed to pressure governments into giving 'out more work to the profession.'[3] He also found the relationship between contractors and architects in Ontario unsatisfactory, preferring the Montreal model, where a general contractor who oversaw all the trades lightened the burden placed on architects. He suggested that engineers' fees be subject to a percentage surcharge to compensate architects for the time and energy they put into directing their work. Lyle had always thought the best way to maintain and raise professional standards was through education rather than legislation, but here he reconsidered his position, saying members of the profession should take steps 'to enact legislation governing the employment of quantity surveyors, a clerk of works, and the registration of architects.'[4]

Opposite page: 3.1 Lyle's watercolour of the Bank of Nova Scotia, Sparks Street, Ottawa, was produced as a diploma work for acceptance into the Royal Canadian Academy.

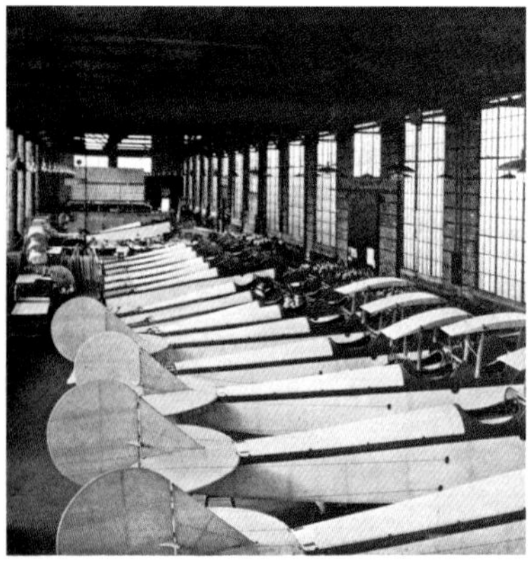

3.2 The Canadian Airplanes Limited factory in Toronto was constructed in sixty-six days.

3.3 Bank of Toronto, College Street, Toronto.

Although his workload was small, Lyle continued to work on several projects during the war, including Union Station, the Bank of Toronto and a number of small branch buildings for the Dominion Bank. Another large but extremely quick commission was the design for a series of factories for the firm of Canadian Airplanes Limited in Toronto, in 1917.

Taking advantage of the new invention of flight, both the British and Canadian governments had set aside large sums of money to purchase airplanes and train fighter pilots for the war. At that time the only airplane manufacturer in the country was the Curtis Aeroplane and Motor Company, founded by American pioneer aviator Glenn Curtis, who had worked with Alexander Graham Bell and the Wright brothers. The firm, which became the biggest aircraft manufacturer during World War I, had large plants in New Jersey and New Brunswick, as well as a small plant on Strachan Avenue in Toronto. Proposing to take over the Canadian arm of the business, the federal government wanted to build a new $2 million facility near Ashbridge's Bay in the eastern part of the city, and Lyle was commissioned to design the plant.

When the site turned out to be ill-suited for the project, a new location on a ten-acre site on Lappin Avenue was obtained. This meant Lyle had to adjust his plans, of course, but he was not allowed to take his time about it. The government was not joking – they needed this plant and they needed it fast. Everyone complied. Groundbreaking for the foundations in the still-frozen winter soil started on February 1, 1917, the very same day the property was purchased, and the plant was completed in an astounding sixty-six days, with portions of the building operational and assembling airplane parts within forty–five days! To achieve this, there was a remarkable degree of co-operation and standardization in design and production. Whenever possible, Lyle used standard lengths of material, especially for the columns, beams and trusses. Delivery to the site was based on the principle of 'supply upon demand,' using both a penalty and a bonus system – financial incentives for the contractors if daily work quotas were met and deductions if they were not. There were ten buildings in the complex, each serving a separate function. Designed so as to permit a flow of raw material and supplies to the manufacturing areas for assemblage, and then allow for the finished product to move from one building to the next or be shipped from the nearby railway line, the complex represented the optimum production efficiency.

After the war, the economy did not immediately return to its robust pre-war state; there was a financial slump that had a negative effect on all sectors of the economy as well as construction starts. Unemployment and inflation led to civic unrest across the country, with general strikes from Vancouver to Halifax. The most dramatic occurred in Winnipeg, where police and strikers clashed, resulting in one death and many injured. The prevailing attitude on the part of national and provincial governments was that economic issues and the primacy of 'market forces' would resolve themselves without intervention. There was a general reluctance to initiate programs during periods of economic downturns. In this environment, unemployment soared and Canadians suffered without a social safety net to provide the basic necessities.

To help kick-start the economy, the architectural community became actively involved on a political level, proposing various plans. One of these was presented in 1921, at the annnual meeting of the Royal Architectural Institute of Canada, where Lyle advocated the adoption of a tax-exemption law similar to the one in effect in New York City as a means to stimulate business activity.

The same year, there were newly elected federal and Ontario provincial governments. The new prime minister was the Liberals' William Lyon Mackenzie King, a former bureaucrat with experience in labour relations, and in Ontario, Ernest Drury, head of the United Farmers party, was elected and served as premier from 1919 to 1923. No doubt wishing to avoid the general strikes then occurring throughout the country, and to help stimulate the local economy, the provincial government was forced into action and proposed to commit $25 million, with $20 million earmarked for construction. These initiatives may have had an effect. By 1922, building starts had surpassed the number of construction starts of a decade earlier, with $35 million worth of building permits being issued in Ontario.

Bank Architecture: Neoclassical Inspiration

Just after the war, Lyle designed a number of single-storey bank branches that were consistent in the simplification of both the exterior and interior treatments and the use of a classical vocabulary of architraves, cornices and, on occasion, pediments. The Bank of Nova Scotia in St. Andrews, New Brunswick, and the Bank of Toronto in Cambridge, Ontario, both of 1920, although almost identical in elevation, exemplify how Lyle adapted his design to meet local conditions. The St. Andrews branch, in keeping with the East Coast's refined Colonial Georgian past, used red brick and period mullion window treatment. The Cambridge branch, on the other hand, is a more robust design with its ashlar facing, window treatment of scrolled keystones, bracketed lintels and pronounced quoins, all features that reflected the influence of the local Scottish limestone masonry. Another interesting design was the Bank of Toronto, College Street branch, Toronto, of 1922, which featured an urban design for an interior lot site with the dominant feature of a centrally located window with geometric-shaped metalwork, and medallions representing commerce on the ashlar facing.

Lyle's last and most successful of these neoclassically inspired temple banks was the Bank of Nova Scotia, on Sparks Street, Ottawa, of 1923. It is significant in his oeuvre because it 'represents the height of Lyle's achievement in Classical design.'[5] It was also a consciousness-raising experience for the architect, moving him forward in his search for an indigenous Canadian style. The Bank of Nova Scotia, which had absorbed the Bank of Ottawa in 1919, wanted a strong presence in the city. It also had to compete against its neighbour, the newly constructed Bank of Commerce. An interior lot site on Sparks Street, the most prominent business and retail area in Ottawa, was purchased. This Ottawa branch bank was a step up over the St. Andrews branch in budget, location and prestige that

3.4, 3.5 Lyle continued to use the classical vocabulary on several banks, including the Bank of Nova Scotia in St. Andrews, New Brunswick, and the Bank of Toronto in Cambridge, Ontario.

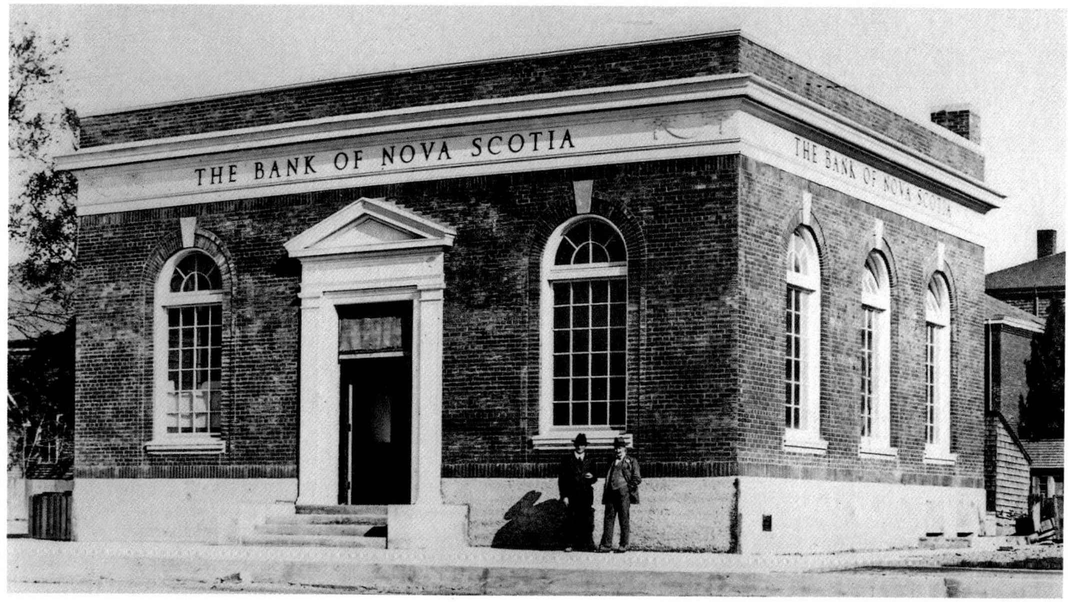

1832
THE BANK OF NOVA SCOTIA
1924

continued to develop a long and fruitful relationship with the Bank of Nova Scotia, a relationship that saw Lyle produce some of his finest work.

The building was designed in what the architect termed a 'modern adaptation of the Grecian Doric.'[6] Throughout the building, from the cornerstone to the electric light fixtures, the spirit of the Grecian Doric prevailed. The Sparks Street elevation was in a cream-coloured Bedford stone, where the ground-floor rusticated masonry provided an ample base for the second storey's four fluted Doric columns supporting the cornice and parapet. A noted feature was the use of niches containing bronze braziers on the facade. These served two purposes: first as decoration, and second, together with a string of floodlights between the columns, they were part of the external lighting scheme that illuminated the building at night with a soft light. This helped to overcome a common criticism by neighbouring retail stores that banks were too gloomy at night and had a negative effect on their businesses. This latter point was an achievement for Lyle, whose watercolour illustration of the building, which he used as his diploma piece for his election into the Royal Canadian Academy in 1925, was deliberately painted at dusk, showing the structure bathed in a soft glow, to convey it as a hub of urban life and activity and a vital link in the streetscape.

The building's mouldings are crisp with slight projections and all-important light-and-shade effect obtained through judicious fenestration placement and the channelling from the ground-floor masonry. The bank contains a rich sculptural program that is not only decorative, with its use of classical motifs of ox skulls and festoons, but also symbolic, in its banking crests, horns of plenty and emblems of agriculture, lumbering, fishing, industry and finance. It also attempts to provide a regional component, anticipating Lyle's later Canadian phases: the column's frieze features imagery of log cabins and wheat sheaves.

The mahogany entrance doors lead into a marble-lined vestibule, then to the bronze doors of the banking hall. The hall is generously proportioned, with a mezzanine floor at the front of the building that uses two types of Tennessee marble, grey for the larger areas and pink for the borders. The mezzanine walls are of a yellowish grey marble, and above them a cast Caen stone was used. The ceiling is plaster, with the frieze below the skylight pierced for ventilation. The counters are of a soft grey St. Genevieve marble with counter screens of bronze, ornamented in low relief. The colour scheme of the banking hall is gold and grey, making for a restful, pleasant atmosphere. The vault was in the basement, accessed by a flight of stairs from the banking hall. The plan is typical for an interior lot, with the main lighting of the banking-room floor provided by large skylights supplemented by light from the mezzanine. Lyle attempted to make the large banking hall as warm and friendly as possible through the interior floors', walls' and ceilings' colour combinations that gives 'the interior a soft radiant glow, almost equivalent to sunshine.'[7]

Lyle had always been a strong advocate for more critical writing on Canadian architecture, hoping it would raise the profile of the profession, stimulate lively debate and engage the public in the issues of the day. He was to get his wish when newly appointed University of Toronto architectural professor Eric Arthur was hired to review the annual awards of the Ontario Association of Architects in the Royal Architectural Institute of Canada's *Journal of the RAIC*. The Bank of Nova Scotia branch received a second-place award in the financial class from the OAA in 1926 and fell into the cross-hairs of criticism from the young scribe. Arthur objected to two aspects of the building: the use of a two-storey exterior when the interior banking room was only one floor, as well as what he deemed the facade's excessive use of ornamentation. Lyle was keen to engage in the critique and defended his 'child' in a letter to the editor. Since he considered the structure to be on a two-storey and basement plan, with the front mezzanine acting as the second level, Lyle's major concerns were how to provide sufficient light for the interior and how to solve the transition from the mezzanine walls to the main banking room. His solution was to open 'the whole banking room, giving air, light and distance, a play of light and shade and particularly sunshine from

Opposite page, left: 3.6, 3.7 Original interior views of the Bank of Nova Scotia, Sparks Street, Ottawa, c. 1923.

Opposite page: 3.8 Bank of Nova Scotia, Sparks Street, Ottawa.

Above: 3.9. One of a set of bronze braziers that are part of the bank's exterior lighting program.

3.10, 3.11 For one of his oldest friends, Clarence A. Bogert, Lyle designed a Georgian-inspired residence on Forest Hill Road, Toronto.

the large front windows.' As to Arthur's second criticism, Lyle dismissed it by saying that buildings should not be slavish copies of the more austere Grecian or Roman temples and that 'some of the most successful of the great modern American banking institutions are sumptuous in their enrichment.'[8]

After closing in the mid-1990s, the building eventually acquired a new lease on life. It was purchased by the federal government and converted into a temporary location for the Library of Parliament, which was also being renovated. This conservation and rehabilitation was undertaken by Lapointe Magne et associés of Montreal with local associates Schoeler & Heaton of Ottawa. They have successfully included a modern interior in the historic shell with five levels of exposed book stacks. A glass facade extension was added onto the north face to provide light into the below-grade work areas and ensure a library standard for environmental controls. This new shell allowed three openings to be punched through the back wall matching the fenestration pattern of Lyle's south facade. Although originally conceived as a temporary measure until the extensive renovations for the Parliament Library were completed in 2002, the design will be retained and adopted for other federal government use.

Residences: Toronto Georgian

Lyle's formal Georgian-inspired residential program came to its conclusion with the Clarence A. Bogert residence on Forest Hill Road, Toronto, in 1923. For his oldest friend, the former president of the Toronto Board of Trade, Lyle designed a suitably impressive house. To take full advantage of the sun and the relatively large city lot, the building was orientated toward the south, turning its primary axis away from the street. This approach was successful in two respects: it increased the amount of daylight into the principal rooms and provided more privacy. Although other architects shied away from this atypical approach, as it detracted from the usual manner in which buildings were supposed to address the street, Lyle proposed it for another residence, for W. C. Lee of Toronto (not built).

The principal elevation of the Bogert residence is north-facing and two storeys high with an attic. The facade has an asymmetrical disposition created by the unusual feature of an entrance porch that extends from the easterly wing. A series of retaining walls and staircases leads to the entrance. Other features on the north facade include a large Palladian window and a projecting gable-end frontispiece with a secondary entrance. The south facade is simply handled with nine bays and a projecting sunroom. The exterior is rendered in red brick with appropriate window dressing of white stone and shutters, and quoins. The house won an honourable mention in the residential category from the OAA. This time Eric Arthur was less critical: 'Lyle gives us a glimpse of the interior of Mr. Clarence Bogert's house, which is evidently of considerable size. It has all the dignity of a mansion and the fireplace in the hall is pleasant feature. Mr. Bogert's "lares and penates" receive a warm resting place on the altar, which cunningly conceals the radiator.'[9]

Competitions and Proposals

The largest and most sensational open competition of the post-war era was the Chicago Tribune Building of 1922. This brilliant piece of self-promotion by the newspaper company was to serve as a prototype for new high-rise construction. It attracted 259 entries from over twenty nations. Some of the most innovative individuals and firms submitted proposals, including German's modernist Walter Gropius, Finland's Eliel Saarinen, who placed second, and the eventual winner, America's Howells & Hood. Four Canadian firms entered into the competition: Hugh Jones of Montreal, H. S. Penlington and Walters & Wilkes of Toronto, and Lyle. *Construction* magazine found all the entries were based on classical forms with an emphasis on horizontal massing, which it rightly thought lessened their chances of placing in the competition. However, *Construction* did congratulate the Canadian entries, hoping the competition would 'raise the standards of our architecture and create a new impetus towards a dignified style of design.'[10] It was an odd choice of phrasing given that Lyle's usually restrained design approach, one of his trademarks, seemed

3.12 An unexcutated residential design for W. C. Lee, Toronto, c. 1923.

to have abandoned him on this project. It was not that he wasn't capable of high-rise design. Several previous hotel proposals displayed the appropriate and elegant tripartite approach. But perhaps sensing that only something eye-popping and spectacular would catch the assessors' attention, Lyle abandoned reason and, going way over the top, proposed a quasi-classical model replete with a cacophony of columns, pediments, temple motifs and a highly excessive sculptural program.

This competition revealed the gulf between the quality of the winning designs and the submissions by the four Canadians. Not that the Canadians were bad designers – on the contrary, all four of the architects that submitted plans were good at what they did, but with little opportunity to design high-rise structures and few local examples to study, they were not in a position to explore the design challenges the medium offered. The opportunity for designing high-rise buildings was far greater in America than anywhere else, and when Lyle was presented with another chance to propose a multi-storeyed structure (for the head office of the Bank of Nova Scotia seven years later), he was better prepared for the project by spending time in New York studying first-hand the most current innovations and stylistic trends.

Sometimes becoming involved at the inception of a project is a surefire way of getting the job. But at other times, even that is no guarantee. In 1919, Lyle prepared plans for a Women's Building, which later became Whitney Hall at the University of Toronto. During the preceding decade the university had significantly expanded and the number of women attending had steadily increased. Having no suitable residential facilities, the women began to lobby for a building of their own. Becoming involved before funds were secured, Lyle designed a Romanesque-style women's residence that was very much in keeping with neighbouring University College. In an attempt to raise awareness and finances for the building, Lyle

3.13, 3.14, 3.15, 3.16, 3.17
Chicago Tribune Building competition proposals, including the winning scheme by Howells & Hood (left), the second-place submission by Finland's Eliel Saarinen (second from left) and three of the four Canadian entries: Lyle (centre), Hugh Jones of Montreal (second from right), Walters & Wilkes of Toronto (far right).

3.18 Lyle's 1919 proposal for a Women's Building, which later became Whitney Hall at the University of Toronto.

3.19 Toronto Regiment C and D Companies, Third Battalion, proposed commemoration memorial, Saint Julien, France, 1919.

Opposite page: 3.20 Memorial Arch, Royal Military College, Kingston, Ontario.

gave a number of public slide presentations, but to no avail. The scheme languished for lack of funds for over a decade. By the time sufficient sums were in place, the choice of architects became Mathers & Haldenby while Lyle had to make do with the title of consulting architect.

Monuments: Commemorating the Fallen

In 1919, Toronto Regiment C and D Companies of the Third Battalion, wishing to commemorate the 2,000 men they lost in a German gas attack, retained Lyle to design a private memorial at Saint Julien, France. Lyle's proposed monument was a classical antique pylon formally placed on a stepped podium. It was a meticulously proportioned structure, with a base, Doric columns framing a commemorative dedication with relief panels, and capped with an entablature and suitably dressed with classical detailing. An illustration of it was featured in *Construction* that year, with a caption by Lyle urging others to follow in the Toronto regiment's footsteps and leave the job of designing such memorials to architects rather than amateurs in order 'to halt the blight of hideous designs executed in a slovenly manner.'[11]

Lyle was not alone in his concerns. Acknowledging the need to commemorate the exploits of Canadian troops overseas, Parliament established a special committee of the House of Commons who proceeded to appoint a Canadian Battlefield Memorials Commission. The military and political appointees of the commission, along with Percy Nobbs as architectural adviser, decided to erect eight memorials on sites where the major battles involving Canadians were fought – Vimy, Bourlon Wood, Le Quesnel, Dury and Courcelette in France and Saint Julien, Hill 62 (Sanctuary Wood), Passchendaele in Belgium. With Saint Julien now a National Monument Site under the jurisdiction of the federal government, Lyle's proposal for a private memorial was quietly dropped.

The commission's grand plans for memorials at all major battlefields became overshadowed, however, by the proposed monument for Vimy Ridge. The battle at Vimy had become such a metaphor for Canadian nationhood that it consumed all the resources of the commission. In 1920, Toronto sculptor Walter S. Allward won an open competition for the war monument when his proposal was selected from 162 submitted designs. The other seven official battle sites were relegated to second place, commemorated by small cenotaphs or memorials.

The architectural forms used prior to World War I for memorial design included Roman columns, triumphal arches and Egyptian obelisks, but the nature and severity of the destruction from the war gave rise to two new forms and approaches to commemorate the dead. First, the cenotaph became a symbol of remembrance of all who had perished and whose bodies were never found. The cenotaph, of Greek origin, is a structure to replace the dead that may have been lost in battle or at sea, where a burial was not possible. It was revived by the French in 1919, at the Paris Victory Parade, where a temporary wooden cenotaph was erected at the Arc de Triomphe for the troops to march past and salute in honour of their dead. The solemn associations of that act appealed to the British, who were mourning over a million of their dead citizenry, and later that same year, they too had a Peace Celebration March, past a temporary cenotaph designed by Sir Edwin Lutyens. That cenotaph was recreated in Portland stone on the same site in 1920. The second new approach, which was to address the 'modern anxiety of erasure,'[12] was the inscribing of names of all the soldiers who had died or were missing in action on all commemorative work.

In Canada, virtually every community across the country that had sent and lost citizens to the war honoured them with structures. These ranged from the very simple, such as Manitoulin District's cenotaph with only four names, to the monumental, such as the Memorial Chamber in the Peace Tower on Parliament Hill in Ottawa, which records the 60,000 Canadians lost in action. One of the most impressive war memorials from this era is Lyle's 1921 Memorial Arch at the Royal Military College in Kingston, Ontario.

Wanting to commemorate those from the RMC Academy who had made the supreme sacrifice for their country, Brigadier-General C. J. Armstrong, RMC commandant

TO THE GLORIOVS MEMORY OF THE EX-CADETS
OF THE ROYAL MILITARY COLLEGE OF CANADA
WHO GAVE THEIR LIVES FOR THE EMPIRE

3.21 *Memorial Arch, Royal Military College, Kingston, Ontario.*

Opposite page: 3.22 The facade facing the college features an inscription from the poet Rupert Brooke.

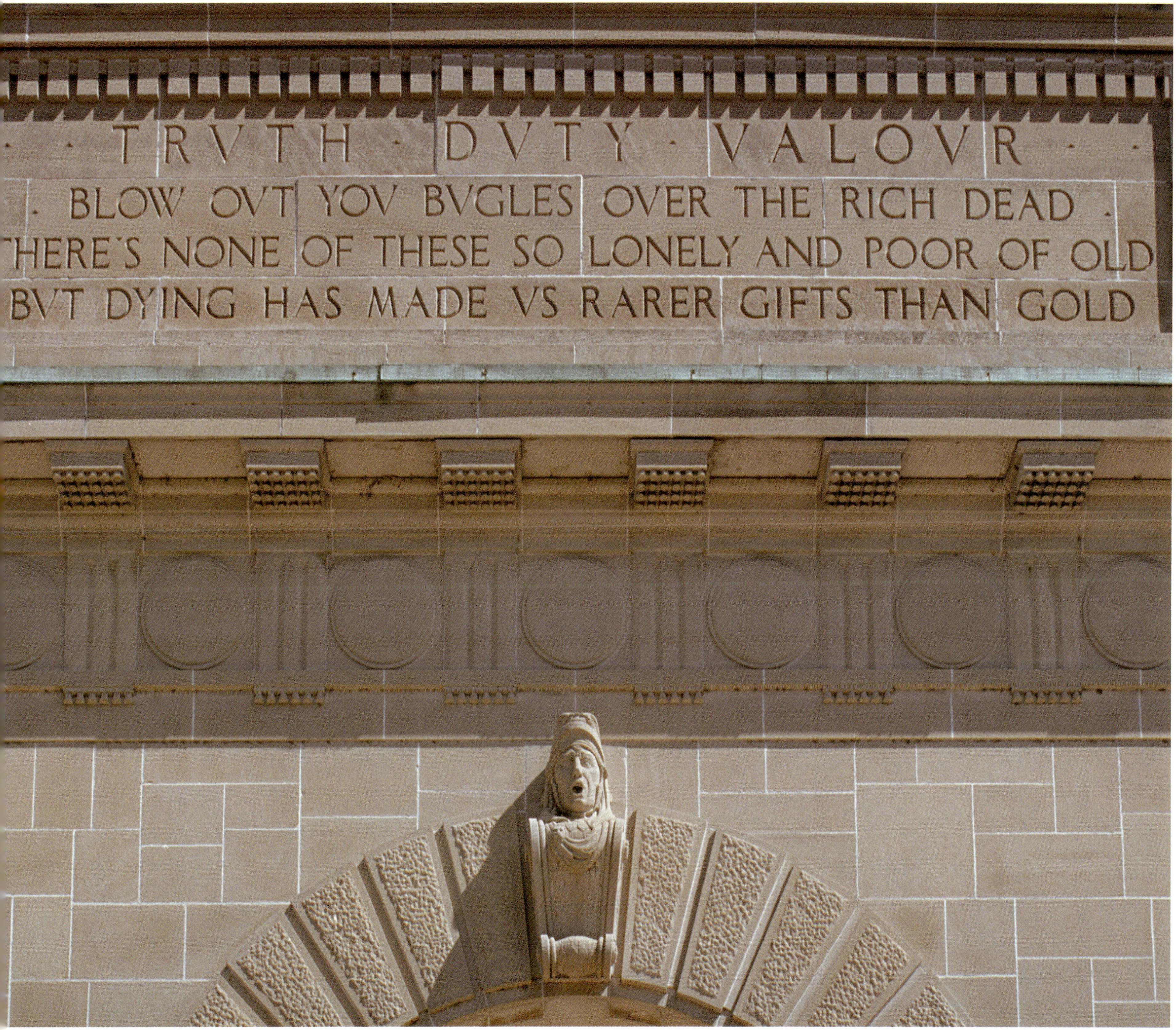
TRVTH · DVTY · VALOVR
BLOW OVT YOV BVGLES OVER THE RICH DEAD
HERE'S NONE OF THESE SO LONELY AND POOR OF OLD
BVT DYING HAS MADE VS RARER GIFTS THAN GOLD

Major-General Sir A. C. Macdonell and members of the 'Old Eighteen,' the first graduates of the college, took up the cause of a suitable memorial. An ex-cadet from Montreal, Louis Amos, was also involved with the organization of the competition and provided a perspective sketch of his vision of the winning design for a widely circulated fundraising pamphlet.

The RMC drew from the War Memorial Commemoration processes established by both the Battlefield Memorials Commission and the Ontario Advisory Committee. They hired Ramsay Traquair, Professor of Architecture at McGill University, as their assessor and prepared the conditions for the competition. The competitors included Sproatt & Rolph and John M. Lyle from Toronto, J. Omer Marchand and Fetherstonhaugh & McDougall from Montreal, as well as three ex-cadets: Montreal's Amos, K. J. Baldwin of Toronto and John Woodman of Winnipeg. The program was outlined to the competitors: '[T]he Memorial Arch is to be placed on or near the site of the present entrance gates to the Royal Military College at Kingston, Ontario. The promoters desire that the arch shall be well seen from the road approaching from Kingston, and for this purpose the Arch may be set back on the angles of the grounds. The existing gate lodge may be removed if necessary, and the expense of this removal will not be included in the cost of the monument. The Arch is to be used as an actual entrance gate, and has to be large enough to take wheeled traffic and infantry column marching in fours and face in the direction of Kingston.'[13] Other conditions were the inclusion of the Royal Arms, the Arms of the Royal Military College, the motto 'Truth, Duty, Valour' and a means for exhibiting 200 names of the fallen in the interior of the arch. Recommending that the memorial be constructed of local Queenston limestone, the committee set the budget at $50,000.

After careful consideration of the proposals, Traquair reported to the committee in 1921 with his assessment of Lyle's design. It was, he said, 'distinguished by fine proportion, a skillful and economical use of delicate detail, an imposing mass and the opportunity for the display of sculpture, should this be desirable at a future date.' Pointing out that the design used 'somewhat austere lines' he thought were well 'suited to a Military school,' he noted that Lyle's straightforward handling of the massing 'should show well as approached from Kingston.'[14] Traquair also suggested that a rough wooden model of the structure be constructed and positioned on the road to ensure the right location, a recommendation the building committee followed.

None of the other designs have survived, although all the proposals were exhibited in the Art Gallery of Toronto. Although the committee requested a design in keeping with the other Collegiate Gothic–style buildings on the campus, Lyle's design drew from ancient Roman military traditions and precedents of arch designs from France and the U.S. These included the Arc de Triomphe du Carrousel, by architects Percier & Fontaine, in 1806–08, and the Arc de Triomphe at Etoile consecrated in 1836, designed by Jean Chalgrin, both in Paris. In the U.S., there was the Soldiers' and Sailors' Memorial Arch at Grand Army Plaza, Brooklyn, built in 1889, and Stanford White's (of McKim, Mead & White) Washington Arch, in Washington Square, New York, from 1892.

Lyle's proposal cleverly incorporated the then-current trend of commemorative design using the form of a cenotaph and leaving space for the names of the fallen, with a classical Roman arch. The memorial consisted of a structure forty-six feet high and forty-two feet wide, with cenotaphs flanking each wing and attached with a low-arced retaining wall that successfully reinforces the sombre nature of the work. Sculpted relief panels of Roman armour shields and a full battle dress act as a base for the rusticated quoins, which terminate at the dentillated cornice of the attic storey. The edges of the structure are sufficiently highlighted with rusticated voussoirs, and the apex of the arch features a keystone of a soldier with headdress in full battle cry. A. F. Harvey's drawings of the sculptural panels were exhibited at *An Exhibition of Architecture and Allied Arts* at the Art Gallery of Toronto in 1927 and that same year reproduced for the front cover of the *Journal of the RAIC*. The firm of Balmers & Blakney executed the plaster models,

3.23 3.24, 3.25, 3.26
Decorative panels, Memorial Arch.

and the carved stonework was produced by the most prominent of Canadian architectural sculptors, Ira Lake.

Commemorative bronze plaques bearing the names of the fallen as well as of the battles were placed in the barrel vault. The attic storey was decorated with swags and shields and bore an inscription on the north side: 'To the glorious memory of the ex-cadets of the Royal Military College of Canada, who gave their lives for the Empire, erected Anno Domini MCMXXII.' Concerned about possible interference from the committee, Lyle wrote, 'We think that it is important, from the designer's point of view, that the inscription should be approximately of the length given in the accompanying data, owing to the fact that these inscriptions bear a direct relation to the design, giving texture and scale to the architecture.' Lyle also commented on the inscription on the attic storey of the Gananoque Road facade, which he thought should be 'descriptive and documentary in character, and that the corresponding inscription towards the college side should be suggestive and poetical in spirit.'[15] Following his advice, the college side features an inscription from the poet Rupert Brooke, reminding cadets of the seriousness of their commitment and the nature of sacrifice: 'The Dead: Blow out, you bugle, over the rich Dead./There's none of these so lonely and poor or old,/But, dying, has made us rarer gifts than gold.'

Deviating from the committee's guidelines, Lyle suggested the monument be built from Indiana limestone, a material he preferred because it could be cut into large blocks and was more suitable for the finely carved details proposed, and for its weathering properties. Ever the patriot, he apologized for his choice: 'The Canadian Architects would, of course, be only too delighted to use a Canadian stone if such were available.'[16] Lyle considered the plaza surrounding the memorial 'most important, as it will lead the eye to the Arch and give a proper vista. It will also afford space for the parading of troops on ceremonial occasions.' Lyle gave special instructions for the landscaping as well: 'Flanking the main plaza entrance would be grass plots surrounded by Japanese Barberry hedges. These grass plots to take the architectural lines as suggested on the

3.27, 3.28 Lyle with top hat and cane amid the military and political dignitaries at the opening ceremony for the Memorial Arch.

drawing, in order to conform to the development on the opposite side of the roadway and to emphasize the architectural lines necessary to lead the eye to the Arch.'[17]

After a few years, the necessary funds were finally raised, and Governor General Lord Byng laid the memorial's cornerstone in a ceremony on June 23, 1923. The arch was formally unveiled on June 15 the following year and Lyle attended the ceremonies with his mother. As they sat watching the proceedings, one of the college's old boys approached and insisted that Lyle join in the activities. Lyle recorded the moment: '[T]here were a great many old cadets, now generals and high ranking officers in the Canadian Army, that came in line after the cadets, so I was hustled along with some of the Committee and joined the march through the Arch.'[18] Beaming with pride and self-satisfaction, Lyle was no doubt happy to join in the celebration of a structure he considered 'one of the highlights of my career as an architect.'[19]

In an article for *Construction* in 1922, based on a speech he had delivered earlier that year and suitably entitled 'Monumental Architecture and Town Planning,' Lyle describes the qualities that good monument work should possess. He writes, '[T]he structure should be distinctly commemorative and suggest the character of the design…be a work of art, beautifully designed and executed… It should be the finest product of the designer's art where, with painstaking and sympathetic care from the foundation to the crowning stone, a structure that would strike the imagination and point the path of duty to generations still unborn, that the youth of our city should be reminded of the sacrifices that have been made in the past so that they might walk abroad in peace and freedom.'[20] These lofty ideals were no doubt what Lyle aspired toward with his design for the Memorial Arch.

Commercial: Exotic at Present

In 1922, having for years been vocal in his disapproval of the appearance of Toronto's busiest commercial street, Lyle got the opportunity to personally address the problem. Up until then, in both his writings and his speeches, Lyle had disparaged Yonge Street's meanness, and its proliferation of false shopfronts that were further defaced by unregulated billboard and store signage, all hidden behind electrical and streetcar poles and wires. Given the opportunity to lead by example in designing Yonge Street's Thornton-Smith Building, Lyle was eager to bring his vision to life.

The Thornton-Smith Building was a three-storey structure, built to accommodate an antique and interior design business. Lyle described its style as a 'modernized Italian treatment of simple character.'[21] Its most prominent features are the five two-storey showroom windows. All architectural elements were designed to show the thinness of the walls with low-relief pilasters and very narrow windows, with few reveals and no trim. The facade stonework, especially around the window voussoirs, was finely pointed. The architect's preoccupation with cast shadows and the interaction of light and dark, and the contrast between his and earlier architects' handling of these issues, is wonderfully illustrated in a period photograph. Reflecting the changed role of the wall, which, having been replaced by the metal substructure, was no longer needed to carry the weight of the building, the contemporary perspective was moving toward flatter exterior features.

The photograph reveals the nineteenth-century approach on the building to the left, whose highly defined ornamental work casts pronounced shadows across the face of the buildings, while the only feature to produce a shadow on the Thornton-Smith Building is the roof overhang. More preoccupied with the shadow of the fenestration voids, Lyle's design features metal window spandrels decorated with swags delineating the first and second floors, while the drapery contained within the round window heads contrasts and softens the transition from the white ashlar facing of the exterior walls to the dark interior spaces within. The remaining trim of the cornice is similarly handled in a thin contemporary manner. A steep pitched roof of red-brown Spanish ceramic tiles caps the festive character of the design.

Lyle's approach to his design found favour with another critic of Yonge Street, Eric Arthur, who wrote, 'Those people who in designing a façade, attach importance to the architecture of surrounding buildings surely have a problem here if they would design their building in the most chaste of the Yonge Street-esque, and that Mr. Lyle acted rightly in wholly ignoring the sordid surroundings of his site, the most ardent of the school would surely agree. It certainly looks rather exotic at present, but we trust the day will come when any of its flanking shops will appear strange and slum-like in a street of well designed buildings.'[22]

In 1926, the Ontario Association of Architects held a large exhibition of its members' work on buildings constructed after the war. At this show Lyle presented the Memorial Arch at the Royal Military College, the Bogert residence and the Thornton-Smith Building. All three structures were singled out. Lyle was awarded a first-place finish for the Memorial Arch, an honourable mention for the residence and another first, this time in the commercial category, for the Thornton-Smith Building. Further acknowledged as the 'finest work on view at the present convention,' Lyle's design for the Yonge Street building received the OAA's first gold-medal award.[23] The building became one of Lyle's portfolio pieces and received a great deal of attention. It was exhibited locally, nationally and internationally, and was written up in architectural journals in London and New York.

Through a convergence of events in 1923, Lyle's position as a leader in the Toronto architectural community had solidified. Eric Arthur, who had emigrated from England in 1923 to take up the post of Professor of Architecture in the Faculty of Applied Science and Engineering at the University of Toronto, was in a good position to observe the city's architectural environment. In a report for the OAA, Arthur noted that the 150 members of the architectural profession located in Toronto in the 1920s were, in the main, divided into two camps. He found this rather unusual for a city of Toronto's size, but reassured his readers that the two camps 'live together in perfect harmony.'[24] The two consisted of 'the traditional Renaissance style, and they are the big majority, led by Mr. John Lyle; and there is that small band which practices Gothic architecture, led by Messrs. Sproatt & Rolph.'[25] The positive reception of a number of high-profile works, including the Thornton-Smith Building, Union Station, the Bank of Nova Scotia's Ottawa branch and the Memorial Arch in Kingston, as well as the respect obtained through his teaching, writing and lecturing on architectural issues, had all contributed to Lyle's growing reputation.

In 1922, Lyle gave a speech and wrote an article on 'American Architecture' that served as both a summation of his work to date and an unintentional epitaph for Beaux-Arts Classicism. He praised the style's proponents for their virtues of scholarship, solidity and simplicity, and for their restraint, execution and handling of monumental work. Having peaked in the pre-war era, the Beaux-Arts style in North America was now on the wane. Its principal exponents, the two New York firms of McKim, Mead & White and Carrère & Hastings, had seen their power and influence diminished. White had died in 1906, McKim in 1909 and Mead had withdrawn from the practice by 1914, leaving the firm in the hands of a new generation of less skilled principals. Likewise, Carrère & Hastings had undergone changes. John M. Carrère died in a car accident in 1911, leaving Thomas Hastings to handle the firm's functions as well as continue as the principal designer until his death in 1929. In Canada, the classical architects like Lyle, Chapman, Marchand and the Maxwell brothers were a generation younger than their American counterparts, and at the peak of their careers. But the need for monumental work financed by expanding governments or large corporations had diminished. The expansive pre-war building program that gave rise to a series of government buildings in the western provinces, monumental railway stations often accompanied by equally grand hotel schemes, and large, impressive head offices for national banks and insurance institutions was never resumed after the war. During the 1920s, although classicism was still the dominant mode, the projects were more modest in scale, fewer in number and generally less innovative in approach.

3.29 Lyle's design for the Thornton-Smith Building, Yonge Street, Toronto, received the OAA *first gold medal award in 1926.*

Chapter 4: 1924–1928

Enthusiastic Propagandist

An Emerging National Style

The theme of nationalistic and regional styles evolving out of our collective cultural past was one Lyle continued to explore in talks, articles and slide presentations during the mid-1920s. In many ways, Lyle was mirroring the rise of a Canadian consciousness that had been surfacing not only on the political front but also in creative fields. In painting, a new art movement that had been maturing and developing during the war years came into full bloom in 1920, with the first exhibition by the Group of Seven at the Art Gallery of Toronto. This joint show featured a panorama of canvases from artists who were searching for and defining distinctive national symbols and forming an indigenous school of Canadian painting. The impact of their work on the public and the creative community was significant, feeding into a new sense of nationalism and finding a Canadian voice that had been stirring since the conclusion of World War I.

In 1916, national concern was focused on Ottawa with the accidental burning of the Parliament Buildings and the subsequent eleven-year reconstruction process of the central block and wings by John Pearson of Darling & Pearson, Toronto, and Montreal's J. Omer Marchand. It was only natural that the reconstruction would be in Gothic Revival, the same style as the original. The Gothic Revival had been widely considered Canada's first national architectural style, the most visible example being the original 1856 Parliament Buildings by Thomas Fuller and Chilion Jones. Many of the country's established and non-conformist ecclesiastical buildings that were erected throughout the nineteenth century were also designed in the same style. It was an obvious choice given its associative and symbolic links to British heritage and the Houses of Parliament at Westminster. But since the 1890s another style had begun to be identified as truly Canadian, sparked by the construction of the Chateau Frontenac in Quebec City by Canadian Pacific Railway's American architect Bruce Price. Price introduced the Chateau Style to the country, employing the characteristic forms of Northern French buildings – steep pitched roofs, pavilions, towers and picturesque silhouettes. This style's success was immediate and began to challenge the Gothic Revival as a national style. From the turn of the twentieth century to the beginning of World War I, the Gothic Revival and Chateau styles were the most dominant forms used for grand hotel schemes, federal government structures, collegiate schools and ecclesiastic buildings. These styles became officially sanctioned when the Holt Commission of 1913–15, whose mandate was to develop a civic plan for Ottawa and Hull, recommended that all new government buildings emulate the style of the most prominent buildings in Ottawa – either the Gothic Revival of the Parliament Buildings or the Chateau Style of the Chateau Laurier.

It wasn't just bureaucrats who were trying to identify a Canadian architectural identity. Other architectural voices had tried to herald the arrival of new and distinctively Canadian national or regional styles, perhaps prematurely. For example, Toronto's Alfred Chapman in 1913 foresaw a new light 'breaking in upon the architecture of the country,' attributing this development to the two distinctive types of architects, with different educational backgrounds, who were practicing in the country. There were the English-trained architects who rose through the apprenticeship programs responsible for producing 'clever individual artists' who, said Chapman, were 'strong in the refined sense of traditional beauty.' And there were those who followed the French/American Beaux-Arts educational models that Chapman called 'modern organizations for producing good architecture.' Writing that these two influences in the country 'should produce the basis of a great architectural development,'[1] Chapman, however, did not speculate as to what form, style or shape this new architecture would take, only that the foundation was there for it to evolve.

After a cross-country tour, Montreal architect Hugh Vallance was in a position to talk about the emergence of regional styles in the country. In 1923, in an address to the OAA, Vallance noted that in the contemporary residences of cities such as Montreal, Toronto and Hamilton, there was a 'development which is not quite English nor is it American.' Other cities he singled out for having an indigenous look

Opposite page: 4.1 A silhouette of the Gage Park Fountain, Hamilton, that Lyle designed in 1926.

included Winnipeg, which he thought had a style that was 'local, but more influenced by the work in neighbouring states,' and Vancouver, whose character he thought was 'largely influenced by the material.'[2]

At the height of his Beaux-Arts success, Lyle took the unusual step of re-evaluating his work and developing a 'critical interest in the Canadian architectural movement.'[3] This was sparked by critiques of his Bank of Nova Scotia building in Ottawa by fellow architects during a series of chance encounters. The first of these took place when Lyle, returning from an inspection of the Ottawa bank, met a long-time friend from the École des Beaux-Arts in Paris, J. Omer Marchand, who was working on the reconstruction of the Parliament Buildings. Marchand greeted Lyle with, '"Hé bien! mon vieux. I have just seen your bank c'est très bien, it is well studied, ç'a le goût Anglais" – so I asked to him do you think it looks like the work of an English architect? "No," he said, "it does not look English, French or American, but it does look like the work of a man trained in the French School – mais! ç'a le goût Anglais."'[4]

After his return, Lyle met fellow Toronto architect Mackenzie Waters, who commented, 'I saw your Bank the other day in Ottawa; it looks like a London street facade. You must have studied Robert Adam when you were developing your design.'[5] Lyle responded that he had never considered the eighteenth-century Englishman Robert Adam's work, but rather his sources of inspiration were Greek and Roman architecture. Sounding somewhat defensive, he added that his usual approach, conditioned by his Beaux-Arts training, was not 'to design a building that would be a replica of any building, but rather a marriage of known motifs and ornament treated in a logical or personal manner.'[6] Struck by these comments, Lyle realized he had unconsciously designed a work that resembled an eighteenth-century English style even though he had modelled it on more ancient sources. This observation triggered an examination of the unconscious creative process that had led him to this design. He also expanded the question to include whether a subconscious architectural taste influenced by architects' education and cultural backgrounds was developing in Canada.

Lyle expected that the emerging Canadian architecture would be a synthesis of the country's founding nationalistic traditions and those of major immigrant populations. Noting that Montreal and Toronto architects were split stylistically along national lines, he carved out a niche for Canada that lay between them: 'The predominant note in Canadian architecture is not English; it is not French; and it is distinctly not American. It has a vigor, a tang, a boldness, an individuality that is Canadian.'[7] He realized that the external conditions such as climate, material and traditions play their part in the forming of a national architecture, but the primary reason was that the country's architects are 'a group of trained men with the background of scholarship.'[8] Lyle noted that these groups 'have unconsciously evolved a phase of architecture characterized by a certain restraint, a certain Anglo-French character that stamps it as personal.'[9]

To support his argument, Lyle presented – at a commemorative banquet honouring Sproatt & Rolph for winning the prestigious American Architectural Association's gold medal in 1926 – a lecture entitled 'Canadian Architecture,' during which he showed about forty slides of buildings across the country. The selection was not his alone, but had been made with the Dean of the University of Toronto's School of Architecture, Brigadier-General C. H. Mitchell, and Professor Eric Arthur. This survey of what the three men considered the best in contemporary design in Canada included Sproatt & Rolph's Hart House and Memorial Tower at the University of Toronto; Darling & Pearson's Sun Life Building, Montreal; Ross & MacFarlane's Chateau Laurier, Ottawa; the Maxwell brothers' Parliament Buildings, Regina; the Herald Building, Calgary; and J. Omer Marchand's Chapel du séminaire de théologie, Montreal. It also included three of Lyle's works: Union Station in Toronto, the Memorial Arch in Kingston and the Bank of Nova Scotia in Ottawa. Focusing on these buildings, Lyle noted the distinct and personal characteristics of the works in an effort to define a truly Canadian architecture.

Left top: 4.2 Ross & MacFarlane, Chateau Laurier, Ottawa.

Left bottom: 4.3 Sproatt & Rolph's Hart House, University of Toronto.

Above: 4.4 Darling & Pearson, Sun Life Building, Montreal.

Above: 4.5 A residence designed by Mathers & Haldenby that Lyle admired for its French and English-Georgian features.

Opposite page: 4.6 Entrance gates to Wynnstay, designed for Hamilton businessman F. F. Dalley in Ancaster, Ontario, in 1925.

He singled out works for praise that were amalgams of many different stylistic sources, including French, English, Scottish and American. Lyle noted the challenges that faced the country's designers in their attempts to define a national style: '[T]here is no such thing as an architectural style being borne over night, but rather is it a gradual growth, known motifs and styles of different periods forming the basis of the designer's inspiration, who, in turn, by reasons of climatic conditions or of cost, through his scholarship and ability is able to impart, consciously or unconsciously, that cache and touch which stamps his building with a personal or national note.'[10]

Residences: Amalgam of Sources

The search for an indigenous Canadian voice in architecture was given a boost with the publication of two academic studies on early built forms in Quebec and Ontario. In 1920, Ramsay Traquair of the Architecture Department at McGill University produced a scholarly volume on early Quebec buildings using his own and his students' drawings as illustrations. In 1925, he also published an article, 'The Old Architecture of Quebec,' in the *Journal of the RAIC* and discussed examples of well-preserved seventeenth- and eighteenth-century architecture, such as the Château de Ramezay and the Ursuline Convent at Trois-Rivières. In Ontario, Eric Arthur and his students worked on a similar study, producing a brochure of measured drawings from local examples of eighteenth- and nineteenth-century Georgian and American Colonial–style houses. In 1927, a series of enthusiastic articles written by Arthur, starting with 'The Early Architecture of the Province of Ontario,' appeared in the *Journal*, confirming and promoting the Georgian as an indigenous native style.

In 1928, W. L. Somerville, the president of the OAA, wrote on current residential trends of the past decade and noted that there were two lines of thought among the province's designers: 'those in favour of what might be called the romantic or picturesque type of house and the other the formal; the latter usually expressed in the Renaissance, English, or the so-called American Colonial predominating. The English Georgian and American Colonial are certainly our rightful heritage in Ontario.'[11] Another reviewer noted that 'quite definitely the Georgian establishes itself still more firmly as the choice of the Toronto architects.' The article added, 'The term "Georgian," however, is so pleasantly broad in its significance and in the long period which it covered that it has acquired a certain dangerous looseness.'[12]

In Lyle's address 'Canadian Architecture,' there were among the body of work discussed six slides of current residences. The work Lyle considered 'the most interesting and individual house that has been recently built in Canada' was a residence on Poplar Plains Road, Toronto, by Mathers & Haldenby. Lyle praised it as a 'distinctively personal building, with a suggestion of French, English-Georgian antecedents.'[13] Perhaps not coincidentally, those characteristics best summarize Lyle's own approach to the residences of this period, a synthesis of English and French cultures, based on Georgian models and infused with the architect's personal touch. This approach was not merely a matter of taste, it was also ideological. Through the union of these styles, Lyle hoped to achieve a truly Canadian architecture.

An example of this fusion of sources can be seen in Lyle's design of Wynnstay, for highly successful Hamilton businessman F. F. Dalley in Ancaster, Ontario, in 1925. A period review of the house noted that 'without unbending adherence to any particular architectural style, yet with a pleasant mingling of the traditions implanted in Canada by the French seigneurs and their British successors, this interesting house may well serve as an example of the new spirit, at once vigorous and gracious, which animates Canadian architecture today.'[14]

Fred Dalley had the business acumen to buy up a number of companies and thus corner the North American market on shoeshine products. His factories that produced the household names Shinola and 2 for 1 were located in Hamilton, Rochester and Brooklyn, with a large plant in Indianapolis. Having made his fortune, however, Dalley tired of the constant travelling to oversee his companies, sold the business to

4.7, 4.8, 4.9 A series of perspective drawings produced in 1924 (opposite page, top) and 1925 (opposite page, bottom, and above) that reflect Wynnstay's exterior and Lyle's preoccupation with the landscape design.

Opposite page, top left: 4.10 One of the hidden joys on the Wynnstay estate is the tea house designed by Dunington-Grubb.

Opposite page, middle left: 4.11 The large central hall connected the principal rooms of the ground floor.

Opposite page, bottom left: 4.12 The library.

Opposite page, top right: 4.13 Aerial view of Wynnstay, c. 1930s.

Opposite page, bottom right: 4.14 The living room was a combination of formality and comfort, and its windows provided a panoramic view of the Dundas Valley.

American interests and retired to Ancaster. There he commissioned Lyle to build his house on the family's 100-acre country estate, a scenic property along the Niagara Escarpment that was described as 'rolling eminence above the picturesque Dundas Valley.'[15]

To achieve architectural unity, the house was planned and located in careful relation to a comprehensive landscape scheme. Lyle's major objective was to design the house in accordance with the demands of the natural setting and take full advantage of the 360-degree panoramic view the site offered. The desired location was the crest of a long ridge, which was the highest point of the estate, with sharp drops on the east and more gentle slopes on the south and west. The house is situated quite a distance from the street entrance and is approached by a long, meandering road through the grounds. To best utilize the site, Lyle designed an asymmetrical plan with each major wing oriented to the views. The pegging of the site for the final placement of the house by client and architect was reflective of how critical the location was. They staked out the house four times in one day, only to be followed by another pegging a few days later. The scheme called for a central block with a formal axis, while a secondary axis at right angles to this connected the dining room to the library, and an additional wing with kitchen, pantries, mechanical rooms and servant quarters connected to the central block.

The scheme for the garden immediately surrounding the building was of primary concern and had to be carefully considered as well. The perspective drawings Lyle produced in 1924 and 1925, while primarily reflecting the house's exterior, also reveal a comprehensive garden plan for the south elevation (which was never built). These included graded terraces, retaining walls, pathways, stairs and plantings that are in sympathy with both the house and its setting and help make a gradual transition from the formality of the architectural lines to the informality of the open fields, woods and distant landscape. These drawings show Lyle's talent for landscape design, especially when it came to working around existing physical conditions. He establishes logical boundaries in the landscape and gardens that are in sympathy with the overall plan, takes full advantage of the differences in elevation, and his sense of scale and placement of plantings neither impede nor obstruct views, either into or away from the house.

The grounds of Wynnstay were landscaped by the firm of H. B. Dunington-Grubb, a successful, Toronto-based husband-and-wife team who had emigrated from England in 1911. Their practice flourished after they established Sheridan Nurseries, which provided them with the ornamental plant material they needed for their residential and urban projects across the province.

A comparison of the two perspective drawings to the finished product reveals the evolution of Lyle's design. The plans were similar, but in place of the main entrance the proposal featured a massive centrally located three-storey tower. This element was eliminated in the next perspective in favour of a continuous roofline, placing more focus on the smaller-hipped roof tower adjacent to the entrance. The built version reduced the central block to three bays and included a projecting right-angled end pavilion. A more local, picturesque and informal look was also suggested by random patterned local fieldstone, which was originally proposed for this purpose, but was rejected in favour of a brick base with a grey stucco finish.

The exterior of the house is markedly French in character, with its asymmetrical massing, steep pitched roofs, segmental dormers and squat tower. The projecting front entrance is arched and framed by pilasters, surmounted by an openwork iron balustrade. The house was constructed in stages, with the living room built a year after the main component was finished. To impart a more picturesque irregularity to the easterly pavilion that houses the library, it was projected slightly forward and oriented at a right angle from the central block, delineating a separate interior function for the room and allowing for better exterior views. The focus of the main facade is the tower, located to the west of the entrance and projecting to the same forward plane as the front porch and easterly pavilion. Its large windows illuminate the interior staircase, and below its roofline is a carved detail of the Dalley family's crest.

The westerly wing also is oriented at a right angle, flanking the central block and enclosing an 'L'-shaped courtyard where a circular driveway serves the front entrance. This wing's lower height and dormers cutting through the roofline signify its subservient status. It accommodates the kitchen, pantry and other service rooms.

One of the hidden highlights of the estate is an outbuilding designed by Lyle. Tucked away in one of the corners of the grounds, half-hidden by evergreens and scrubs, a bellcast-roofed tea house overlooks a tranquil pond that slowly drains down a cascading brook over layered stones, through woodlands, until it reaches the valley stream below. In 1926, Lyle's words of advice when viewing the year-end projects of his architectural students was that they display in their designs 'more restraint,' which he considered 'a great architectural quality.'[16] He practiced what he preached, and even an affluent project such as Wynnstay is restrained in character, with all projections, decorative elements, carved stonework and pilasters simply handled, and with less three-dimensional relief. In terms of character, finishes and furnishings, the interior was decidedly more English than the exterior. The principal rooms of the ground floor consist of the living room, library and dining room, all connected by the large central hall. These rooms are bright and spacious and have large, uninterrupted wall areas without any intrusions such as columns. They are well-lit by numerous, generously proportioned windows and have strategically located fireplaces that create focal points.

Continuing his attempt to achieve 'homogeneous units,' Lyle selected, arranged and coloured all the elements of each room. The living room, a combination of formality and comfort, occupied one wing of the building and its east-facing Palladian window commanded a panoramic view of the countryside on both sides of the Dundas Valley. The walls of the room were painted in a soft ivory parchment, with cornice and mouldings in an antique glazed salmon-pink colour. The eighteenth-century English theme was carried through with furniture groupings of Chippendale, Hepplewhite and Sheraton pieces, and a mantel in the style of the Adam Brothers. The dining room was warm and intimate, with rich, glowing colours – green wall panelling and gold-highlighted mouldings and cornice. It was furnished with a Sheraton table, sideboards and Chippendale chairs upholstered in a mustard-coloured Queen Anne floral pattern. Over the mantel hung a painting with an equestrian theme by the English painter George Stubbs. The ladies' powder room and washroom were light and lively. A large mirror dominated one wall and was decorated in the decoupage manner, with flowers, trees and chimpanzees. The floor was a patterned black-and-white marble, the wall and curtain in a scheme of soft pinks, while the washroom fittings were black marble and gold.

Lavish residences on this scale, with building costs alone over $110,000, were a rare phenomenon for Canada. The only other examples in the province at the time include Vincent Massey's Batterwood House in Canton, designed by Mathers & Haldenby in 1927–28, and the Gerald D. Larkin house built in 1926, on Castle Frank Road in Toronto, by the architectural firm of George, Moorhouse & King.

Lyle's quest for an authentically Canadian architecture through the synthesis of English and French sources can be more fully appreciated by comparing his 1926–27 design for the R. J. Christie residence on Frybrook Road in Toronto to an almost identical house designed for Lt.-Col. Norman D. Perry by Mathers & Haldenby. Both houses are similar in their use of forms, featuring a central block of three bays, two storeys high, with a steeply pitched roof with dormers and projecting end pavilions. Where they differ is in their use of materials and the stylistic source from which the forms were derived. The Perry house replicates the classical features of a Georgian house, with forms that are true to the period, and material, which is red brick with white dressings and keystones around the windows, and a pronounced dentillated cornice under the roofline.

Using the same vocabulary of architectural elements, the Christie house playfully interacts with its French, English and Italian sources, revealing a more imaginative use of material. The exterior walls are finished in smooth grey stucco, which

4.15, 4.16 Above: A residence designed by Mathers & Haldenby, for Lt.-Col. Norman D. Perry, Toronto, that used a massing scheme similar to that of Lyle's Christie Residence, Toronto (left).

Above: 4.17. R. J. Christie Residence, interior main hall, c. 1930.

Right: 4.18. Detail of stucco and brick wall treatment, with shutters.

contrasts well against the grey-green window shutters, whose ground-floor pairs exhibit a fanciful cut-out pattern. The stringcourse, quoins and chimneys feature exposed brick and stonework, and to impart a local character to the design, Toronto's indigenous grey brick was used. Although the forms were similar, the combination of different stylistic sources, coupled with the architect's individual touch and sympathetic use of material, elevates Lyle's design. For Lyle, a habitual use of the same forms, sources and material was archaeology, not architecture, and he found that most Canadian architects did not try to solve each new problem in a personal and individual manner, but relied heavily on or copied what had been achieved before, both in plan and detail. The Perry house, for example, is a handsome but archaeological reproduction of an eighteenth-century American colonial house that would not have been out of place in the then heavily publicized restoration and reconstruction of Williamsburg, Virginia.

The same imaginative use of combined styles and materials was carried through the interior of the Christie house. The entrance hall is paved in black Missisquoi and Kasota gold marble laid in the Italian manner, while the fireplace is framed in a black marble richly veined with gold. The grand and leisurely staircase has black Missisquoi marble treads with terrazzo risers and a wrought-iron rail with brushed steel and gold ornamentation. The stairwell ceiling is coffered in the Italian manner and decorated in blues, greys and deep ivories, while large, south-facing windows wash the interior with light. In the living room, Canadian knotty white pine panelling was used with classical features of channelled pilasters and a dentillated cornice. The bedroom was designed in a Georgian style and the library in a French Provincial with soft grey-toned oak panelling. For the dining room, a modernized version of the Louis XVI style is evident in detail and trim, which featured a Verde antique marble fireplace and polished steel surround complemented by jade-green walls.

Contemporary architects and writers such as W. L. Somerville were aware of Lyle's efforts and singled out his work for noteworthy praise in a period *Journal of the RAIC* article entitled 'Is Our Domestic Architecture Mediocre?' that featured illustrations and reviews of both the Perry and Christie houses. The title was misleading since Somerville thought highly of both houses – perhaps they were exceptions to the rule. Somerville called the Perry house an 'excellent example of what one might call Toronto Georgian,' but he singled out Lyle's work on the Christie house as 'an imaginative piece of clever design. Mr. Lyle has evidently had in mind some of the early Canadian houses of Upper Canada. It is thoroughly Canadian and a real contribution to our domestic architecture.'[17]

Another example of Lyle's use of Georgian forms in combination with indigenous Ontario features is the Dr. King Smith residence on Highland Avenue, Toronto, in 1925. Lyle and local architect Mackenzie Waters made a few attempts at the use of the two-toned brickwork, a local characteristic feature used by nineteenth-century architects. Lyle used this technique successfully at the King Smith residence on Highland Avenue, and Waters on a house on Park Road. Eric Arthur noted these attempts and congratulated the architects for being 'more successful with it than our 19th century builders.'[18] The front facade of the King Smith house has a main entrance framed with banded pilasters, supporting a scrolled broken pediment that has an urn in the apex and a Palladian window above it. The walls are constructed out of red brick with Indiana limestone trim for both the doorway and the Palladian window. The other windows on the facade and the roofline's stepped corbel gable are highlighted with grey brick.

An impressive but odd commission of this period was a Cotswold-type residence for T. C. Cowan, on Teddington Park Avenue, in Toronto in 1928. This popular subtype of the Tudor Revival house was English country style, based on the cottages built since medieval times in the Cotswold region of southwestern England. It became fashionable in North America through the 1920s, due in part to Henry Ford, the auto manufacturer, who brought a complete sixteenth-century Cotswold stone cottage house back from England and placed it in his outdoor museum in Greenfield

Top: 4.19. Dr. King Smith Residence, Highland Avenue, Toronto.

Bottom: 4.20. A residence designed by Mackenzie Waters, Park Road, Toronto.

Village, Dearborn, Michigan. This informal and romantic style featured stone facing, asymmetry, a steep, complex roofline, floor plans that tended to include small, irregularly shaped rooms, and upper rooms with sloping walls and dormers. The home might have had a sloping, slate or cedar roof that mimicked the look of thatch. A massive chimney often dominated the front or one side of the house.

Lyle designed a two-storey, asymmetrical building with a projecting gable-ended frontispiece. The stone house had a steep pitched slate roof with dormers, and windows highlighted with stone dressings and glazed with multi-paned glass. A pair of tall chimney stacks on either side framed the house and imparted a picturesque element to the composition. The east facade opened gracefully to the grounds, providing access from the main living and dining rooms that offered panoramic views of the ravine and the Rosedale Golf & Country Club.

The owner of this house, heir to the Cowan family fortune, had manufacturing and financial interests that included the Ontario Savings and Loan Bank in Oshawa, a bank Lyle was to design a year later. In contrast to all of Lyle's other residential works of this period, the Cowan house was neither exhibited by Lyle nor reviewed by the local architectural press. Presumably Lyle was not pleased with the results or perhaps he had to design to his client's specifications, putting aside his own preference for more indigenous Canadian architectural forms, and therefore felt little kinship to the work.

Banks: A Transitional Work

In the mid-twenties, when construction starts had picked up after a post-war recession, Lyle continued to work on several smaller, one-storey bank branch buildings, mostly for the Dominion Bank. His largest commission of this period was for the Dominion Bank on Bleury Street at St. Catherine in Montreal, in 1926. The modern tendency toward the use of flatter forms that Lyle explored in the Thornton-Smith Building in Toronto are continued here. The significance of this bank building in Lyle's oeuvre is that it's a transitional work, taking him from his Beaux-Arts classicism toward an awakening to the possibilities of the modern movement. Although he used a classical decorative program here, he also incorporated a flatter wall treatment, in an attempt to suggest the building's substructure.

The bank's exterior featured subtle projections of the facade, with the rounded corner entrance being slightly recessed. The fenestrations were classically handled: the window, doors and building edges were appropriately articulated through the use of rusticated quoins and sculpted keystones. The clock over the main entrance was treated in a classical manner with scrolls, columns, garlands and a curved pediment.

The unusually exaggerated proportions and height of the building meant this two-storey branch dwarfed similar neighbouring structures. The resulting brighter interiors, and the possibilities opened up by the corner entrance, allowed for a different approach to the plan. The high-ceilinged banking hall accommodated offices and a mezzanine, while the tellers' counters were placed on the outside walls. This created brighter work areas for the employees and still provided an attractive space for the bank's customers.

The design of the bank was not a smooth process, since its personnel were unusually fussy. Typically Lyle had to propose only one design to his clients for approval; on this occasion, however, the abundance of opinions on a building committee that consisted of general manager Clarence Bogert, the Montreal branch manager, the bank's in-staff architect and other high-ranking company officials meant a prolonged process. The bank manager, who was determined to have a corner entrance, did not even look at Lyle's original proposal. It took three series of plans before they all agreed on one and finally approved it in fall 1926. However, it was now the turn of the building's neighbours, who, unhappy with the proposed plan, held up construction with a court injunction. When it was finally time to begin, tenders for the project exceeded the bank's budget, leading to revisions, alterations and compromises before it was eventually completed. Perhaps due to the disjointed selection process,

Opposite page: 4.21 T. C. Cowan residence, Teddington Park Avenue, Toronto, with a later addition on the left.

Top: 4.22 Dominion Bank on Bleury Street at St. Catherine in Montreal.

Above: 4.23 The two-storey branch provided a bright interior, offices and a mezzanine.

Right: 4.24 Dominion Bank on Bleury Street at St. Catherine in Montreal features an embellished corner entrance.

the building has its faults, chiefly a lack of cohesiveness that was pointed out by one critic who thought the bank was 'more interesting as a detail and corner treatment than as a compo-sition,' and that he 'like[d] the facade to the cornice immensely, but the high attic storey with the balustrade seems too high. It would have been better without the balustrade

Commercial: High Traditions

American novelist Ernest Hemingway, a reporter for the *Toronto Star* newspaper from 1920 to 1924, wrote articles about the sporting life of the city, including its inhabitants' particular inclination toward betting on horse racing. He noted that there were, according to a horseman source who remained anonymous, '10,000 people in Toronto who bet on the races' with 'over $100,000 played each day,' and that 'for years Toronto has been known all over the world as the biggest betting town in North America.'[20] These bets were placed through various bookmakers in the city on races that occurred throughout the continent, but during the local racing season these activities took place at the city's only track, the Woodbine Race Course. This organization opened in 1874 on what were then the eastern outskirts of Toronto on a spacious tract of land that overlooked the Beaches neighbourhood and Lake Ontario. It changed its name in 1956 to Old Woodbine and then to Greenwood in the spring of 1963. When it was demolished in 1993, it brought an end to an era.

The Ontario Jockey Club's philosophy about racetrack policy and programming was to follow the 'high traditions of English racing.'[21] Those traditions also applied to the social environment at Woodbine, which was for decades a hub for the city's high society, a place to promenade one's fineries and mingle socially, and to see and be seen. Social columns in local papers reported on the latest news and gossip with headlines such as 'Society at The Woodbine [...] was the mecca towards which the social world flocked in hundreds on Saturday afternoon.'[22] The Woodbine was home to the Queen's Plate, North America's oldest annual horse race, a regal pageant to which the Lieutenant Governor of Ontario arrived in an open horse-drawn carriage with a royal guard as escort, and which was attended by men dressed in tails and top hats and women bedecked in their finest jewellery, silk dresses and spring hats.

The pomp, ceremony and social environment of the racetrack was one Lyle would have been right at home with. The executive board of the racetrack included Gooderham, Seagram, King Smith and Hendrie, members of the province's richest and most powerful families. Some of these individuals Lyle had known and socialized with since childhood and others he had designed private residences for.

To deal with overcrowding in the grandstands, as well as some deteriorating older buildings around the track, the Woodbine's executive board decided on an extensive building program that called for a new jockeys' room, a covered paddock, a directors' room and a members' stand. Lyle was commissioned to help determine the best course of action for the proposed structures. Along with Ontario Jockey Club secretary W. P. Fraser, they went on an extended research trip to the racecourses at Lincoln Fields, Chicago, and Churchill Downs and Latonia, in Kentucky. The final proposal contained a synthesis of ideas developed through what Lyle claimed to be a 'study of French, English and American tracks' and 'adopted from these three countries together with certain traditions of the old Woodbine Track plus some original ideas of the last Secretary – Mr. W. Fraser – and our own.'[23]

The new stand was constructed using reinforced concrete over a steel skeleton. Its lower level was devoted to 130 private boxes, with a large, centrally placed semi-circular Royal Box complete with a prominently displayed coat of arms made especially for the Lieutenant Governor of Ontario or other representatives of the crown. The upper level had one row of boxes and general seating behind it. Its roofs were cantilevered, with no columns to interfere with visibility. For those more interested in socializing than horse racing, there were wide corridors at the rear of each section that could accommodate a small orchestra, as well as washrooms, tea rooms, a bar and ladies' cloakrooms. To accommodate its inhabitants' prolific

Above: 4.25 Detail of the Royal Box, Woodbine Race Course, Queen Street East, Toronto.

Right top: 4.26 Directors' Building and Members' Stand.

Right bottom: 4.27 Interior of the paddock.

Opposite page: 4.28 Woodbine Race Course, perspective watercolour signed lower right, 'S. M. Maw,' signed lower left 'John M. Lyle', architect,' Queen Street East, Toronto.

betting habits, the parimutuel betting facilities were also located in the corridors but were segregated so as not to interfere with the 'holiday and social atmosphere' that made 'this track unique in America.'[24] In front of the stands, flower boxes gave plenty of brilliant bloom and colour to both the spring and fall events. The two-storey Directors' Building was a fashionable contemporary Georgian Revival–inspired design with private lounge rooms, kitchen and serving pantries, an executive boardroom and an upper verandah giving a panoramic view of the track. The open-air paddock was designed so that the jockeys and horses no longer had to parade in front of the crowds in adverse weather conditions; instead, the horses could be saddled in sheltered comfort and spectators given free access to view them before race time. This was the first such paddock in North America.

Monuments: Spouting Forth

A large, sixty-acre farm belonging to Hamilton's once-prominent Gage family, originally on the city's outskirts, was, by the early twentieth century, engulfed by new residential construction. When the Hamilton Parks Department proposed to buy the farm and convert it into a park, the last surviving member of the Gage family retained the name, in exchange for a $20,000 donation to be used for a memorial fountain. City Council purchased the Gage property in October 1917 and transferred Gage Park to the Parks Board in 1922. The landscaping firm of H. B. Dunington-Grubb was hired to design the overall concept of the park, and in 1926 Lyle was commissioned to design the Gage Memorial Fountain. The park was laid out by Dunington-Grubb in a scenic fashion, with large open areas in the centre of the grounds offset by asymmetrical groupings of trees and plantings along the bordering streets. To counter this informal setting and give a focal point, Lyle designed a series of formal walkways, garden beds and cascading pools, and a terrace and fountain on the north end of the park.

Lyle's approach, typical of Beaux-Arts architects when extending into garden or park design, meant there was a strong reliance on architecture, a symmetrical plan, careful attention to detail and proportion, and a masterful use of three-dimensional space. Conscious of the setting, Lyle was meticulous in his choices of placement and scale. Striving to balance the horizontal and vertical forms of the fountain with the natural elements of sky, earth and water, he located it at a strategic distance from the street. From the foot of the water pool, one's eye is led, by means of the cascading pools, to the central focus of the fountain. The composition is framed on a north-south axis by a pair of heavy retaining walls bracketing the elevated terrace and is terminated by the escarpment. The height of the terrace was consciously set at eye level to increase the horizontal perspective. The size of the fountain is overwhelming, reaching a height of about ten metres. This was calculated to ensure that the fountain would act as the vertical focal point breaking above the horizontal plane of the background escarpment.

A two-tier basin design, the fountain itself was not unusual for its time; similarly styled fountains could be seen at Gore Park in Hamilton or at the Canadian National Exhibition grounds in Toronto. Positioned in the middle of an elevated terrace, and reached by two large open staircases, a deeply inscribed dedication to the Gage family members runs along the fountain's base, and above it, the drum features a classically stylized group of cherub-like children dancing (since removed). Miss Gage made this latter suggestion during a meeting with Lyle, and also asked for a prominent display of her family's coat of arms, an idea that was quietly discarded. The figures were sculpted by M. Donald Cree and modelled by Florence Wyle. At the peak of the fountain, the water leaps skyward before cascading into a first-tier basin that, when full, spills over into the second level. From the fountain base and outside retaining wall, Lyle incorporated secondary sources of spouting water from four bronze turtles and ducks that interact with the cascading water.

Designing a fountain was a rare opportunity for an architect and one for which Lyle certainly rose to the occasion. This work was so highly regarded that it was awarded first prize in the Memorial category – over Chapman & Oxley's Princes'

4.29, 4.30 Gage Memorial Fountain, Gage Park, Hamilton, c. 1927. The drum section (since removed) featured a classically stylized group of cherub-like children dancing. The figures were sculpted by M. Donald Cree and modelled by Florence Wyle.

4.31, 4.32 To counter the informal setting of Gage Park and to give a focal point, Lyle designed a series of formal walkways, garden beds, cascading pools, and a terrace and fountain at the north end of the park.

4.33 The Diet Kitchen School – including (standing, from left to right) Lyle, Mackenzie Waters, C. B. Cleveland, (seated, from left to right) L. Somerville, Martin Baldwin, Eric W. Haldenby, A. H. Gregg, A. S. Mathers and (missing from photograph) Bruce H. Wright – was seen by the media of the day to be the architectural equivalent of the Group of Seven.

Gate for the Canadian National Exhibition – at the second Exhibition of Architecture and Allied Arts held in 1929. Eric Arthur, reviewing the piece, noted, 'Lyle has made the most of an opportunity rarely given an architect today of designing a fountain which is large enough to dominate a park. One may stand in pensive mood and gaze into a basin of the Gage fountain and see reflected in the water all the spouting monstrosities in cast iron or terra cotta of thirty or forty years ago, and feel a certain pride in the achievement of our time.'[25]

Enthusiastic Propagandist

A group of Toronto architects, led by Lyle, were inspired by two major artistic events of 1925 – the New York Architectural and Allied Arts Exposition and the Exposition Internationale des Arts Décoratifs et Industriels Modernes in Paris. Lyle had acted as an adjudicator of the Canadian submissions to the New York show, which also included work from the U.S., England and France, and displayed several of his own pieces, including the Bank of Nova Scotia, Ottawa, and the Thornton-Smith Building and Union Station, Toronto. The Paris exhibition was the more historically significant of the two events because it introduced the world to the art deco style and showcased contemporary French design in architecture, the allied arts, interior design and fashion.

In the spirit of these shows, and to further their own interests, Lyle and his group decided to hold a similar event in Toronto. This group, who frequented a local lunchtime spot, evolved into a loosely knit organization named after their favourite Bloor Street eatery, the Diet Kitchen. The Diet Kitchen School of Architecture – including Martin Baldwin, C. B. Cleveland, A. H. Gregg, Eric W. Haldenby, A. S. Mathers, W. L. Somerville, Mackenzie Waters, Bruce H. Wright and Lyle – was seen by the media of the day as the architectural equivalent of the Group of Seven. The driving force and spokesperson, Lyle wrote that 'painters have a lot of trick names for themselves. There is the Barbizon School, the Glasgow School and the School of Seven. So why shouldn't the architects have some trick names, too? I think you will agree that the designation Diet Kitchen School, has quite a toothsome sound.'[26] The organization was a tongue-in-cheek attempt to inject spirit and debate into the architectural community and come to terms with the ever-changing and radical new forces shaping current architectural trends. Until the beginning of World War II, the Diet Kitchen remained a location for lively architectural debate and a source of local news.

In 1927, the group organized an exhibition, the first of its kind in Canada to feature both architecture and the allied arts, at the Art Gallery of Toronto. Prominently featured alongside the photographs, drawings and architectural models were the decorative arts, crafts and manufactured items of fabrics, furniture, metal and glasswork, painting and sculpture. The objectives of the exhibition were threefold: to showcase the quality and standard of contemporary design and craft in Canada; to strengthen a co-operation between architecture and the allied arts; and to promote local design and continue developing a distinctively Canadian style. The show also included contributions from Europe and the U.S., with the metalwork from firms such as Samuel Yellin in Philadelphia and Edgar Brandt in Paris. Sculpture was well-represented with memorial pieces, decorative friezes and fountains carved by some of the country's most prominent practitioners – Florence Wyle, Frances Loring, Merle Foster, Gustav Hahn and Scott Carter. The exhibition proved a huge success, with over 29,000 visitors over a two-week period, an attendance surpassing the seminal exhibitions of the Group of Seven.

One member of the Diet Kitchen group, Martin Baldwin of Baldwin & Greene, took the spirit and objectives of the exhibition and applied them to architectural projects in the city. For the Concourse Building on Adelaide Street West, a speculative office building in 1928, the firm utilized a decorative program that included sculptural cast stonework and ceramic mosaics. The mosaics were created by Group of Seven painter and graphic designer J. E. H. MacDonald and his son Thoreau. This collaboration between architect and artists produced a unique work of local Canadian character. The mosaics were concentrated in the round-arched entrance to the building, and the ceiling was decorated with panels depicting airplanes, ships and other modes of modern transportation. A semi-circular abstract frieze dominates the entrance with an image of a flaming sun that enriches and nourishes the natural elements under its domain. (That same year, MacDonald was involved in another architectural collaboration when he designed a painted decorative mural of abstracted patterns loosely based on native Indian motifs for the foyer beams and ceiling at the Claridge Apartments in Toronto.)

More than any other architect in the country, Lyle actively promoted the profession through teaching, public lectures, slide presentations and articles. His energy and efforts were singled out by several appreciative sources. In 1927, during the annual OAA executive meeting, the organization's secretary, R. B. Wolsey, acknowledged two outstanding features of the year that brought 'our Association before the Public more than anything that has been accomplished during the thirty-seven years of its existence, I refer to the Architectural and Allied Arts Exhibition that has been assembled in the Toronto Art Gallery [sic] under the auspices of the Toronto Chapter and the address given before the Canadian Club by John Lyle.' He further acknowledged that the association owed Lyle a debt of gratitude, 'for in the eloquent address and able criticism he gave before the Canadian Club he has, single-handedly, aroused the interest of our people and created an appreciation of the fact that Architecture is a fine Art. We cannot have recognition or appreciation without criticism and that criticism is just as necessary for the Architect's good as it is for the public's education as to what constitutes good and bad Architecture.'[27]

Eric Arthur's review of the annual RAIC exhibition in 1927 compared Lyle to an Italian Renaissance preacher known for his passionate and eloquent sermons: '[I]n Toronto Mr. John M. Lyle like a Savonarola has fired thousands with an enthusiasm for the Art which he represents, who had all their lives considered Architecture but a necessary evil. That so practical a thing as building might be beautiful, and that Toronto might be a better place to live in if more people employed architects were news that must have set many people thinking.'[28]

Lyle also pressed ahead with his attempts at improving Toronto's urban landscape, giving a number of talks on civic improvements. He was at this point mostly concerned with the visual clutter resulting from the unregulated placement of hydro and telephone poles, as well as the retail shopfronts and signage, along the city's main streets. In an article on the front page of the leading daily in Toronto, Lyle strongly criticized the appearance of the city's retail business streets: 'I doubt if any city in the world of a similar size can show a shabbier street than Yonge Street, a meaner lot of shops, or a worse conglomeration of false fronts.'[29] Trying to appeal to the commercial interests of the storeowners, he stated that 'beauty has a cash value' and that it was in the business community's best economic interests to have visually appealing shops, neighbourhoods and districts in the attempt to attract more business. Lyle offered several suggestions for the improvement of these areas, including a proposal that the city's business community offer awards for the best-designed shop, and that all poles and projecting overhead signs be abolished. He also recommended the appointment of a civic art commission to oversee matters that affected the aesthetic life of the community.

The article served its purpose in generating energy and discussion, garnering responses from the paper's editor as well as its readers. Some claimed that Lyle 'was not far wrong,' while those who defended the city charged him with being 'unfair to Toronto.' In 1928, Lyle expanded on these themes in an address to the Toronto Board of Trade entitled 'Civic Beautification,' which was later published in the *Journal of the RAIC*. Once again, Lyle attempted to inspire his audience by urging them to realize the commercial value of a well-planned city with beautiful streetscapes, attractive buildings and fashionable storefronts. Acknowledging Lyle's unstinting efforts in the cause of his profession, the *Journal* editorial stated, 'The architectural profession in Canada needs more enthusiastic propagandists of the type of John M. Lyle…and urge that more architects in every community follow his example.'[30]

Lyle's contribution to the field of architecture and the high standard of his design work did not go unnoticed or unrewarded

Left: 4.34 Exhibition of Architecture and Allied Arts included works from Europe and the U.S., featuring metalwork from firms such as Samuel Yellin in Philadelphia and Edgar Brandt in Paris.

Right: 4.35 Lyle showed several works in the exhibition, including a dining room cabinet.

by professional institutions both at home and abroad. In 1925, he was elected into the Royal Canadian Academy, an honour bestowed upon the country's leading practitioners in the visual arts. This organization had always maintained a limited number of members, but opened itself to a group of architects that year that included H. G. Jones, Hugh Vallance, J. Omer Marchand, Ernest Cormier, all from Montreal, and Toronto's Alfred Chapman. Among the conditions of acceptance into the institution is a diploma work that is donated to the RCA permanent collection housed in the National Gallery of Canada. Lyle obliged and produced a watercolour of the Bank of Nova Scotia, Sparks Street Branch, in Ottawa. Three years later he was elected a fellow of the Royal Institute of British Architects, an honour that had been bestowed on only five other Canadian architects: C. B. Cleveland, V. D. Horsburgh, John A. Pearson, Ernest R. Rolph and Henry Sproatt. This award by the RIBA was a major acknowledgement of Lyle's professional achievements because it was given to the rare individual who not only had an outstanding track record of architectural merit in his country but whose work transcended it and had an influence that would provide inspiration for other architects and professionals.

Chapter 5: 1929–1931

Response to Modernism, Toward a Canadian Architecture

European Influences

The influential work of European Modernists was, by the mid-1920s, spreading throughout France, Germany, Holland and Scandinavia. It was also being introduced to North America through the New York–based architectural publications that kept abreast of current trends. In Canada, however, the conservative and reserved *Journal of the RAIC*, the architectural community's chief publication, had turned a blind eye toward European Modernism. It was not until 1929, with Lyle's article 'Address on Architecture,' that the modern movement found its way into the publication. The article was based on a talk Lyle had given at the annual convention of the Royal Architectural Institute of Canada. Lyle's lecture recounted his previous summer's ten-week excursion to France and England, undertaken primarily because he was 'anxious to study the modern movement in architecture, which is now sweeping over the world.'[1]

The origins and early influences of the twentieth century modern movement in architecture were multifarious. By the early 1900s, a number of architects in America and Europe had begun to develop new architectural visions to interpret the demands being placed upon them by emerging technologies, new materials and changing social conditions. Frank Lloyd Wright and Irving J. Gill in America, Victor Horta and Henry van de Velde in Brussels, Antoni Gaudi in Barcelona, Otto Wagner in Vienna and Charles Rennie Mackintosh in Glasgow were some of the architects seeking new interpretations and voices.

It was just after World War I that the search for a new architecture intensified and crystallized into a more formal doctrine. There were several different schools of thought with their own themes, philosophies and inspiration, but they could be roughly broken down into three broad categories: decorative, functionalist and regionalist.

The decorative camp was best seen through the work of French architect Robert Mallet-Stevens. Mallet-Stevens emerged after World War I as a fashionable avant-garde designer with important early commissions – the villa of the Vicomte de Noailles at Hyères of 1924; the Pavillon du Tourisme at the Exposition Internationale des Arts Décoratifs et Industriels Modernes; and terrace housing known as Wohnhaus, Paris, in 1926–27 (the street this housing was built on was later named rue Mallet-Stevens to commemorate the work of the architect). Mallet-Stevens' work was a sophisticated synthesis of cubist forms and decorative art deco detailing, using metal framing, reinforced concrete and wide expanses of glass.

The functionalist groups (whose work would later be dubbed the International Style) started to form independently of each other in three pockets of activity, with the Dutch De Stijl movement in the Netherlands, the work of Le Corbusier in France and the Bauhaus school in Germany. The De Stijl movement started primarily with a group of painters who attempted to express a spiritual harmony and utopian ideals by means of compositional reduction of all forms and colours to their bare essentials. They used simplified visual constructions of vertical and horizontal elements, with a colour scheme featuring the primary colours plus black, grey and white. The most significant architectural work produced under this style was the Schröder House, at Utrecht, Netherlands, in 1924 by Gerrit Rietveld.

In France, part painter, part architect Le Corbusier was publisher of a small monthly review, *L'Esprit nouveau*, in which he aired his ideas, which were gathered into his seminal work, *Vers une architecture*, published in 1923. Quickly translated into English, the work preached a new aesthetic based on technology and functional structures such as grain elevators, ocean liners, motor cars and airplanes. Le Corbusier's theories of a house being 'a machine for living in' took physical form in residential buildings constructed in and around Paris, including the Ozenfant house, av. Reille, in 1922.

In Germany, the need to consolidate the various craft traditions with the new industrial technologies resulted in the forming of the Bauhaus school in Weimar (later moving to Dessau, then Berlin) that operated from 1919 to 1933. Walter Gropius founded the school with the intention of combining architecture, more traditional forms of craft, and painting and

Opposite page: 5.1 Grillework at the Bank of Nova Scotia, Halifax, featuring local maritime imagery.

sculpture. He believed a new era had emerged from the ashes of the war and he wanted to create a new design style far removed from previous historic periods. This style, to be applied to all of the disciplines, would be based on functional considerations, inexpensive materials and potential for mass production. From its inception until the Great Depression, the Bauhaus style was a major influential force in European Modernist architecture, peaking at the housing exhibition of 'Die Wohnung,' organized by the Deutscher Werkbund, in Stuttgart in 1927.

A regional perspective to the tenets of the new Modernism was characterized by the architecture of a handful of Scandinavian designers including Sweden's Erik Gunnar Asplund and Eliel Saarinen of Finland. In 1928, Asplund designed the Stockholm City Library using the basic forms of a circular rotunda with a dome protruding from a rectangular base and a rigid fenestration pattern dressed with plain brick surfaces. The design transcended traditions – it was neoclassical in spirit but reminiscent of the functionalist and had a strong regional feel deriving from the use of local conditions and resources. Saarinen was addressing similar concerns of how to embrace Modernism and contextualize it with the local Nordic vernacular traditions. His best example is the Helsinki Central Railway Station of 1904–14, in which the modern streamlined exterior and bold architectural appearance is expressed through local masonry techniques and an elaborate sculptural program. These Scandinavian architects were open to outside influences, but combined them with their local environments and traditions, creating work that was modern, original and national.

Before his trip to France, Lyle's impression of the new architecture, based on pictures and photographs, had been that the 'style moderne is cubist in essence and made up of parallel and interlocking geometric forms…the impression that was given through publications that illustrate the most extreme types.'[2] After actually viewing some of the works, however, Lyle described modern architecture as possessing 'a simplicity of wall surface, both of the exterior and interior, a use of parallel lines or concentric curves, a use of incised relief ornament with semi-flat surfaces, a daring use of modern materials such as the combinations of metal and glass, wood and metal, an altogether charming use of what might be termed sunshine colours, their interiors being keyed to a lighter, gayer note.'[3] Although he did not single out any particular architect or building for praise and was not impressed with some of the work he studied, Lyle did find many aspects of the movement to be sound and beautiful.

One of the modern movement's more interesting aspects was that it represented a revolt against archaeology in architecture. This was particularly relevant for Lyle, who had long felt that Canadian architects did not try to solve each new design problem in a personal and individual manner, but relied heavily on Roman and Greek antecedents. Lyle was certainly not as dismissive of historical tradition as the principal exponents of the modern movement were – he did not believe that any new style could be born overnight, but that development would have to be gradual, with tradition as a background. He did concede, however, that the designers in the 'modern manner are blazing a trail that we must recognize as having great possibilities,' and encouraged Canadian architects to take advantage of the possibilities the movement had to offer.[4] Other Canadian architects were beginning to arrive at the same conclusion. In 1930, Percy Nobbs highlighted new German and Dutch work in a *Journal* article, and while he condemned it for its 'adverse influence,' he surely realized which way the wind was blowing since the 'architectural realists of Europe may have an enormous influence for the good on our future work, that is, if we keep our heads, accept so much of their doctrines as will help us, and solve our own problems in our own way, with a weather eye on our climate.'[5]

Addressing another of his pet concerns, Lyle warned that Modernism without regionalism would lead to an architecture that was international and generic in style. He encouraged Canadian architects to follow paths similar to those of countries such as Sweden, whose architects he considered to be 'developing their modern architecture along national Swedish traditional lines.'[6] And returning to his favourite topic –

national architectural traditions – he wrote, 'You say that we have no traditions in Canada – I do not agree. There are the traditions of lower French Canada; the colonial architecture of New Brunswick, Nova Scotia and Ontario: the two-coloured brick architecture of our own province, and for decorative motifs and ornaments we have the Indian traditions and our own native flowers, fruit, animals and trees.'[7]

Not all Canadian architects agreed with Lyle's approach to either regionalism or modernism. The younger generation, such as Montreal's Ernest Cormier, who in 1908 had studied at the atelier Jean-Louis Pascal at the École des Beaux-Arts, was quicker to embrace all aspects of Modernism. Asked by a journalist to give his opinion on regional architecture, Cormier declared, 'Regional architectures are vanishing. Differences between countries are diminishing, thanks to the speed of communications and our present means of locomotion. On the contrary, everything is moving toward standardization… Why should we go looking for a regional style?'[8]

An aspect of the Modernist movement Lyle did not agree with was the aesthetic of functionalism, whose principal concern was to have buildings work and flow as a machine. Referring to 'the modernist who thinks of architecture in terms of geometry,' Lyle disagreed with the rationale that because he and his contemporaries were living in a 'machine age,' their architecture should look like and function as a machine.[9] He believed architecture began where functionalism ended. Efficiency was desirable but should not be the overriding principle. Lyle felt the ultimate responsibility of architecture was beauty, which he feared would become, in the hands of the modernists, the 'Orphan Annie of the architectural world.'[10]

What Lyle approved of in the modern movement was the freedom it offered, since he considered any dogmatic architectural theory, historical or contemporary, too limiting and a handicap to the creative process: 'It should be considered rather as a spirit of design, and a release from the historical styles of the past – it is probably the only movement since Gothic architecture was born that possesses a germ of greatness.'[11] His question was how to apply this new spirit of architecture to his work – should it be through the use of new forms or through ornamentation? Taking his cues from the Canadian Group of Seven painters and Scandinavian architects such as Saarinen and Sweden's Ragnar Östberg, Lyle decided to strike a modern Canadian note in architecture without dealing with formal concerns, which he considered an area unlikely to yield any radical new thought, by focusing on a building's ornamental program. It was in this area that he saw 'a rich field of inspiration lying dormant in the fauna, flora and marine life of Canada.'[12]

Lyle took to the new cause of establishing an authentically Canadian architecture with the zeal of the newly converted. He and his office began to 'accumulate data in the forms of Canadian flowers, fruits, trees, birds, animals, grain, marine life and Indian motifs. I sent a man to the Royal Ontario Museum to make colour drawings of Indian forms. My office staff at first was but mildly interested and it was not much travail that we where able to translate the natural forms into conventionalized ornament. The staff is now enthusiastic in its interest…they adopted new forms or old forms in new combinations trying to create a new language based on Canadian forms, the only criteria was that any form had to pass the test of beauty.'[13]

Lyle's buildings from this period – 1929 to 1931 – exhibit an amalgam of modernism, nationalism and regionalism that was innovative, dynamic and full of creative potential. We see it in his work for W. R. Johnston, a summer residence on Lake Couchiching near Orillia, Ontario; in his design for the Runnymede Library, Bloor Street West, Toronto; and in the limited design program on the High Level Bridge in Hamilton.

Although they varied greatly in shape, proportion and treatment of detail, the placement and forms used in the decorative sculptural program on Lyle's buildings from this era were all classically based. But sculpture had to be an organic part of the structure and not draw undue attention to itself, and its function was to soften the transitions of a building's various parts and do so in an understated manner. Since the current

trend in architecture was toward thinner and flatter walls, the decorative program had to follow suit. Therefore, as one period critic pointed out, 'for wall decoration, it is obvious that designs of a geometric character in low relief, or even incised in the stone, are better suited to the flat surfaces of modern buildings than the high reliefs of classical and baroque styles.'[14]

Lyle's newly discovered Canadian style was embraced by the most conservative of his client base, the banking community. This surprising twist speaks volumes about the position and respect Lyle commanded and the creative freedom this afforded him. The first manifestations of Lyle's new style appeared in his designs in 1929 for the Bank of Nova Scotia, Calgary; Toronto's Dominion Bank branch at Yonge and Gerrard; and to a lesser degree the Central Canada Savings and Loan Company, on Simcoe Street in Oshawa, Ontario. But its most evocative form was the Bank of Nova Scotia's head office in Halifax, in 1930.

Bank Architecture: A Radical Departure

In size, exterior massing and type, the Bank of Nova Scotia in Calgary resembles the same bank's 1923 branch in Ottawa. Both are constructed on interior lots and use the same classical vocabulary of ground-floor base supporting an architrave and cornice surmounted by a parapet, although the Calgary branch was handled in a more contemporary, flattened manner. In terms of formal elements, the building is similar in many ways to the Dominion branch in Montreal with its thin exterior walls. A new and what Lyle considered to be 'radical departure' was the handling of the first-floor pilasters that were slightly curved instead of being flat.[15] These elements reflect his shift toward the design vocabulary of the modern movement.

The building's elaborate regional sculptural program revealed Lyle's 'passionate attempt to use local symbols to give a humane and familiar face to a traditionally imposing national institution – the bank.'[16] As such, it was a virtual catalogue of the region's history, environment, demographics and economy.

On the ground floor, the crest of the Bank of Nova Scotia is carved on the keystone over the central entrance. The architrave

5.2, 5.3, 5.4, 5.5 The Bank of Nova Scotia, Eighth Avenue SW, Calgary, Alberta, has an elaborate regional sculptural program that is a virtual catalogue of the region's history, environment, demographics and economy.

Above: 5.6, 5.7, 5.8 The three economic pillars of the region: oil, farming and ranching.

Right: 5.9 The window jamb's decorative panels depict two periods of Western Canada's history.

framing the main doorway is stylized with flower motifs of the sunflower, lily, marsh marigold and pitcher plant, separated by the Indian symbol of progress, the inverted triangle. The window jambs on either side of the entrance are splayed with decorative panels depicting two periods of Western Canada's history. The panels feature a buffalo head, tools and implements, and a vase containing just a few grains, representing Indian life, while on the other panel, the guns, cowboy Stetson and a vase overflowing with an abundance of grain depict the supposed advantages of Western colonization. Carved into the lintel soffit panels are symbolic birds in full flight overseeing this historic transformation, while scenes over the first-floor windows depict the three economic pillars of the West. The ranching scene features a saddle and fence with the Rocky Mountains in the background; the second, a wheat sheaf with a radiant sunset; and the third, a gushing Turner Valley oil derrick showering down financial fortune. The building's storeys are demarcated with a stringcourse of an Indian dogtooth pattern, and the main cornice has a waterleaf motif. A stylized western eagle is the central decorative motif in the pilaster's capital. Even the bronze window grillework offers an elaborate decorative program, with Indian arrow and inverted triangle motifs, wheat sheaves, tassels and inserts of maple leaves, roses, thistles, shamrocks, leeks and the fleur-de-lys, representing the dominant cultures of the region's population. In the interior, the pilasters are reeded instead of fluted, with alternating capitals of a wheat-sheaf motif, as well as anvils, gears and governors typifying the mechanical industries. The counters' and ceiling's focus is more organic, with themes of floral growth and movement.

Toronto was next to receive one of Lyle's Canadian-inspired works – the Dominion Bank, Yonge and Gerrard streets. It was situated to take advantage of the anticipated economic shift of the city's retail centre, which was expected to occur with the construction of Ross & Macdonald's massive commercial project for Eaton's College Street department store. The Dominion Bank commissioned Lyle to design a two-storey branch bank on a site adjacent to the store. The Eaton's project was planned to consume a whole city block and the building was set back to allow for the widening of Yonge Street from Gerrard to College, providing a grand, tree-lined boulevard. During the construction of the bank, there was a ten-day delay and the project was almost cancelled when city planners debated the merits of widening Gerrard Street as well. The bank's site, a narrow Yonge Street frontage and a long north side on Gerrard, meant Lyle had to change his customary plan and shift the interior counter's placement to the window side. This would allow the customers, when dealing with the teller, to look northward onto the Eaton's development. The large ceiling height and five north-facing windows enliven the interior banking room, making it as bright as possible for a two-storey branch. In spite of the site's challenges, the plan was described as 'one of Toronto's most successful banking rooms.'[17]

The exterior of the Dominion Bank is less exuberant than the Calgary branch and possesses a more self-assured dignity. Lyle's solution to providing a focus for the narrow Yonge Street facade was to use a tall entrance and transom window that act as a single unit indicating the height of the banking hall within. Enlivening the entrance were a pair of bronze doors and scrolled open-work pediment embellished with a florid arrangement of indigenous flowers and cornucopia supporting a centrally placed clock (since removed). Framing the entrance is a pair of quarter-round columns that rise from the building's base, terminating at the entablature. This element is embellished with bronze lettering of the bank's name, while the cornice is decorated with a heavy chevron and semi-circle motif. On either side of the second-storey three-bayed window are enlarged French and English coins.

On the Gerrard Street facade, a strong emphasis is given to the horizontal elements, which are counterbalanced by quarter-round columns, pilasters and sculptural elements. The fenestration treatment is particularly interesting. All vertical transitions from wall to void have gently stepped elements, whereas the tops and bottoms are unadorned, giving the design a sharp horizontal crispness. The ornamentation is based on

Top: 5.10 The Dominion Bank, Yonge and Gerrard streets, has enlarged French and English coins on either side of the second-storey windows.

Bottom: 5.11 The ornamentation was based on Canadian themes, with flowering balsam root on the cast bronze panel doors.

Above: 5.12 The Dominion Bank, interior, c. 1930.

Right: 5.13 The interior furnishings included custom-designed writing desks and chairs for the bank's clients.

Left: 5.14 The Gerrard Street facade of the Dominion Bank.

Above: 5.15 A stone-carved decorative panel of a busy harbour scene.

5.16 The front facade of the Central Canada Savings and Loan, Oshawa, Ontario.

Canadian themes, with flowering balsam root on the cast bronze panel doors (since removed) and owls with lilies and sunflowers for the capitals. The local flowers in the second-floor vases are riverbank gentian, trumpet creeper, pine cone, may-apple, spatterdock, hedge bindweed, charlock and sunflower. The lily and the sunflower also appear in the capitals of the reeded window jambs, while the birds in the capitals alternate between herons and turkeys. The window grilles above the side entrance are in cast and wrought iron, again adorned with a wheat-tassel motif. Two hexagonal panels on the Gerrard Street facade depict local industrial, commercial activities and high-light a busy harbour scene. The quality of the stone carvings was singled out for praise by *Construction* as 'showing all the vitality and strength without the sacrifice of delicacy which are so characteristic of the very best in modern work.'[18]

Lyle's newly formed decorative program, used for a facade makeover of the existing building of the Central Canada Savings and Loan, Oshawa, Ontario, 1929, won first prize at the OAA annual awards in 1931. Like the Dominion Bank, it was a post-and-lintel-style construction with large bronze panels set between and contrasting with the warm Indiana limestone pilasters. Canadian imagery reflecting the local economy of agriculture and industry adorned the facade, with two coins of early Ontario scenes framing the bank's name on the lintel. Native birds and floral motifs were applied to the spandrels; the window grilles had wheat-tassel motifs; and, to acknowledge the largest and most successful local industry – General Motors – automobile gears were used in the pilaster capital's swags.

Lyle's Canadian decorative program reached its apex in the Bank of Nova Scotia, Halifax, in 1930. To acknowledge its place of founding and ensure a lasting presence, the bank had purchased a conspicuous location at Hollis and Princess streets, on the site of Cyrus Thomas's 1860 Italianate-styled Union Bank and across from Halifax's most iconic structure, Province House. Sensitive to the location, Lyle was 'anxious to strike a modern note but owing to the fact that the Parliament Building [Province House] was just across the street we felt that certain characteristics of this very fine building should be echoed in the new building.'[19] This approach was evidently successful for, as the *Halifax Star* noted, the building 'fits gracefully into its surroundings as if it had always been there.'[20] Percy Nobbs, reviewing the building in the *Journal*, was also impressed. 'Here is a building,' he wrote, 'that hangs remarkably well together with an all pervading substantiality. It does not pretend to have been born when Halifax was young, far less to have been fathered centuries before Halifax was dreamed of. There is scholarship in it, there is originality in it and it takes place amidst surroundings imposingly but not vociferously.'[21]

The bank, whose principal facade faces Hollis Street, has all the earmarks of a classical design, with a base, cornice, suit-able corner and edge treatments and articulated forms, but all handled in a contemporary manner with an emphasis on the flattening of the elements to reveal the shallowness of the exte-rior facing. The design program called for a banking hall and four storeys of rental office space above. Lyle truthfully reflects the interior usage in the exterior massing. The Princess Street facade's ground-to-ceiling windows indicating the bank hall, and the Hollis Street's ground-floor fenestration pattern, reflect the mezzanine and vestibule contained within. The main entrance is framed with carvings of stylized local fruits and flowers, and the bank's crest is surmounted over the bronze door. The Hollis Street facade has a slightly projecting three-bay frontispiece with rusticated masonry supporting fluted pediments that rise four storeys to support the cornice. The cornice frieze is simply decorated with medallions of old French, English, Canadian and Nova Scotian coins. The same pattern is repeated on the Princess Street facade, except that the projection contains five bays.

The sculptural program included three themes important to the maritime communities: history, economy and natural habitat. The strength and success of the decorative work is due to Lyle's ability to convince Ira Lake, the country's most prominent architectural sculptor, who had previously worked with him on the carvings for the Memorial Arch in Kingston,

5.17 Bank of Nova Scotia (right), Halifax, is situated at Hollis and Princess streets, overlooking the city's most iconic structure, Province House.

Above: 5.18 Lyle's perspective drawing of the Bank of Nova Scotia.

Right: 5.19 Interior banking hall.

5.20 Located in the main banking hall are a pair of spectacular bronze doors decorated with snakes, beavers, birds, squirrels and local fauna.

Above: 5.21 Exterior decorative panel, Bank of Nova Scotia, Halifax.

Right: 5.22 Bank of Nova Scotia, interior banking hall ceiling panel.

to come out of retirement. According to Lyle, eighty-six different motifs were incorporated in the program, 'from the small trailing arbutus – the floral emblem of Nova Scotia – to the sunflower, and from the seagull to the Canadian goose, the bear, the silver fox, the codfish and crab… In every case, we studied forms, translating them into conventionalized ornament for wood, stone, plaster, bronze or iron. The ornament on the exterior stonework was treated in the modern manner, quite flat with softened arises with occasional crisp, sharp notes as accents. The effect of this treatment in the wall is to make the ornament plastic in character and married to the wall surface without undue play of light and shade.'[22] As Percy Nobbs noted, '[W]e have an exterior in which Mr. Lyle has been enjoying himself immensely. And it is all to the good, for it is nice to feel oneself infected by the exuberance of vegetable forms with a touch of the baroque, and a hint of horned Pan; especially in these days when rising costs and falling incomes compel most of us to emasculate our facades to the verge of inanity.'[23]

The bank's ground-floor plan was a departure from the customary symmetrical type. To accommodate a light well on the interior wall of the banking hall, thereby permitting illumination from three sides of the room, the ground-floor axis was pushed off-centre from the building's entrance. This presented a tricky problem that Lyle solved by adding a vestibule that would accommodate a row of elevators and placing it to the left of the main doors, then creating an off-axis entrance into the main banking hall. The vestibule itself is a fitting introduction to the lavish material usage and decorative program throughout the bank's interior. The walls are panelled to the ceiling in marble, with floors of Roman travertine and bronze doors. Marine motifs of fish and shells are depicted in the surrounds of the manager's door and the decorative metalwork. Screens of floor-to-ceiling glass divide the vestibule from the banking hall.

The floor of the banking-hall entrance features a large circular metal coat of arms, and above the door a colourful mosaic plaque designed by Robert McCausland of Toronto and assembled in England depicts the 1831 arrival in Halifax of the Cunard steamship *Britannia* on her maiden transatlantic voyage. The use of travertine walls is continued in the banking hall, while the floors, counters and banded dados are of a red marble Levanto and Lorada Chiaro. The ten-metre-high banking-hall ceiling is one of the highlights of the building and a 'breath-taking piece of masterful plaster-work,'[24] with a colour scheme consisting of two tones of green, a light red, chrome and white. The ceiling is divided by a series of plaster beams that span the room, and the intervening spaces are decorated with five flat-sided octagons, each side depicting a Canadian bird or animal. The ceiling demanded a high degree of skill on the part of the plasterers and painters, and to meet the clients' demanding production schedule, Lyle spent two months in Halifax attending to the details. He noted that 'practically all the daylight hours, and often the early evening ones, were spent at the building… I spent days on the scaffold during the erection of the plaster and again when they were painting.'[25]

The manager's room and the second-floor boardroom are more intimate in scale and in materials. They reflect a quiet elegance, with floor-to-ceiling wood-panelled walls, bird's-eye maple and walnut furniture for the manager's office, while the boardroom is in pine with a cove ceiling. The same fine detailing is evident in the wood and metalwork of the fire gratings, wall lamps and fireplace.

Along with Barott and Blackader's Bank of Montreal in Ottawa of the same year, which won the RAIC's gold medal in 1932, Lyle's Bank of Nova Scotia represents the passing of an era. It was, as Susan Wagg wrote in 1990, 'one of the last opportunities in Canada to work in a traditional, handcrafted manner using the full gamut of architectural arts.'[26] The financial and political events of the Depression and World War II limited construction of works on this scale and of such splendour, and when building programs of this magnitude resumed in the fifties, the Modernist agenda provided different solutions. It is appropriate and ironic that the Bank of Nova Scotia is located across the street from the Province House, as the two buildings act as bookends to the classical period in Canada. As architectural historian Alan Gowans noted, Province House is where 'the British classical tradition began, we should see it in a sense coming to an end,' while at the Bank of Nova Scotia, 'the classical forms here are vestigial; they do not articulate the building or define its form, but are simply and obviously applied decoration – the classical spirit, in short, is gone, and its forms will soon follow.'[27]

Residences: French in Spirit

The only residence where Lyle could fully embrace his Canadian style was a summer house for W. R. Johnston, on Lake Couchiching, Orillia, Ontario. Johnston was an old client and associate of Lyle who had commissioned the architect to design a fence and living room addition to his original Toronto residence in 1908, and during World War I worked alongside him and Sir Glenholme Falconbridge on the executive of the Toronto Chapter for the Secours National. In 1929, Johnston asked Lyle to design a summer residence for him in the style of a French-Canadian cottage. Lyle responded that he would not replicate the style but would gladly 'take the spirit of French Canada and modernize it to fit the site and the type of life which he proposed to lead in his summer house.'[28]

The house is five bays wide, single-storeyed with a steeply pitched hipped roof of dark blue-green painted cedar shingles and attic dormers that cut through the bellcast eaves. The required rustic, primitive Canadian theme is achieved through the choice of local material, colour and details. The exterior stonework consists of material selected from neighbouring fields and old broken-down walls. The rough-textured stone is mostly granite in variegated reds, blues, yellows and blacks. The odd sizes and shapes necessitated a random pattern with wide parging of the mortar joints. A dogtooth-patterned cornice echoes the one Lyle used at the Runnymede Library in Toronto, but here it is put to greater effect in unifying the

Left: 5.23 W. R. Johnston residence on Lake Couchiching, Orillia, Ontario.

Above: 5.24 Lyle extended his living room to accommodate a series of nineteenth-century French decorative wallpaper panels.

dormer windows. The ground-floor window shutters were painted in bold diagonal bands of white and dark blue-green that matched the roof colour. In contrast to these more primitive elements, the principal entrance is framed with classical white Doric columns and the two verandahs feature a delicate lattice treatment.

The interior continues the same combination of rustic and classical elements. The large central living-dining room was designed in an eighteenth-century French Norman style with cottonwood panelling from British Columbia and the fireplace and hardware all furnished in the same style. The ground-floor plan called for a central hall with living and dining rooms on either side, each accessing a covered verandah that was used as a summer dining area.

Another residential work of note for this period, although it did not fit his favourite Canadian theme, was Lyle's extension of the living room of his own house in 1930 to accommodate a unique series of wallpaper panels. These panels were created by French artists Merry-Joseph Blondel and Louis Laffitte, and were printed for Joseph Dufour et Compagnie in Paris in 1815 at the request of Napoleon I. These fine Empire-style works, entitled *Les Amours de Psyché et Cupidon* and depicting the story of the mythological couple, were printed by hand using approximately 1,500 different wooden blocks and featured thirty-three shades of grey requiring the same number of different impressions. Matching the colour of one of the panels, the walls were painted a warm grey, then over-glazed to produce an antique finish, while the capote was a deep sapphire blue and the curtains a grey-gold. Artfully placed antique period furniture completed the room and included a mahogany Sheraton table and sideboard, as well as a screen designed by Lyle in the Empire manner with a grey, blue and gold background.

Public Architecture: A Gateway to Hamilton

Lyle's second opportunity to design a bridge (his first was an unexecuted 1909 plan prepared for Toronto's Civic Improvement Committee) arose from the City of Hamilton's decision to replace its crumbling bridge and beautify the northwest entrance. In the fall of 1927, the Hamilton Board of Park Management held a limited open competition, entered by twelve firms. To act as assessors, the board hired Eric Arthur, Hamilton architect W. P. Witton and T. D. LeMay, the City of Toronto surveyor. The site of the bridge was a narrow spit of land called 'the Causeway,' which spanned Hamilton Bay and contained road, rail and canal links to the communities along the northern shoreline. This elevated causeway offered excellent views: to the west a marsh stretched out toward Dundas, to the east there was the bay, to the north there were fields and woodlands, and to the south lay Hamilton. This unique location presented the perfect opportunity to develop a gateway to the city, and the competitors were encouraged to include such features as pavilions, tea houses, balustrades, fountains, lamp standards and places for public gathering and walking.

The proposals varied widely, from purely architectural plans to those dominated by landscaping, with the structures playing a secondary role. The most important criteria for the assessors included how the northern and southern approaches were handled; the design of the bridge; the treatment of the highway with regard to both traffic flow and scenic prospects; the development and access to low-lying lands; and the location of buildings and parking space. The winning plan had to demonstrate not only the architect's ability to develop and improve the site but provide 'an adequate and dignified entrance highway…[making sure] that the purpose is not only to advertise the city, but also to provide enjoyment and pleasure for its citizens.'[29]

The winning design was a group entry by three firms, Wilson, Bunnell & Borgstrom, consulting engineers and landscape architects, along with Harkness, Louden & Hertzberg, engineers, and architect Earle Sheppard of Toronto. Lyle placed third behind the joint entry of Dunington-Grubb, landscapers, and architect W. A. Watson of Toronto. The dominant features of the winning design included a symmetrical pairing of classically styled entrance gateways featuring columns, with offices and a centrally placed obelisk in the middle of the roadway. The assessors declared that if carried to a conclusion this

Opposite page: 5.25 Hamilton High Level Bridge pylons and lanterns.

scheme would 'provide Hamilton with an entrance [that is] useful, dignified and beautiful.'[30] The second-place entry was more landscape-based and dealt with the issue of providing a prominent entrance by discarding all architectural forms in favour of pylons erected on either side of the highway to put the required focus on the bridge. Lyle's design, in contrast, was based on strong architectural forms and featured little landscaping so as not to impede the naturally scenic panorama of the site. His proposal also included a futuristic clock tower and carillon with provisions for searchlights and revolving airplane beacons. Other highlights were an open-air bandstand, a French flower mosaic, tea rooms, gasoline stations, a zoo and aquarium, water gardens and, to emphasize the importance of the bridge, a decorative colonnade between pylons with statues of leading Canadians placed in the voids.

The parks board retained the right to adopt the best features of any plans submitted and could appoint any architect or engineer to execute the final design. Acting out the well-known pejorative phrase 'design by committee,' the board combined its favourite features into the final proposal. From the first-place design they retained the lowering of the grade of the bridge and its approaches, which broadened out the ridge, and from the second- and third-place submissions, the use of architectural pylons. Carl Borgstrom, the engineer of the winning design, continued to advocate for his plan, architect and engineer to be used on the project. But Lyle had a strong supporter in Eric Arthur, who advocated for his inclusion as architect. Arthur did not have a very high opinion of the winning architect, Earle Sheppard, when he wrote to the head of the parks board, 'Keen as I am to see Lyle appointed architect, and only his intense interest in the scheme would tempt him to do it, I think the method, which Gore suggested, of leaving Shephard [sic] with the work and having Witton or myself, pull his stuff to pieces during the process of designing, would be a far safer way of ensuring a good job. If there is no hope of getting Lyle in, I should push for that. I honestly wouldn't leave Shepherd [sic] with a lamp post to design without close supervision.'[31] Arthur's persuasive argument convinced the board not to leave the project in the inexperienced hands of the younger architect and, in 1931, Lyle was officially appointed 'the consulting architect responsible for the architectural features throughout.'[32] The structural component of the project was then awarded to the consulting engineers James, Proctor & Redfern in conjunction with the city's engineering department.

Lyle had to redesign the bridge to accommodate the more restrictive budget imposed on the project by city officials in face of the economic conditions brought on by the Depression. The final plan included few of the grand public spaces originally envisioned by all of the entries; although the pylons were retained, they were greatly reduced in both size and spirit. After receiving tenders for the revised plans, the municipal authorities, trying to reduce the overall cost, proposed to omit the architectural details altogether. This angered the local citizens, who had been promised a grand entrance into the city. The Hamilton Chapter of the OAA and the Wentworth Historical Society rallied around Lyle's design and lobbied the city councillors to maintain the pylons. The *Hamilton Spectator* also came out in full support, writing, 'In one moment the Board of Control dissipates the dream of cultured Hamiltonians. In a high tone, a tone of almost moral indignation, it orders the removal of these artistic appendages.'[33] With strong vocal support, the city council overruled the mayor and the Board of Control and the architectural details and pylons were retained.

These four imposing, lozenge-shaped pylons are located at both entrances to the bridge and frame the northwest approach into the city. The forms are simplified and flattened, and detailed with inverted triangle and semi-circle motifs. The inner faces of the pylons have sculptural niches that were never filled, and a low-relief carving of Hamilton's crest surmounted above. The piers, abutments and upper deck of the bridge were constructed of reinforced concrete with steel trusses for the spans, while the pylons and railing supports were from Queenston limestone. The metalwork for the railings was a curvilinear design that contrasted with the more austere pylons

Left top and bottom: 5.26, 5.27 Lyle's third-place design for the Hamilton High Level Bridge competition.

Above: 5.28 The winning proposal was a group entry by three firms: Wilson, Bunnell & Borgstrom, consulting engineers and landscape architects, along with Harkness, Louden & Hertzberg, engineers, and architect Earle Sheppard of Toronto.

Above: 5.29 Lyle's proposal included a futuristic clock tower and carillon with provisions for searchlights and revolving airplane beacons.

Right: 5.30 Aerial view of Hamilton High Level Bridge, c. 1933.

Opposite page: 5.31 Hamilton High Level Bridge in the evening.

and provided a lighter, airy feeling. Twelve oversized ornamental cast-iron lanterns were part of a special lighting scheme that illuminated the bridge at night.

The bridge met with instant critical success. Percy Nobbs, one of the losing competitors, gave no evidence of sour grapes when he wrote, '[W]hat a difference it makes when an architect is graciously permitted to take a hand in a bridge project… [M]ost of our Canadian bridge engineers would be the better off having an architect to help them when they invade the landscape.'[34] In 1933, the bridge won second place in the annual North America–wide competition sponsored by the International Institute of Steel Construction, and an honourable mention in the public-building class of the RAIC awards. Although Eric Arthur found the bridge 'so much better than most of our engineers' bridges in Canada,' he strongly objected to the relationship between the pylons' lamps and the street lamps that he considered too thin in comparison, and noted that 'the major fault lies in the pylons themselves. It is an established modern practice (if not an ancient one, as in Wren's entrance to Greenwich Hospital) to indicate by asymmetrical masses that a gateway is but an entrance to something beyond. The bridge, however fine cannot, or should not, stand as a thing in itself. Hamilton, after all, is the goal.'[35]

Lyle responded in a letter to the *Journal*'s editor, writing that he had little control over the size of the lanterns by the pylons, which were designed to provide vertical and horizontal floodlighting and were kept as small as possible. As for Arthur's second criticism, Lyle claimed (disregarding the spirit of the original competition) that the bridge was not a gateway to Hamilton but rather 'an isolated thoroughfare.' He also noted the bridge's location on a narrow escarpment with precipitous drops on all four sides necessitated a symmetrical approach.[36]

Institutional: A Personal and Canadian Note

The design for the Runnymede Library, on Bloor Street West at Glendonwynne Road, Toronto, in 1929, born in the midst of Lyle's most creative and fertile Canadian-style period, is one of his most enduring works. The library shares many of the same features as his other buildings in this style and, like them, drew its inspiration from indigenous forms, materials and details.

Opposite page: 5.32 Lyle's Bloor Street elevation drawing of Runnymede Library, Toronto.

Libraries had changed drastically since the first wave of classically designed Carnegie buildings swept the continent at the turn of the century. The societal impact of the new technologies of radio and moving pictures meant libraries were no longer 'a mere storage house for books…but rather the intellectual home of the community in which it is placed.'[37] As a result, there was much greater emphasis on programming. Children in particular required special spaces or club rooms for their activities, which included the popular Saturday-afternoon story hour. Branch libraries were to feature a flexible floor plan that could be easily and economically monitored, and provide space for adult education programs and private lecture rooms.

In 1929, as part of an ongoing building program aimed at meeting the ever-expanding population of the city, the Toronto Public Library Board requested two new branches from local architects. The buildings were to have a semi-public character featuring a residential and club atmosphere and were to be styled in the Elizabethan or Jacobean manner. The board asked Lyle and another Toronto architectural firm, George, Moorhouse & King, to provide them with new designs. George, Moorhouse & King complied with designs for the Danforth Branch that were in the half-timbered Elizabethan mode, but Lyle, in the throes of his new-found mission, responded by saying, '[W]hy go back to the 15th and 16th centuries, why not try something more modern and endeavor to strike a personal and Canadian note into the design of this building?'[38]

In a bold and unusual step, the board approved Lyle's suggestion and design, a tasteful synthesis of French, English and Native elements married into an invigorating and daring composition. Lyle described some of the attributes of the design: '[T]he high, pitched roof of French Canada has been used, as it has a particularly northern significance as against the flatter or more southern type roof. The ordinary small black slate similar to that used in France has been adopted… The central entrance motif is Indian in its inspiration, as the totem pole

RUNNYMEDE BRANCH LIBRARY
STREET ELEVATION
RUNNYMEDE BRANCH LIBRARY
JOHN M. LYLE ARCHITECT

5.33, 5.34 Runnymede Library, Toronto.

PUBLIC LIBRARY
RUNNYMEDE BRANCH

idea has been taken and married to the ordinary Classic lintel treatment. The cornice of this entrance has Indian decorative motifs treated in a naïve manner to echo the totem pole motifs which support this cornice. The totem poles have at the top the raven, then the beaver, and at the bottom the bear, significant of Canadian bird and animal life.'[39]

The dominant features of the building are the steeply pitched black-slate roof with bellcast eaves inspired by French-Canadian form, the variegated walls of local red and yellow Credit Valley limestone and the dressed-stone main entrance. This doorway is framed with totem poles and the Native theme is continued in the building's ironwork, which includes the inverted triangle and the arrowhead pattern, while the cornice is decorated with the dogtooth pattern. A palette of 'primitive' colours, such as green, yellow ochre and Cobalt blues in the exterior wooden doors and shutters, maintains the theme. Other Canadian motifs highlighted in the stonework are the Canadian lily, pinecones, and keystones of squirrels and Indian heads.

The plan separates the users' functions. The lower floor, with the main entrance on Bloor Street, was designated for adults. It features a large open space for the reading room, with the book stacks against the walls and staff quarters in the rear. Large, low windows supply ample interior light and give the building an open, inviting feeling. The west elevation on Glendonwynne Road is for younger children and is less formal, with a separate entrance and a staircase leading to the second-floor reading area. The large chimney stacks that would have framed the composition and provided a picturesque element were eliminated by budget cuts.

The building has been described as 'one of the most beautiful branch libraries in Canada,'[40] and in 1989 it took its rightful place in the pantheon of nationally significant architecture as part of Canada Post's high-value postage-stamp series 'Our Nation's Buildings.' The corporation's advisory committee selected buildings from a diverse range of architectural styles, periods, regions and types, with the only proviso that the buildings be in good repair and in current use. The first to be honoured in this series, because of its uniquely modified modern style, and Canadian themes that incorporated a rich array of French, English and West Coast Indian carved-stone motifs, was the Runnymede Library.

The Canadian phase of buildings brought Lyle well-deserved recognition and attention. Both the local and national press had produced numerous illustrated articles highlighting his work and the international architectural press had also taken notice. In a series of booklets on architectural decoration in contemporary buildings, published by *American Architect*, Lyle's work was included in a portfolio of sculptured eagles alongside American architects of the stature of McKim, Mead & White, Cass Gilbert and New York City's Empire State Building architects John De Cesare, Shreve, Lamb & Harmon. The English *Architectural Review*, one of the world's most prominent architectural magazines of the period, devoted four pages to Lyle's buildings, highlighting the Canadian themes of the four banks.

Not all critics were impressed by Lyle's attempts at defining a new Canadian architecture, however. Eric Arthur, in 'Architecture in Canada,' written for the *Yearbook of the Arts in Canada*, noted:

> We have in the East made no attempt, so far as I have noticed, to force a national style. The painters I believe hatched one overnight. If they have been successful we have to admit that we have not been so fortunate or that in architecture we do not admit the possibility. Some slight obvious contributions have been made, but only in ornament. The maple leaf is certainly to be preferred to the egg and dart, but a gopher or squirrel on a keystone does not make a building as national in character as the Parthenon. There must be something other than ornament… I believe it will take a thousand years to develop a national style in Canada, but I do see a light in the west over a grain elevator.[41]

Left: 5.35 The front entrance door with totem poles have a raven (top), beaver (middle) and bear (bottom).

Above: 3.36 The boys-and-girls side entrance was for younger children and led to the second-floor reading area.

Chapter 6: 1932–1940

BANK
NOVA SCOTIA
Join the
Royal Canadian Air Force

Modern – But Not Crazy

A New Spirit

When Eric Arthur referred to seeing a light in the west over a grain elevator, he was suggesting that the ideals and forms of the European Modernists (who were inspired by functional structures such as grain elevators) were potentially the path toward a new Canadian architectural style. The word *modern* began to take on a new meaning in the second quarter of the twentieth century. Until then, when an architect or designer used *modern* to describe a building or object, its meaning was strictly chronological. It meant contemporary, or of its time, without wider stylistic or philosophical implications. It was not until the 1920s when, in an attempt to create a new order, a group of European architects rejected all historic references in their work, the word became associated with a set of specific values. The modern movement, or Modernism, was interpreted in many different ways, and it took many forms, including Art Deco, Moderne and the International Style.

In 1932, historian and critic Henry-Russell Hitchcock and architect Philip Johnson assembled an exhibition at the Museum of Modern Art in New York that showcased the most minimal form of Modernism in architecture, as exemplified by the work of Walter Gropius, Le Corbusier, Ludwig Mies van der Rohe and Jacobus Oud. The curators codified the principles of modern architecture and named the movement the International Style. The basic features of this work were a focus on volume, regularity of design as opposed to symmetry, the use of materials in such a way as to bring out their intrinsic qualities, and a rejection of all historical references.

That same year, Lyle gave a lecture at the twenty-fifth annual meeting of the RAIC in Lucerne, Quebec, entitled 'Canadian Decorative Forms,' in which he addressed the issue of Modernism and national identity in Canadian architecture. He started by asking his audience about the nature of Canadian architecture: 'Is there such a thing? Has it any national characteristics or is it merely a repetition of historical forms and ornament, or prevailing modes of Paris, London or New York? What road will it travel, towards a modernism based on international forms and ornament or on Canadian forms and ornament – or is it to remain a dead thing chained to the moss-grown chariot of Rome or to the mystic spirit of the middle ages?' Lyle concluded that Canadian architecture needed 'a tonic and I see signs that a few of us have been at the bottle – some take it in moderation, others have been more reckless, while others again claim that it is more nauseating than castor-oil. This new medicine is called "Modernism," and it seems to make the old young and the young frantic.'[1]

Lyle reiterated the position he had put forward a few years earlier with regards to what he considered an extreme form of the modern movement – the Internationalists, whose practitioner is 'equally at fault with the extreme traditionalist, in that he is trying to tie up architecture to a definite set of formulas. Surely you must keep it free if you wish to keep it alive. If however, you look at the modern movement as a new spirit of design and a release from the historical styles of the past, then I see a germ of greatness which offers rewards to the skillful designer.'[2] Lyle's mode of Modernism, which was both a reaction to these more extreme forms as well as a search for a national style, was based on an elaborate Canadian decorative program. However, several forces that shaped architectural trends in Canada doomed his efforts. These included the influence of European Modernism, the fiscal restrictions imposed by the Great Depression that reduced a building program to its bare essentials, and the impact of the federal government's Public Works Construction Act.

The New York stock market's crash on Black Tuesday in 1929 triggered a chain of events that plunged the Western world into a decade-long depression that hit its lowest point in 1932 and ended only with the outbreak of World War II. It was estimated that Canadian stocks lost a total value of $5 billion and that, by the mid-1930s, the value of stocks for the fifty leading companies had fallen by over 50 percent from their peaks in 1929. In that year the Canadian construction industry employed over 300,000 people, plus an additional 70,000 whose factory work was indirectly linked to construction. This represented about one-eighth of the country's population. By early 1932, the industry was operating at

Opposite page: 6.1 Lyle's intentions for the Bank of Nova Scotia, Saint John, New Brunswick, were 'to design an interior which is modern but not crazy.'

about 10 percent of its 1929 capacity, and with building starts at an all-time low, that figure was 'diminishing rapidly and (was) quickly approaching the zero point.'[3] The *Journal* reported that 'practically every municipality, as well as Provincial and Dominion Governments, have indicated that in the year 1933 no capital expenditures will take place. This policy of retrenchment we have so far never severely criticized, but we are today firmly convinced that its continuation will only lead to disaster.'[4]

Others had similar views – in late November of that same year, Prime Minister Richard B. Bennett announced in a radio broadcast to the nation the Canadian government's version of Roosevelt's New Deal. Bennett said, '[W]hile at the moment it is difficult to forecast with any degree of assurance what the future may be, the steady improvement of the past few months, in our opinion, warrants the view that we may be able, with the return of spring, to undertake a reasonable policy of public works in every province of the Dominion that will substantially assist in stimulating private enterprise, increase purchasing power, provide employment, and hasten the return of prosperity.'[5] The federal government inaugurated a Public Works Construction Act with a budget of $55 million, of which approximately $40 million was designated for new public buildings. The federal government had its own Department of Public Works, and its chief architects Thomas Fuller and Charles Sutherland and a large staff of designers were responsible for almost all federal construction. Through the lobbying of the RAIC, the government agreed to commission architects in private practice for sixty-seven buildings, costing approximately $16 million. These included post offices, customs departments and other multi-use government structures, and the federal government became the largest patron of the industry.

The form these large public buildings took during the thirties was still based on classical themes. Architectural historian Janet Wright described the style: '[T]he new federal architecture of the mid and late 1930s was not the revolutionary modernism of the International Style, but represented a reinterpretation of established building types in the light of current values of modernism and nationalism.'[6] They were mostly tripartite compositions of base, middle storeys with pilasters and a cornice, symmetrical facades and flat roofs, constructed using local materials often with white stone or artificial cast stone. There was a continued movement toward expressing the thinness of the wall, emphasizing its volume rather than mass. When the budget permitted, a decorative program was used. This program, in terms of form and placement, was still based on classical precedent, although architectural features were flattened and highly stylized. Designs for banks tended to exclude freestanding classical columns holding up a pediment, replaced by stylized pilasters, and the once-prominent cornice became a narrow band or disappeared entirely. In the interior, the engaged column that was used to break up wall spaces gave way to flat pilasters without bases or caps, and the coffered ceiling was replaced by plain surfaces enlivened by colour. To obtain cleaner and brighter interiors, the contemporary material included nickel or aluminum alloys for counter screens and doors, rubber or mastic tile flooring, noise-absorbing materials in ceilings, ply and veneer woods, indirect and floodlighting in illumination and air conditioning in the ventilation scheme. This style is known by several different names, including Stripped Classical or Depression Moderne, but architectural historians prefer Modern Classicism.

Bank Architecture: Surviving the Thirties

The crowning touch to Lyle's career would have been the twenty-three-storey General Office Building for the Bank of Nova Scotia at King and Bay streets, in Toronto. The location was in the heart of the financial district on the northeast corner, where the William Cawthra house was situated, and across the street from Carrère & Hastings's Toronto Bank (1911–13). The Canadian Bank of Commerce, located on the southeast corner, designed by New York architects York & Sawyer with local associates Darling & Pearson, had the good fortune of breaking ground before the Wall Street Crash and was far

6.2 Lyle's Bay Street elevation proposal for a twenty-three-storey General Office Building for the Bank of Nova Scotia at King and Bay streets, in Toronto.

enough along that construction continued through to completion in 1931. The Bank of Nova Scotia's timing, however, was not as fortunate. The project was originally proposed in 1929, just a month after the market crash. Assuming that the economic conditions were just a temporary slump and that the crash was just a market correction, the bank's executive instructed Lyle to go ahead with the project.

In July 1930, Lyle went to New York with Arthur Eadie, a junior designer in the office, to study first-hand the latest architectural developments. The design they proposed for the Bank of Nova Scotia was based on current New York trends, which were shaped by two events, the city's 1916 zoning bylaw and the *Chicago Tribune*'s 1922 office-tower competition. New York's 1916 ordinance was implemented primarily because of the construction of the Equitable Building on Broadway in 1912, designed by Ernest R. Graham. This massive structure occupied a whole block, and its density and height caused a public outcry that forced city officials to respond. Since the primary concern was the blockage of sunlight from the street, new zoning regulations were introduced to restrict the shape of tall buildings. New setback restrictions meant buildings could no longer be sheer vertical walls – after a certain number of stories, tiers had to be set back from the block below, causing a stepped or ziggurat form. This zoning code successfully reduced the buildings' shadows and allowed for more sunlight at street level. A secondary benefit was the distinctive character this lent to the city's architecture. This set-back form was copied widely, and high-rise buildings in cities that never implemented these zoning restrictions began to sport the familiar shape.

In 1922, the *Chicago Tribune* held an open competition to replace its outdated headquarters with a new design that would define the modern skyscraper. John Howells and Raymond Hood won the competition, but it was the second-place design that exerted the most influence on subsequent high-rise development in North America. These plans were submitted by Finnish architect Eliel Saarinen, who struck a successful balance between the progressive and the traditional with a design that used a series of setbacks emphasizing the structure's verticality and incorporating an ornamental program based on historical precedents. Saarinen's design was to change the image of 'modern skyscraper from corniced block to tapered, soaring ziggurat,' according to American architectural historian Leland Roth.[7] In New York by the mid-twenties, a number of Saarinen-inspired structures were being constructed, including William Van Alen's Chrysler Building in 1928–30, and Reinhard & Hofmeister with H. W. Corbett and R. Hood's Rockefeller Center, 1927–35. In Canada, the set-back style was used by York & Sawyer with associates Darling & Pearson at the head offices for the Canadian Bank of Commerce, Toronto, of 1929–31, and Ernest I. Barott's Aldred Building, Montreal, of 1929–31.

The Bank of Nova Scotia's design program called for a building of twenty-three storeys, a ground-floor banking hall and sufficient room for the bank's corporate headquarters. The cost was limited to $6 million. The design process continued throughout 1930, with preliminary plans being approved by the directors, and building permits obtained, along with the selection of a construction contractor. Lyle made another trip to New York, with another junior associate, J. J. Beck, as well as bank officials and contractors, to further study construction methods and details. However, client changes and alterations drove up the overall projected costs of the project to $8 million, and in all areas drastic cost-cutting measures were attempted. By the summer of 1931, the effects of the Depression were more acutely felt with every passing month, and the board of directors decided that because of the higher costs, a slower approach was called for. Design revisions continued for another year, and in July 1932 Lyle delivered the first set of finished plans to the bank and had them promptly placed in the vault for safekeeping.

The bank's 'go slow and wait-and-see' approach was a prudent attempt to avoid the controversy or embarrassment of a failed building project. Two New York companies, City Bank Farmers Trust and the Metropolitan Life Insurance, both had their head-office construction compromised due to the Depression. The Metropolitan Life Insurance Tower was the most spectacular failure. Its original 1929 plans had called for

Opposite page, left: 6.3 Angle view from King and Bay streets, Bank of Nova Scotia.

Opposite page, right: 6.4 North elevation proposal, Bank of Nova Scotia.

Above: 6.5 York & Sawyer with associates Darling & Pearson, head office for the Canadian Bank of Commerce, Toronto, 1929–31.

6.6 Bank of Nova Scotia, Saint John, New Brunswick, was a simple rectangular structure with no articulation of mass, and flat wall surfaces with crisp, shallow window reveals.

the world's tallest building, consisting of approximately 100 storeys, but work halted in 1933 with only twenty-nine floors constructed.

Revisions for the Bank of Nova Scotia continued for another year, which was a blessing for Lyle, who had little work and had to lay off most of his staff. Those who remained, including his secretary and his associates Beck and Eadie, all had their salaries greatly reduced. Things looked so bleak that Lyle had even contemplated closing his office altogether. While during normal times the approach of the Nova Scotia bank would have been frustrating, during these lean years, it kept him in business. As Beck noted in his daily work diary, the ongoing Bank of Nova Scotia job 'contributes nicely to Mr. Lyle's depleted treasury.'[8]

For several years, the project lay dormant, although there was talk of incorporating the Toronto Stock Exchange, which was looking for new and larger premises, into the building. Then in summer 1936, the bank requested another series of revisions and plans, only to put off the decision for another year. Again, a year later the plans resurfaced and were once more put on hold until fall, when the possibility of a smaller building was to be explored.

It was not that major changes to the Nova Scotia bank were contemplated. The alterations to the original plans were primarily concerned with finishes and material usage. The main design of a contemporary building, based on the set-back model with a strong emphasis placed on a soaring verticality, was still intact. It featured a base, four storeys in height, with two front entrances on King Street. These entrances led into the main lobby, which gave access to the banking hall or to the elevators that serviced the upper floors. The banking hall ran parallel to Bay Street and connected to the upper levels through a series of piers that set back with each tier. The sculptural program was rich and lavish, consisting of the bank's coat of arms, coins and medallions, individual figures and complex group settings, as well as a row of symbolic urns on the banking-hall piers, signifying the storage of wealth.

Compared to other sectors of the economy and other national financial institutions, the Bank of Nova Scotia weathered the Depression relatively well. During the 1930s, it closed down fifty-one branches, mostly in the western provinces and Ontario. During the same period four banks were constructed, two in outlying areas of Toronto, one near Timmins, Ontario, and one in Prince Edward Island. By the late thirties, thinking the worst was over, the bank resumed a more substantial building program. In 1939, it constructed two impressive new branches, one on each coast. In the west, a one-storey branch in New Westminster, B.C., was designed by Toronto architect Murray Brown and featured a regional sculptural program based on the local economies, fishing and forestry. The bank's optimistic belief in the east coast's economy was reflected by an impressive four-storey branch in Saint John, New Brunswick, designed by Lyle. In the use of form, the Bank of Nova Scotia in Saint John was similar in some respects to Lyle's Halifax design. It was a simple rectangular structure with no articulation of mass and flat wall surfaces with crisp shallow window reveals, indicating the thinness of the exterior walls. The front elevation that faces onto Charlotte Street consists of three bays with an entrance and windows above on the mezzanine level. Two additional storeys rise from the base, separated from the attic by a thin cornice. The decorative program includes a carved stone crest of the bank above the front entrance and a pair of protective lions each standing on its hind legs, framing the window jamb. Above them, looking down on the streetscape below, are two solitary figures representing local cultural and financial themes.

The King's Square facade is ten bays wide and consists of banking-hall windows rising to the full two-storey height, divided by fluted pilasters with no base or capital. To reinforce the horizontal theme, the second- and third-storey windows over the banking hall are tied together with an extended sill. The sculptural program continues above the windows, featuring highly stylized symbolic images of the region's agriculture, industry and indigenous peoples.

The interior's 'U'-shaped plan calls for the bank manager's office to be strategically placed to the right of the entrance

6.7 Bank of Nova Scotia, King's Square facade.

Opposite page left: *6.8 The winning design for the Dominion Housing Act Small House Competition was awarded to William Ralston of Toronto.*

Opposite page right: 6.9 Ontario Government Housing Competition included two categories, a class 'A' for designs for a family of five and a class 'B' for a family of eight. The winning design in the 'A' category was awarded to Harold Greensides (opposite right) and in 'B,' William Ralston. Greensides had worked in Lyle's office during the 1930s.

vestibule, with the elevator and stairwell on the opposite side. The banking hall is two storeys high with unadorned walls, but brightly painted for a light and airy feeling and featuring vertically grained, wood-veneered low counters and teller screens and other metalwork.

Willa Cather, the Pulitzer Prize–winning author from New York who summered in the nearby Grand Manan region, was a client of the bank. 'I do not know any bank interior in New York which seems to me so completely satisfying,' she told the bank manager. 'Your architect managed to make an interior which is modernistic and yet not inhuman. I concluded that the architect must be a brilliant youth.'[9] Informed that Lyle was sixty-seven, and older than she, Cather wrote to Lyle, saying his work confirmed her belief that 'it is the people who were trained in the old styles of art who can most successfully adapt themselves to the new.'[10] In his response, Lyle outlined his intentions for the bank – 'to design an interior which is modern but not crazy'[11] – and explained the theory that underlay his work: 'We should not throw all traditions overboard but rather profit by the mistakes of the past and at the same time grasp what I consider the essentials in the modern movement – that is, simplification of form, the elimination of meaningless ornament and release from the strictly historical styles.'[12] Lyle concluded by stating that for 'a movement to be permanent and of value [it] must possess beauty of form, of line and colour.'[13]

Residences: Moderne Solutions

During the Depression, the large numbers of people moving from rural areas to urban centres like Toronto in search of work made housing a hot political issue on the national, provincial and municipal levels. In his report of 1934 the Lieutenant Governor of Ontario, Dr. Herbert Bruce, described the deplorable conditions of overcrowding that the city's poor had to endure, and its concomitant health-related and social problems. Bruce recommended that a City Planning Commission for Toronto be established, that all existing unfit houses and slums should be razed and that the city should work with the provincial and federal governments to replace them with low-cost housing.

The humanitarian theme of housing reform coincided with the interests of the construction industry and was duly picked up on by the National Construction Council of Canada, a newly formed lobbying body representing the concerns of architects, engineers and contractors. At the annual meeting of the RAIC, the NCCC stated that it intended to take forward to the federal government a proposal entitled 'Brief on Housing and Slum Clearance,' which contained many ideas from the Bruce Report. In the discussions that followed, architect W. L. Somerville stressed the need of government involvement in low-income housing, and Lyle also contributed to the debate by saying that 'the committee might consider the advisability of suggesting to the Prime Minister that the Government should aid in establishing building and loan societies such as they have in England from whom money to the value of 90% of the value of the house could be borrowed at an interest rate of 2.5%.'[14]

In 1935, Lyle took up the issue of urban and social housing again, in a talk on 'Street Architecture,' part of a series of radio broadcasts entitled 'Architecture in the Modern Life,' organized by the Toronto Chapter of the OAA. This series covered areas of domestic architecture, civic design and the modern movement, with each subject authored by a different architect. Lyle's talk dealt with aesthetic coherence, urban density, suburban sprawl, terrace housing and slum clearing. He recommended the use of row or terrace projects as a solution to the housing problem in urban centres. His proposed scheme featured a terrace plan 'that can be broken up at intervals by garden areas,' which, when coupled with advances in building technologies, could produce interiors that 'would have vastly more light than the conventional houses of the past.'[15]

After receiving input from residential and community groups across the country, an eighteen-member committee, appointed by Prime Minister Richard B. Bennett to look at the housing issue, put forward its recommendations. As a

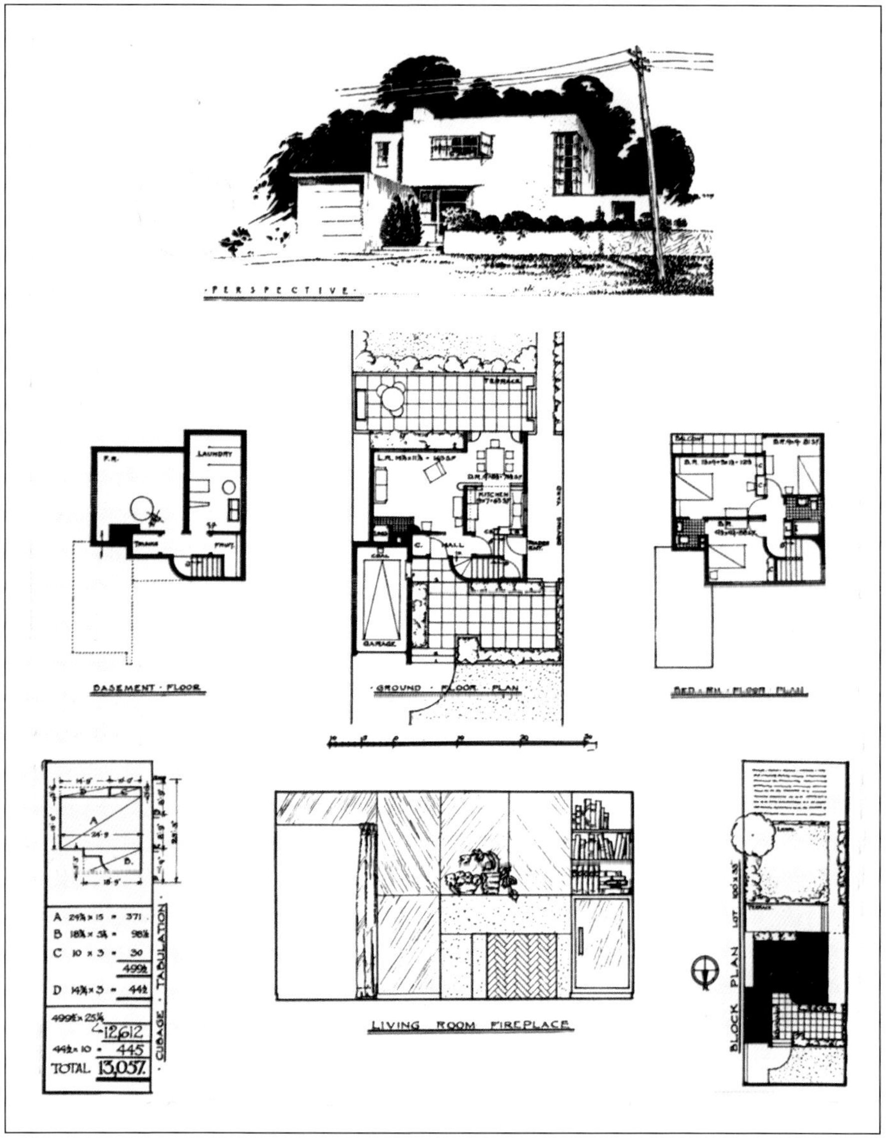
PERSPECTIVE
BASEMENT · FLOOR
GROUND · FLOOR · PLAN
BED · RM · FLOOR · PLAN
LIVING ROOM FIREPLACE
CUBAGE · TABULATION
TOTAL 13,057
BLOCK PLAN

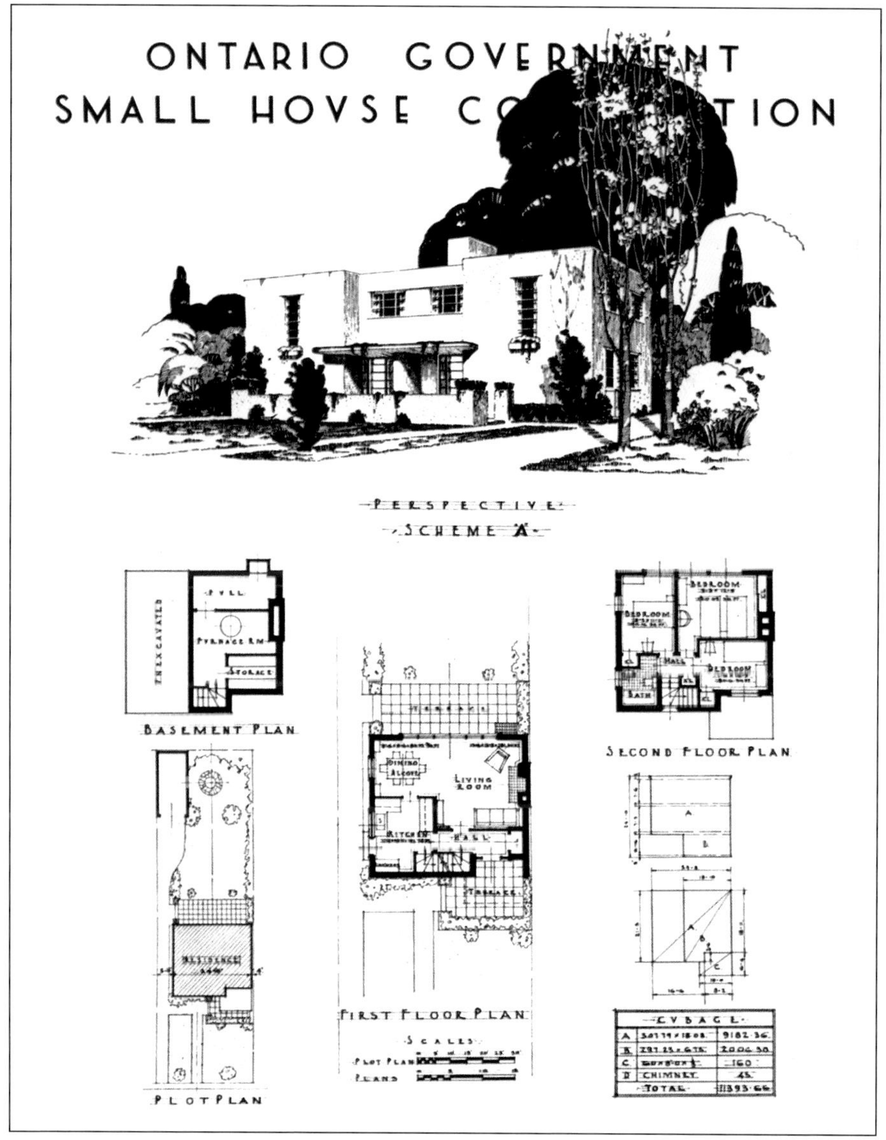
ONTARIO GOVERN
SMALL HOVSE CO
PERSPECTIVE
SCHEME 'A'
BASEMENT PLAN
FIRST FLOOR PLAN
SECOND FLOOR PLAN
PLOT PLAN
CVBAGE

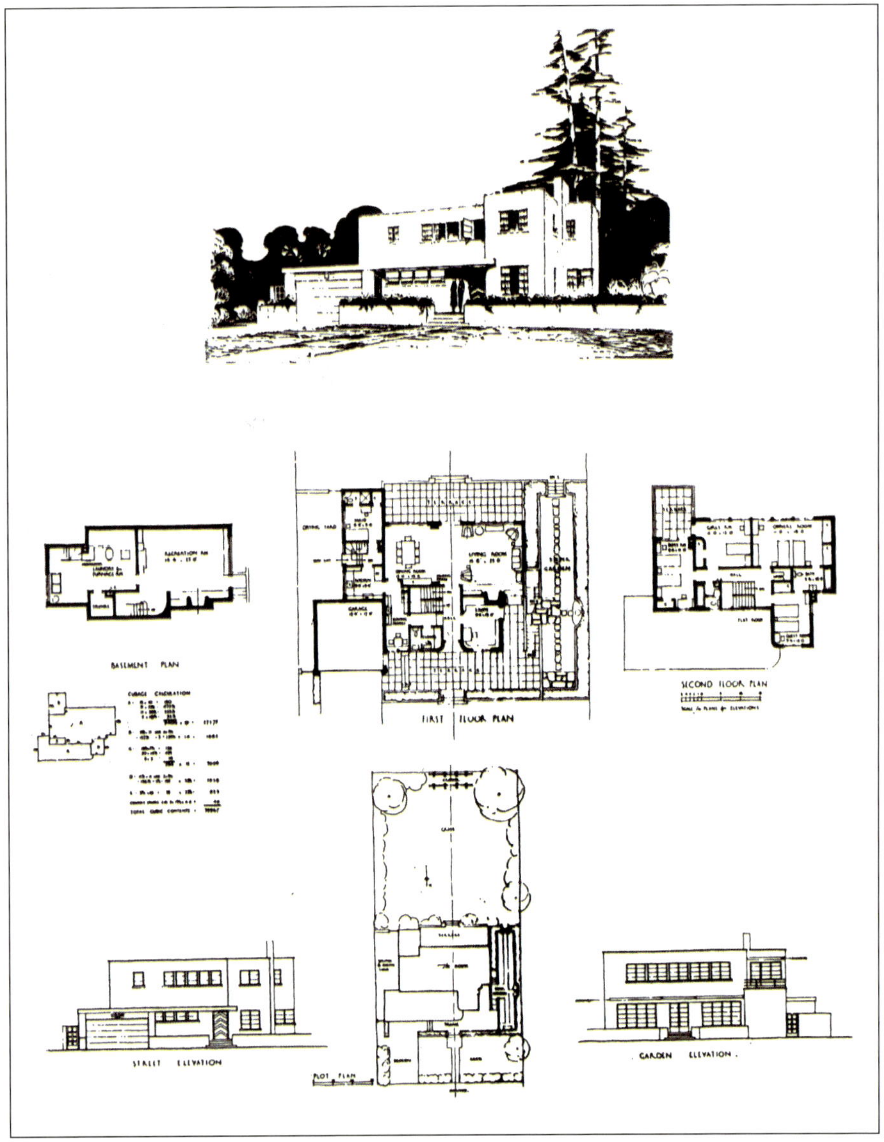
BASEMENT PLAN
FIRST FLOOR PLAN
SECOND FLOOR PLAN
STREET ELEVATION
PLOT PLAN
GARDEN ELEVATION

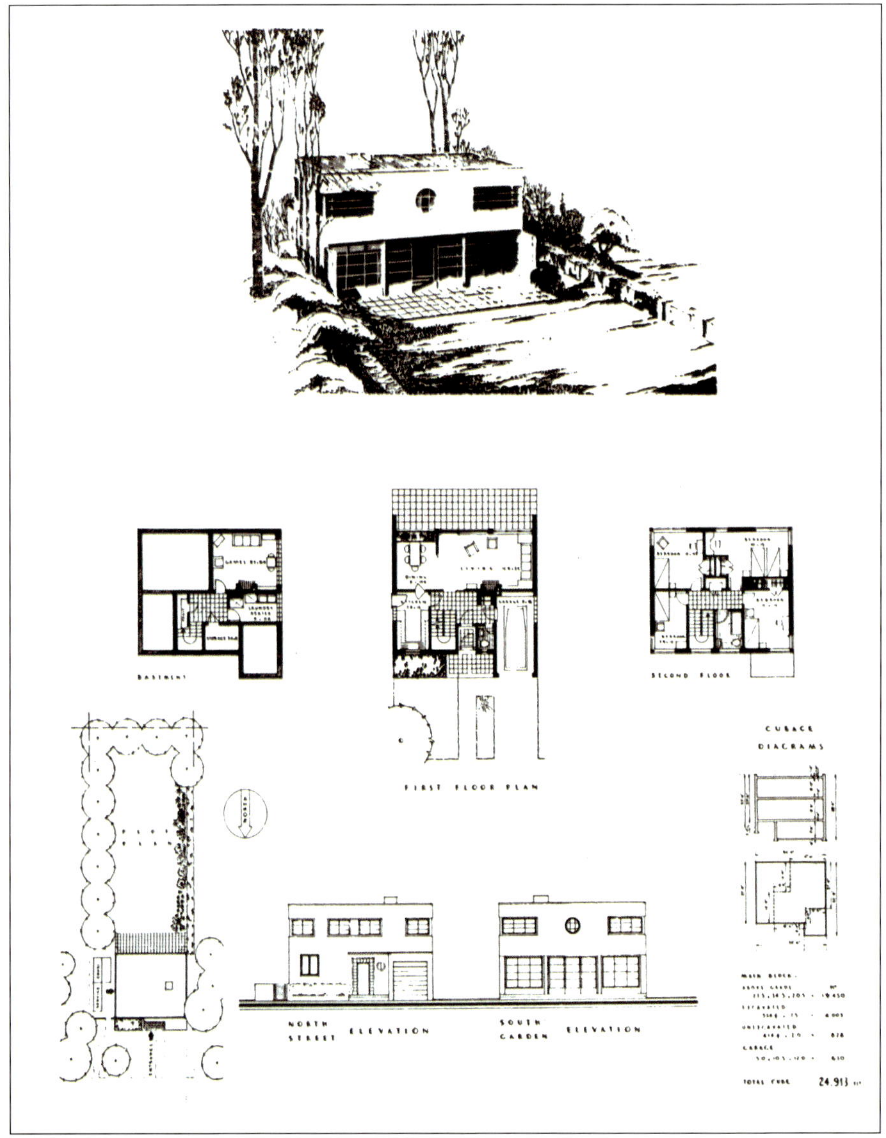
BASEMENT
FIRST FLOOR PLAN
SECOND FLOOR
CUBAGE DIAGRAMS
NORTH STREET ELEVATION
SOUTH GARDEN ELEVATION

result, the federal government, in 1935, introduced legislation to stimulate the recovery of the residential housing sector. The Dominion Housing Act completely ignored the social issues of housing for the poor and slum clearing in favour of providing financing for lower- to middle-class residences. Under this bill the minimum down payment required for a house purchase was cut by one-half, from 40 to 20 percent. The term of the loan was changed from five to ten years, coupled with the right of the borrower to renew the mortgage for an additional ten years. Also, blended equal monthly payments of interest and principal were provided under the legislation, establishing the amortization of mortgages as a standard.

To promote its legislation, a year later the federal government sponsored the Dominion Housing Act Small House Competition, an architectural competition for low-cost housing designs that could be built according to the minimum standards of the construction industry and be eligible for financing under the Dominion Housing Act. The program and conditions were approved by the RAIC and the jury consisted of eight of the institute's members, including the president, W. L. Somerville. The 526 designs submitted from every province contained 'the best elements to be found in recent domestic work.'[16] The winning design was awarded to William Ralston of Toronto, and there were two-second place finishes: Harold Greensides of Toronto and John Fish of Montreal.

Acting in conjunction with the federal government, the Province also attempted to stimulate the economy by announcing the Ontario Government Housing Competition. This contest was larger in scope and included two categories, a class 'A' for designs for a family of five and a class 'B' for a family of eight. The jurors were Murray Brown, president of the OAA, and two University of Toronto architecture professors, H. H. Madill and Eric Arthur. The winning design in the 'A' category was awarded to Harold Greensides and in 'B,' William Ralston was first and Greensides placed second, with J. H. Hoffa in third. Both Greensides and Hoffa had worked in Lyle's office during the mid-thirties.

Jumping on the bandwagon in 1935, the private sector in Toronto announced the Eaton's Model Home Competition as their contribution to kick-starting the economy. In an internal office memo, R. Y. Eaton, president of the T. Eaton Company, suggested the competition was 'something Lyle could be consulted on, as knowing what would best appeal to the architects.'[17] Lyle had just completed extensive renovations to their Queen Street store, and the company hired him as the head juror to help organize the event. The Eaton's management had originally wanted to model the format of the competition after the recently completed General Motors public survey, in which the car manufacturer had given the public an opportunity to select their favourite from several different models. Eaton's management reasoned that this method 'would aid architects and builders in determining what type of house would be the most popular.'[18] Lyle's first response was to suggest a limited competition with six to eight architects and stipulate the type of house or a variety of types, which would then be judged.

Eaton's and the government used the same architectural competition format. A design program was created and publicized to the architectural community who submitted their proposals by a deadline, and a panel of well-established architects evaluated the entries according to the criteria. In all three competitions the winning submissions were announced and the winners received remuneration for their efforts. The Dominion Housing Act Administration offered a total of $1,600 in prizes, the Province of Ontario $1,000 and the T. Eaton Company $5,000. These competitions were intended as a means of exchanging ideas and design developments between architects, juries and the public, in an effort to create activity in the dormant housing industry. However, Eaton's motivation was more self-serving. The president of the store hoped to awaken and stimulate the retail economy and exploit the interest in domestic product. As an internal company correspondent noted, the competition 'would cost the Co. several thousand dollars, but if it went over well, the money would come back in a twelve month in better profits.'[19]

Lyle's position on the jury meant that, as well as judging the submissions, he and architects Mackenzie Waters and

Opposite page: 6.10, 6.11 The winners of the Eaton's Model Home Competition. First prize in the medium-house category was awarded to W. F. Williams of Nelson, British Columbia (left). In the small-house category there were two designs chosen, Kent Barker (right) and Wilkes & Fisher, both of Toronto.

Above: 6.12 An exhibition at the Eaton's Queen Street store highlighted a model of W. F. Williams' winning design.

Bruce H. Wright were responsible for setting the budget and writing the terms and conditions of the competition. Lyle was also responsible for drafting the assessors' report, and had to prepare the working drawings, write the specifications, receive tenders and supervise the construction. The construction budget was set at $7,500 for the smaller house and $12,000 for the medium-sized house. First prize in the medium-house category went to W. F. Williams of Nelson, B.C., and in the small-house category two plans were chosen, those by Kent Barker and Wilkes & Fisher, both of Toronto. An honourable mention in the latter category was given to another architect working in Lyle's office at the time, Wilfred Whaley.

Eaton's had secured a building lot on Strathallan Wood in the city in preparation for the construction of the house to W. F. Williams' plans. Lyle's office prepared the final working drawings and specifications for construction. Tenders were requested from various contractors and the bids came in at around $22,000 plus $2,500 in extras, instead of the specified $12,000. Lyle used every cost-cutting device he could think of to bring the price down. When the second tenders came back at $16,000, the project was cancelled because the company did not want to be embarrassed by failing to construct the house at the advertised price. The tenders for the small-house category also came in at double the budget; however, its architect, F. A. Fisher of Wilkes & Fisher, decided to go ahead and independently build his design on Bennington Heights Drive at a cost of $15,000.

This was not the first time Eaton's had run an open architectural competition. In 1929, they sponsored one entitled the 'Ideal Ontario Home,' seeking a style that could be called a typical Ontario house. Of the 239 plans submitted, all featured historical revival styles with the notable exception of one complex three-storey Modernist design supplied by E. M. Forbes of Toronto, which placed fifth in the competition. The winning entry, a Georgian-inspired design, was constructed inside the new College Street store.

The battle between Modernist and traditionalist architecture was becoming a topic of debate in Toronto, but as W. L. Somerville observed in the *Journal*, 'regarding the various styles of architecture suitable for Canadian domestic architecture. The romantic versus formal, modern versus traditional. Having regard to the predilections of our clients, the traditionalists have much the better of the modernists.' (And, in typical Canadian fashion, he proposed that a 'traditional modernist' would be a satisfactory compromise.)[20] However, as Lyle noted in his report for the Eaton's 1935 Model Home competition, for which there were no stylistic restrictions, of the 149 submissions, the majority were in the modern style, displaying an interesting shift in architectural tastes in the country. A journalist reporting on the results of the three competitions observed that the winning spot in each case 'was given to a design entirely unlike any small home in the Dominion. Not only this, but a large majority of the designs submitted were equally unprecedented.'[21]

This was not quite true. There had been a few modern-style houses constructed in Canada. In Toronto, Group of Seven painter Lawren Harris had a house on Ava Crescent, constructed in 1930–31, designed by Russian-émigré architect Alexandra Biriukova. Originally from St. Petersburg, Biriukova had arrived in Toronto via Rome in 1929, and became the first woman to join the OAA. But the Harris house was her only commission, and she left the profession in 1934 to train as a nurse. Before embarking on the construction of his house, which he wanted to be representative of the latest in Modernist design, Harris visited Werkbund's Modernist housing exhibition in Stuttgart, Germany. This exhibition featured the whole range of modern expression, from the simple single-family dwelling by Hans Scharoun to the more complex programs of row housing by Jacobus Oud and Ludwig Mies van der Rohe, and to Le Corbusier's forceful illustration of the five points of architecture in his design for an apartment block. Compared to the rigid geometric structures of the European Modernists, the Harris house has a more personal expressionistic character. It retains some of the classical spirit with its symmetrical massing, two-storey round-arched window in the central block and wrought-iron balcony.

6.13, 6.14, 6.15 Early examples of modern-style houses in Canada included Group of Seven painter Lawren Harris, house on Ava Crescent, Toronto (top left), and Ernest Cormier's house, on avenue des Pins, Montreal (bottom left and top right), both constructed in 1930–31.

Its very personal character is reflected in the interior plan that called for odd, geometrically shaped rooms.

The most influential modern design in Canada at this time was undoubtedly Ernest Cormier's house, on avenue des Pins in Montreal, 1930–31. Widely illustrated in period magazines, Cormier's work in general – and his house in particular – came to represent the modern face of architecture in the country. His work was not as ideologically driven as that of his European counterparts; Cormier arrived at a highly idiosyncratic style by blending Modernist forms with classical grandeur. He described his design approach for the University of Montreal, noting that 'the buildings are modern in design yet not modernistic. They have been designed from the point of view of practicability, and nothing has been done purely for the sake of aspect.'[22] In his residence there is the same interplay of style and practicality, a building where art deco and European Modernism fuse into a grand theatrical statement.

Lyle knew and admired Cormier both as a person and an architect. He publicly singled him out for praise on two occasions, the first being when he presented Cormier with a bronze metal at the RAIC awards dinner in 1933. Lyle spoke to the audience in French: 'We all regret that Mr. Cormier is not with us this evening. Will you please tell him that we, his fellow architects, are very proud of him, and at the same time very jealous! Think of this! Here is an architect so competent, so clever and also so rich that he has marble columns in his vestibule. It is something extraordinary – but Cormier is an extraordinary man, he reminds me of the great artists of the Italian Renaissance. He is an architect of the first order, he is very musical, he speaks four languages, he is an outstanding watercolour painter and also an engineer of parts; he knows how to design a water-closet or make the structural steel drawings for a skyscraper. What a man!'[23] The second instance was in a letter to the editor after the RAIC annual exhibition of 1933, to defend his work from Eric Arthur's criticisms. In this response Lyle makes several tongue-in-cheek comments about Arthur going 'modern': 'I have always admired Cormier's ability as a creative artist but now I see him in the new role of missionary. If it took only four bottles of "Cormier 1933" to ginger Arthur up, I am all for the RAIC paying the expenses of some of our more serious confreres in order that they can drink at the Cormier fountain.'[24]

Not surprisingly, given the design environment and the predominance of all things modern, when Lyle was given the opportunity to design another residence for himself, he chose to experiment in that style. For the design of Highfields, in Nashville, Ontario, in 1935–36, Lyle seemed to follow the advice of friend and fellow architect Mackenzie Waters, who commented that 'the architect when building for himself seizes the opportunity to try out some of the many ideas that he is unable to submit to his client.'[25] For this planned retirement home, Lyle purchased 200 acres of property overlooking the Humber River, north of Toronto, in a small rural town, and proceeded to make plans, quickly dubbing the project the 'shack.' Also included in the scheme were plans for a stable, pool and gatehouse, the latter being the only structure that was actually constructed.

Thirty plans and elevations for this project have survived, offering an insight into the methodology of Lyle's design process. These drawings reveal the working and reworking of ideas, a typical process involving changes to size, scale, detail and budget, all of which needed to be worked through before arriving at a final solution. The preliminary sketches from 1935 show, for example, that the size of the house was reduced from a very generous 5,400 square feet to a modest residence of about half those dimensions. Although the overall scale was adjusted throughout the series of drawings, the basic vocabulary of the Modernist style remained, with one exception. The central starting point in Lyle's design approach had always been the plan, and the sketched layouts for Highfields show little of the Modernist approach in this area. The European Modernists had preferred a freer-flowing plan with an open concept, with rooms delineated by means of a change in colour, built-in furniture or drapery. Lyle's layout of Highfields was more traditional, featuring a symmetrical arrangement, with the central entrance flanked by the living-dining areas on

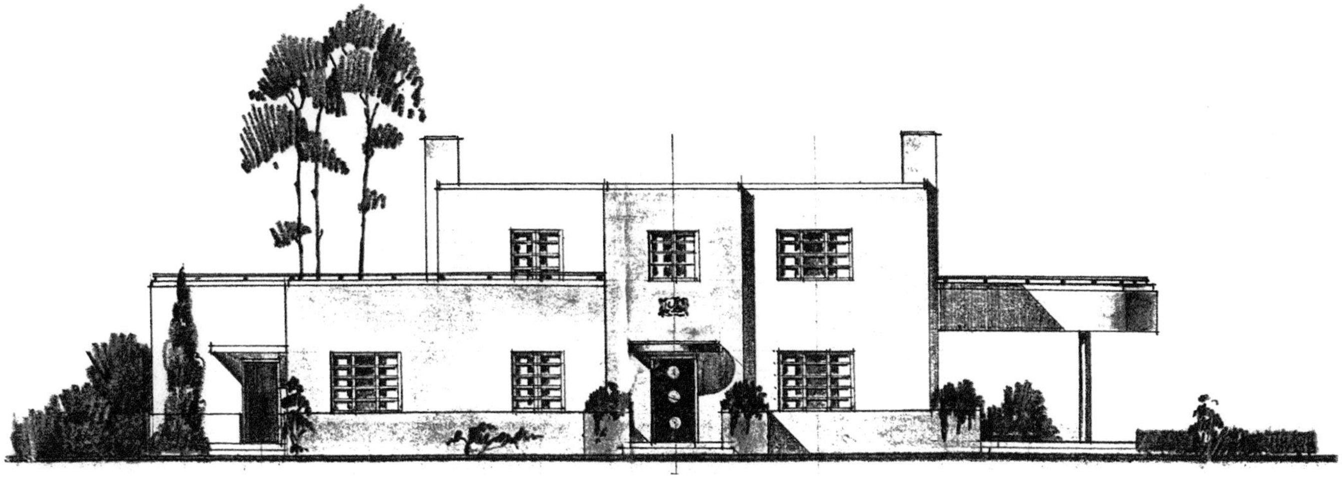

6.16, 6.17, 6.18 For his planned retirement home, Highfields, in Nashville, Ontario, Lyle produced a series of designs showing an exploration of form and mass, in an attempt to bring down construction costs.

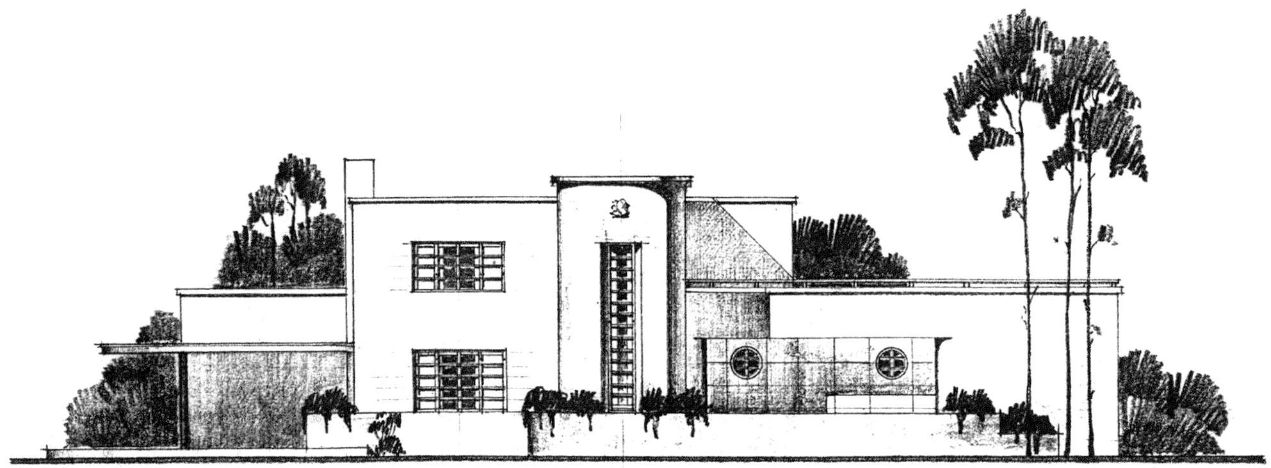

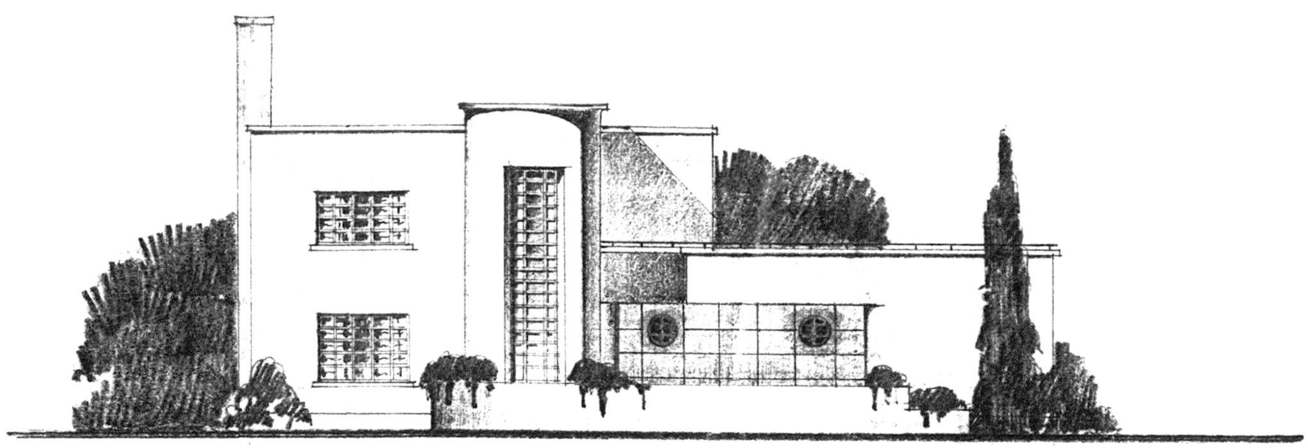

6.19, 6.20, 6.21 Highfields, Nashville, Ontario.

the one side and the kitchen on the other. Each room is a self-contained unit accessed through the main hall.

The elevation of Highfields is more Modernist in tone, revealing interesting combinations of diverse geometric forms that are contrasted with one another, with rigid cubist shapes offset by the gentle curves of the projecting bombé, housing the stairwell and oblong balcony. There is an emphasis on the horizontal through the use of flat roofs, unarticulated walls, the striped window mullion and outdoor terraces.

One influence on the design of Highfields was probably a book by the English architect F. R. S. Yorke. In *The Modern House*, published in 1934, Yorke diluted the more radical social and political ideas of European Modernism and applied them in a practical manner, emphasizing form over content. Lyle owned a copy of this book and likely studied it thoroughly.

Lyle's last opportunity to design in the modern style was for Col. R. S. McLaughlin's bedroom, bathroom and art gallery at Parkwood in Oshawa, in 1940. The only interior Lyle designed that is still intact with all of the original furnishings and finishings, it gives us an example of the homogeneous effect he strove for in his interiors. It remains preserved in its original condition as part of the Parkwood Estate, whose fifty-five-room house and twelve-acre grounds are a National Historic Site open to the public as a museum.

The south-facing bedroom overlooks the estate and the Lyle-designed Formal Garden. The room is a thoroughly modern statement in spite of being housed within Darling & Pearson's 1917 Georgian Revival building. Conspicuously located above the fireplace and dominating the room is a highly stylized pictorial scene, carved in low relief by Donald Stuart, of a standing buck and a reclining doe beside a white pine tree on a flowing river's edge. The relief is directly across from McLaughlin's bed and its symbolic reference can only be guessed at, but it must have held a strong meaning for the owner. The sculpted panel is rendered in the typical fashion of the period, in low relief with simple decorative patterning, and enlivened through the repetitive, simplified motif of pine cones and water treatment.

6.22 R. S. McLaughlin's bedroom fireplace and wall sculpture, Parkwood, Oshawa.

Opposite page: 6.23 R. S. McLaughlin's bedroom, Parkwood, Oshawa.

6.24, 6.25 R. S. McLaughlin's bathroom.

Top: 6.26 Eaton's College Street store was designed by Ross & Macdonald along with the firm of Sproatt & Rolph.

Above: 6.27 René Cera, a French-trained architect, designed the ground-floor interior using the most fashionable materials and art deco forms.

Lyle designed a complete bedroom suite for the room, using exotic woods of pollard oak, brown oak and chestnut, lush material of gold silk damask for the three open-arm occasional chairs, ivory leather for the boudoir stools and polished cream marble tops for the commode drawers and side tables. Repeating designs of Greek key and a stylized leaf motif in two tones of wood are carried through the furniture as well as in valences, door panels and fireplace implements.

Commercial: Eaton's Moderne

Eaton's, the innovator of the Canadian retail industry since its founding by Timothy Eaton in the mid-nineteenth century, had, by the beginning of the twentieth century, come to dominate the middle- and working-class markets in the country. Following the founder's death in 1907, John C. Eaton succeeded his father as president and wanted to expand the store's target audience to include wealthier consumers, hoping to attract them with new lines of stylish merchandise. Assisted by the president's wife, Flora, Eaton's started to pattern itself after department stores such as Harrods of London and its American counterparts, Altman's in New York and Montgomery Ward in Chicago. Since an upscale look was essential, architecture and design played an important role in the new corporate image. The collection of structures at their Queen Street location in Toronto was renovated and consolidated with a rebuilding program by Sproatt & Rolph that continued over twenty-five years. In 1923, René Cera, a French-trained architect, was hired to head up the interior design department. One of his first functions was to transform the store's coffee-counter eateries into the most fashionable dining room in the city, with the elegant, classically designed Georgian Room.

In 1926, 400 items from the Exposition Internationale des Arts Décoratifs et Industriels Modernes, including many household products, toured eight American cities and concluded at the Metropolitan Museum of Art in New York. This sparked a race among the American department stores to introduce the new vogue of art deco design to the marketplace and caused a rash of in-store displays and exhibitions, each trying to outdo the others in size and range of products. In Canada, the department stores consisted of the Hudson's Bay, Robert Simpson's and Ogilvie's in Montreal and the T. Eaton Company. Eaton's was the first Canadian retailer to see the potential of marketing the moderne style and art deco consumable products. In 1928, inside the Calgary store, Cera created a small house entitled 'Canadian House of Today,' which contained the stylish furniture and accessories he considered emblematic of 'the broad principle of Canadian moderne.'[26]

Eaton's ongoing expansion in Toronto culminated with the project located at Yonge and College streets. Planning for this monumental project, designed by Ross & Macdonald along with the firm of Sproatt & Rolph, originally started in 1916, but construction did not begin until 1928, and the structure took two years to build. Originally intended as a corporate landmark for Eaton's, the scale of the project was gargantuan, with a projected retail floor space and administrative office complex to exceed 4 million square feet, or roughly the size of the Rockefeller Centre in New York. The first and only phase of the project to be completed was the seven-storey block on the southwest corner of Yonge and Gerrard streets. Cera designed the ground-floor interior, a lavish exercise in the most fashionable materials and art deco forms. The warm travertine floors contrasted with the cool aluminum metal used for the lighting fixtures and stair rails. The forms were simple and scaled to overwhelm the store's customers with the use of sophisticated smooth-curved surfaces and elongated exotic tulip-shaped lighting fixtures. One of the most prominent features was the elevator concourse that ran along the Yonge Street facade, which gave access to one of the country's art deco showpieces, Jacques Carlu's seventh-floor Auditorium and Round Room restaurant.

The economic depression had stalled Eaton's completion of the College Street store, which meant the Queen Street store remained its largest retail outlet. However, compared to the sophisticated modern-style design of the uptown store, it was looking rather dowdy and dated. In 1934, Lyle was

6.28, 6.29 Alterations to the ground-floor interior of Eaton's Queen Street store consisted of updating the entrances, the lighting program and the display areas with the art deco stylings of the College Street store.

commissioned to address this concern with extensive alterations to the ground-floor interior of Eaton's Queen Street store. The work consisted of updating the 1922 ground-floor entrances, lighting program and display areas. To supplement the excellent local examples of the latest art deco styling at the College Street store, Lyle, with junior architect Arthur Eadie, travelled to see the trends in New York City and Philadelphia.

The renovation turned out to be extensive, with all alterations involving a movement toward more modern features, brighter colours, richer material usage and a contrasting use of metal and glass. The lighting program included large, two-tiered tulip-shaped aluminum ceiling fixtures, and similar table lamps were located on the display cases. The floors were replaced with a warm beige travertine marble that contrasted with the display case's dark vertical-grained wood bases and glass metal frames. The end walls were clad in white Carrara marble, dramatically lit. All in-store signage was in a modern sans serif typeface. The aluminum railing to the basement stairs was beautifully crafted, with large octagonal medallions depicting a scantily dressed dancing female figure rendered in a simple, elegant style. Lyle included these features in his renovations to the store's north entrance along Albert Street two years later. The work was well-received. The 1934 alterations won an honourable mention at the 1938 exhibition of the Toronto Chapter Ontario Society of Architects and the 1937 Albert Street work was also honoured a year later.

Below: 6.30 Lyle's preliminary sketch for the garden.

Opposite page: 6.31 The Formal Garden at R. S. McLaughlin's Parkwood Estate in Oshawa.

Monuments: Grand Classical Garden

In 1935, Lyle was commissioned to design the Formal Garden at Robert S. McLaughlin's Parkwood Estate in Oshawa. The twelve-acre estate had included several different types of gardens. There was a small, enclosed, meditative Italian Garden, just off McLaughlin's private library, a Sundial Garden, complete with a summer house, and, to the south of the main house, a large informal area called the Great Lawn, designed by Dunington-Grubb. To replace a horse arena complex on the south corner of the estate, McLaughlin commissioned Lyle to design the theatrical and dramatic formal garden. Why McLaughlin chose Lyle over Dunington-Grubb is a mystery. Lyle, perhaps aware of this rare opportunity and afraid he might lose it to the landscape firm, had his office staff keep everything about the project a complete secret.

Some landscape architects in Europe had attempted to parallel in their work the features of the modern movement. As early as 1912, André Vera published *Le Nouveau Jardin*, becoming the leading theoretical voice for the development of the modern garden in France. On the practical side, Gabriel Guevrekian designed many modern gardens, including a 1923 work at the Vicomte de Noailles villa at Hyères, which was to complement the Robert Mallet-Stevens–designed house. In 1925, the Paris Exposition Internationale des Arts Décoratifs et Industriels Modernes featured several experimental cubist gardens with blocks of flowers and concrete trees. Another pioneer of the modern garden style was Canadian-born Christopher Tunnard, who had relocated to Britain in 1928. Following the example of Le Corbusier, Tunnard published a manifesto, *Gardens in the Modern Landscape*, in 1938.

Opposite page: 6.34 The Formal Garden at dusk.

Tunnard's major concerns were functionalism, the simplicity and traditions of Japanese architecture and garden design, and that a garden should be a work of art.

Either Lyle was unaware of these efforts or he didn't wish to emulate them. Taking instead the same approach he had with the Gage Fountain in Hamilton, he designed a classically styled garden based on French prototypes, respecting the principles of logic, order, discipline and beauty. The first three components were to be displayed by a rigid, generally symmetrical garden layout and the last was to be expressed by the arrangement of plants within the design. The different foliage within these beds was arranged to complement and contrast with each other in shade, hue, colour, height and texture. The gardens followed definite geometric patterns and called for specific dimensions and precise ways of planting. Planting beds were to be of equal size, either square or rectangle and separated by a system of wide paths. These surfaces were then further divided into smaller, exact sections that often featured mirror images. All the rules and dimensions of this formal approach to garden planning were to be found in Louis Liger's *La Nouvelle Maison Rustique,* published in France during the eighteenth century.

Lyle's approach was typical of many Beaux-Arts architects, relying strongly on garden architecture, and featuring a symmetrical plan, a meticulous attention to detail and proportion and a masterful use of three-dimensional space. His design is formal, with a central axis and cross axes and plantings all set within a symmetrically arranged geometric grid. All architectural forms are white and the garden is punctuated with oversized urns. From the commanding view of the upper terrace, the scene is dominated by a seventy-metre-long rectangular pool of water containing six small waterspouts. These establish a rhythm that leads to the focal point of the main fountain. The vista is terminated on the western end by a single-storey tea house consisting of a central block containing a vestibule, coatroom, washroom, pantry and kitchen behind large glass doors. A pair of unadorned columns support a simple entablature framed with projecting pavilions whose niches hold large urns. The upper terrace, accessed by a pair of flanking two-tier staircases, features an open balustrade. A pair of piers frame a terrace wall fountain with the head of Neptune spouting forth into a rectangular pool that allows the water to cascade down a pair of semi-circular tiers to the ground-level basin. Flanking the scene on the rectangular pool retaining walls are a pair of stone-carved Canadian geese striking a territorial pose with outstretched curvilinear wings, projecting necks and hissing beaks, carved by German-born and newly immigrated sculptor Friedrich Winkler. Running parallel to the pool are narrow, colourful beds framed by Japanese yews containing standard hydrangeas, while a series of pyramidal cedars create the necessary vertical accents. Flanking the fountain and accessed by flights of stairs are raised beds consisting of four areas separated by gravel paths. Each of these beds consists of a low border of Japanese yews, a grassed area and geometrically shaped areas for annual plantings.

During the construction of the project, Lyle had introduced McLaughlin to the well-known Swedish sculptor Carl Milles. Milles had been director of the Sculpture Department and resident sculptor at the Cranbrook Academy of Art in Bloomfield Hills, Michigan, where his work graced buildings designed by the President of the Academy, Eliel Saarinen. Lyle, who had often visited Milles at Cranbrook, had hoped McLaughlin would commission him to design a fountain, either within the Formal Garden or somewhere else on the estate. Unfortunately, nothing came of the meeting.

A formal garden of this size and expense was unprecedented in the country, and what prompted McLaughlin to build it in the height of the Great Depression can only be speculated upon. But there is no doubt about the garden's serene harmony, achieved through the controlled flow of space created by the Beaux-Arts axial plan, the virtuosic use of modern classical architectural forms that are proportioned to dominate but not overwhelm and a fascinating garden planting that is restrained in form and variety of species. The masterful combination of these elements makes Parkwood a unique garden statement in North America.

Opposite page: 6.32 The terrace wall fountain has a spouting head of Neptune with a pair of bronze Canadian geese, carved by Friedrich Winkler.

Left: 6.33 View looking east toward the main fountain from the tea house.

Tunnard's major concerns were functionalism, the simplicity and traditions of Japanese architecture and garden design, and that a garden should be a work of art.

Either Lyle was unaware of these efforts or he didn't wish to emulate them. Taking instead the same approach he had with the Gage Fountain in Hamilton, he designed a classically styled garden based on French prototypes, respecting the principles of logic, order, discipline and beauty. The first three components were to be displayed by a rigid, generally symmetrical garden layout and the last was to be expressed by the arrangement of plants within the design. The different foliage within these beds was arranged to complement and contrast with each other in shade, hue, colour, height and texture. The gardens followed definite geometric patterns and called for specific dimensions and precise ways of planting. Planting beds were to be of equal size, either square or rectangle and separated by a system of wide paths. These surfaces were then further divided into smaller, exact sections that often featured mirror images. All the rules and dimensions of this formal approach to garden planning were to be found in Louis Liger's *La Nouvelle Maison Rustique,* published in France during the eighteenth century.

Lyle's approach was typical of many Beaux-Arts architects, relying strongly on garden architecture, and featuring a symmetrical plan, a meticulous attention to detail and proportion and a masterful use of three-dimensional space. His design is formal, with a central axis and cross axes and plantings all set within a symmetrically arranged geometric grid. All architectural forms are white and the garden is punctuated with oversized urns. From the commanding view of the upper terrace, the scene is dominated by a seventy-metre-long rectangular pool of water containing six small waterspouts. These establish a rhythm that leads to the focal point of the main fountain. The vista is terminated on the western end by a single-storey tea house consisting of a central block containing a vestibule, coatroom, washroom, pantry and kitchen behind large glass doors. A pair of unadorned columns support a simple entablature framed with projecting pavilions whose niches hold large urns. The upper terrace, accessed by a pair of flanking two-tier staircases, features an open balustrade. A pair of piers frame a terrace wall fountain with the head of Neptune spouting forth into a rectangular pool that allows the water to cascade down a pair of semi-circular tiers to the ground-level basin. Flanking the scene on the rectangular pool retaining walls are a pair of stone-carved Canadian geese striking a territorial pose with outstretched curvilinear wings, projecting necks and hissing beaks, carved by German-born and newly immigrated sculptor Friedrich Winkler. Running parallel to the pool are narrow, colourful beds framed by Japanese yews containing standard hydrangeas, while a series of pyramidal cedars create the necessary vertical accents. Flanking the fountain and accessed by flights of stairs are raised beds consisting of four areas separated by gravel paths. Each of these beds consists of a low border of Japanese yews, a grassed area and geometrically shaped areas for annual plantings.

During the construction of the project, Lyle had introduced McLaughlin to the well-known Swedish sculptor Carl Milles. Milles had been director of the Sculpture Department and resident sculptor at the Cranbrook Academy of Art in Bloomfield Hills, Michigan, where his work graced buildings designed by the President of the Academy, Eliel Saarinen. Lyle, who had often visited Milles at Cranbrook, had hoped McLaughlin would commission him to design a fountain, either within the Formal Garden or somewhere else on the estate. Unfortunately, nothing came of the meeting.

A formal garden of this size and expense was unprecedented in the country, and what prompted McLaughlin to build it in the height of the Great Depression can only be speculated upon. But there is no doubt about the garden's serene harmony, achieved through the controlled flow of space created by the Beaux-Arts axial plan, the virtuosic use of modern classical architectural forms that are proportioned to dominate but not overwhelm and a fascinating garden planting that is restrained in form and variety of species. The masterful combination of these elements makes Parkwood a unique garden statement in North America.

Opposite page: 6.34 The Formal Garden at dusk.

Chapter 7: 1941–1945

TRAVEL FUNDS
FOREIGN EXCHANGE
COLLECTIONS
ACCOUNTANCY
RECEIVING TELLERS

Inspiration for the Future

Cultural Contribution

In September 1939, while the opening of Lyle's new Bank of Nova Scotia branch in Saint John, New Brunswick, was being reported on the inside pages of the local newspapers, the front covers ran banner headlines about the German invasion of Poland. Europe was at war, and Canada threw itself full into the conflict. The architectural community was quick to respond as well, and a few months after the outbreak of hostilities, an overseas unit led by Maj. Eric Haldenby embarked for Europe. The country's construction industry again came to a virtual standstill as all material resources and labour were directed toward the war effort. By 1941, however, some construction was underway, mostly small residences being built under the National Housing Act and industrial construction for companies producing military goods.

Given the grim atmosphere, the last known architectural work by Lyle was, ironically, a 1940 sketch for a mausoleum for R. S. McLaughlin. The project did not get beyond the preliminary stages under Lyle and was eventually completed by Beck & Eadie (who formed a partnership after Lyle's retirement). With no prospect of work, Lyle was forced to make other plans. He did not officially retire from practice until 1943, but a year earlier he had already rented out his office to another business and started to look around for the right institution to donate his extensive architectural library to.

Even in this state of war-induced architectural limbo, however, Lyle was still making significant contributions to both artistic and cultural activities in the city. Throughout his life, Lyle had been actively engaged in the promotion of Canadian painting and sculpture. He had written many reviews and articles on group exhibitions or individual artists and had been an elected member of the Art Gallery of Toronto from 1927 through 1939. The gallery, one of the largest in the country, served in a provincial and national capacity. Located in the art centre of English Canada, the Art Gallery of Toronto (it became the Art Gallery of Ontario in 1966 to reflect its changing provincial role) had some of the finest works by contemporary Canadian artists, including Tom Thomson, the Group of Seven and Emily Carr. Its permanent collection proudly boasted an extensive European component as well, including sixteenth- and seventeenth-century Dutch masters, eighteenth-century English landscapes, and works from various French schools, including the Impressionists Monet, Pissaro and Renoir.

Lyle served as vice-president of the gallery for two years, until he was elected president, a role he held from 1941 until 1945. Other members on the executive council included the pillars of the nation's social and financial communities: Vincent Massey, Col. R. Y. Eaton, R. S. McLaughlin and J. S. McLean. Directing and overseeing the functions of the institution during this critical juncture was a challenging and important activity. When asked why the gallery should remain open during the war, for example, Lyle defended the decision by stating, '[W]e stand for the preservation of our intellectual and spiritual resources. Art is the visible and imperishable expression of free minds and, therefore, typifies one of the great goals that we are fighting for. It is an escape from the present and a source of inspiration for the future.'[1]

Lyle's activities at the gallery during this period were extremely proactive and he worked toward making the institution 'a great one in a provincial and national sense, with a membership drawn from every walk of life and from the towns and cities of Ontario as well as the rural areas. In this way we would be a great "people's Gallery" and fulfill our destiny.'[2] To this end, some of the initiatives Lyle oversaw were innovative educational programs. These outreach programs were an attempt to appeal to a broader audience and included a series of evening events devoted to high school students. Additionally, the gallery was opened one night a week for visitors and introduced a circulating exhibition policy for touring shows throughout the province.

Many of the monthly exhibitions held at the gallery had wartime themes, such as the Allied Merchant Seamen's and the Red Cross Exhibition, intended to bolster the public's morale. Several other exhibitions were held in collaboration with the Museum of Modern Art in New York. In 1942, the gallery implemented a highly successful program featuring silkscreened

Opposite page: 7.1 Using Lyle's original plan, Mathers & Haldenby, architects, along with Beck & Eadie as associates completed the Bank of Nova Scotia, King Street, Toronto, in 1951.

Top: 7.2 Lyle (middle) with unidentified guests at an exhibition opening at the Art Gallery of Toronto.

Above: 7.3 Lyle's Ex Libris design for the architectural books that he donated to the Hamilton Public Library.

reproductions of scenes from Canadian art, directed toward the national armed services to promote the country's art while supporting the military effort. The gallery had Group of Seven painters A. Y. Jackson and A. J. Casson produce this series, which continued through the war, printing over 15,000 pictures that were distributed both at home and abroad to the troops.

One of the high points of Lyle's tenure was the special dinner organized for Jackson. In 1942, Queen's University had awarded an honorary degree to the painter, and Lyle, always ready to celebrate the creative genius of others, put together the event, which was a great success. Jackson wrote Lyle, thanking him, as 'such an occasion was beyond even an artist's power to visualize, and will remain in the heart and memory indelible as long as *le bon dieu* allows me to linger on his beautiful earth.'[3]

When Lyle stepped down as president in spring 1945 because of failing health, he had successfully provided stewardship for the institution and seen it through one of its most dark and trying times.

Lyle also made a lasting cultural contribution to the City of Hamilton, and to the institution his father was instrumental in founding, when he donated his architectural books to the local public library. The titles included works from all architectural periods, with an emphasis on traditional styles, showing both Lyle's natural bias as well as the influence of his training. The training of a Beaux-Arts architect meant that students had to study classical monuments, the orders and the rules of formal composition, so every architect had to either have access to a comprehensive library or own one.

Lyle's library was a very busy place, used both for his own reference as well as by the other designers in his office. When he was teaching, the library was open to his students, a fact borne out by pages heavily coated with graphite, suggesting their use by students at Lyle's ateliers.

In 1942, Lyle donated to the Hamilton Public Library 182 books he had acquired from England, France, Germany, Italy, the U.S. and Canada over a fifty-year period. The value of this gift was not insignificant, estimated to be worth about $1,500, the equivalent of the price of a 1942 luxury Cadillac. Lyle proudly claimed, 'I have seen a great many architectural libraries in Canada but I have never seen any that are comparable to the library that we have given to you.'[4]

To identify the books as part of the donated collection, Lyle designed a special bookplate using a simplified silhouette of the Central Presbyterian Church, a fitting gesture that would link 'my Father's name and career to one of our own early architectural efforts.'[5] The church facade appears over the *Ex Libris* inscription, followed by a dedication: 'This book was presented by John M. Lyle F.R.I.B.A. R.C.A. F.R.A.I.C. in memory of his father The Reverend Samuel Lyle B.D. D.D.' Among the books in the collection was an 1892 gift from Samuel to his son, *A Short History of Art*. This gift at the beginning of Lyle's architectural training acquired increasing significance for him, especially as it returned to support and strengthen the institution his father help create. Lyle's donation was a heartfelt commemorative gesture showing his admiration of the father who nurtured and financially supported his pursuit of an architectural career.

The 'Big Job'

Lyle died in his residence on December 19, 1945, at seventy-three, from natural causes; however, his architectural career did not end there. A few months after his death, in spring 1946, the 'Big Job' Lyle had spent over a decade working on for the Bank of Nova Scotia's head office in Toronto was resurrected when the economic conditions were finally right to proceed. Since its previous reworking in 1937, most of the project's principal players had passed on as well, including the structural and mechanical engineers, while retirement had also removed most of the bank's principal officers, with the exception of George Speirs, who had worked with Lyle.

Faced with these losses, the bank appointed Mathers & Haldenby as architects and hired Beck & Eadie, who were familiar with the history and the design of the building, as associates. Since the building's inception in 1929, there had been many innovations in both technical and mechanical areas, as well architectural style, so the project required a total

7.4 Bank of Nova Scotia, King Street, Toronto, 1929–51.

7.5, 7.6 The elevator corridor (above) and the banking hall main entrance windows with stairwell (right), Bank of Nova Scotia, Toronto.

review of Lyle's working drawings and specifications. After a thorough study of the design problem and the restrictions imposed by the site and the client's special requirements, Mathers concluded that Lyle's thinking was sound and his plan exceptional. Using the methodical approach conditioned by his Beaux-Arts training, Lyle had solved the core needs of the building's plan first, and the design was so successful that Mathers and his associates could not improve upon it. Mathers conceded that the fundamentals of Lyle's design were 'the best solution of the problems.'[6]

With the basic plan settled, Mathers' next task was to decide on the interior details and choice of materials as well as plan for the mechanical requirements. In this regard, Lyle's design also proved flexible enough to incorporate and conceal all the new electrical, heating and venting services without losing any ceiling height or requiring the enlargement of columns, beams and wall furrings. Some of the decisions Mathers made, however, did influence the building's exterior appearance. To allow for maximum flexibility in the location of the interior walls on the floors that were to be rented out, single windows – rather than Lyle's proposed continuous sash – were adopted. Mathers also streamlined the exterior massing and did away with some of Lyle's setbacks. His choice of equal-sized piers used to separate the windows created a more austere appearance, but also gave the building a soaring verticality.

The Canadian sculptural program Lyle had used in previous projects for the Bank of Nova Scotia, and one with which the bank had so strongly identified, also changed. Originally conceived at the height of his Canadian phase, Lyle's plans called for a decorative program as elaborate as the bank's Halifax building. However, when the Bank of Montreal, a major competitor located across the street, used a Canadian decorative program for its new building in 1948, Lyle's program no longer seemed appropriate. For the exterior of the Bank of Nova Scotia, Mathers chose classic mythological themes rendered in a curvilinear style of heroic realism. The overall decorative program was greatly reduced so that 'ornament was sparingly used and where employed was concentrated for emphasis of certain elements in the design.'[7] Lyle's Canadian themes can be seen in the interior, however, especially on the rear banking-hall wall that terminates the north-south axis. A large relief sculptured panel by Jacobine Jones depicts regional themes and the country's economic foundations of fishing, lumbering, mining, industry and agriculture. To mark the Bank of Nova Scotia's expansion into the Caribbean, a woman harvesting a banana crop is included. Other East Coast design motifs are used sparingly throughout the interior ground floor of the building.

The ground-floor plan is where Lyle's presence is most keenly felt. The major and minor axes of the plan created highly functional and visually stunning spaces. A series of controlled secondary spaces leads to the primary focus of the banking hall. Making the space so dramatic are the room's ceiling height; the lighting, both natural – from the six westerly bays – and artificial – from the ceiling lamps; the glass-and-metal-grid south wall; and the marble sculptured north wall. The Bank of Nova Scotia building is a fitting tribute to Lyle's skills as a designer and one for which he should be properly credited, but the local newspapers covering the opening of the building identified Mathers & Haldenby as the architects with no mention of Lyle. This oversight continues to this day in most historical accounts as well as descriptions of the building.

A Lasting Contribution

The quality and significance of the buildings Lyle designed would have ensured him an elevated position in the pantheon of Canadian architecture, but when combined with his other achievements to the field and the cultural milieu of the country, his status is greatly enhanced. Lyle's professional career and his contribution to Canadian architecture can be divided into three areas: the buildings he designed, the influence he exerted on the profession, and his teaching and training of the next generation of architects.

Lyle was an eclectic architect who did not specialize in any particular building type; unlike most of his colleagues, he was equally enthusiastic designing a piece of interior furniture and a bridge, and applied proportional amounts of craft and energy

7.7 The Bank of Nova Scotia maintained Lyle's regional decorative program in the interior of the building with a large sculpture panel by Jacobine Jones.

in each effort. Throughout his career, Lyle was a traditionalist who never completely abandoned the basic tenets of his Beaux-Arts education and his belief in the beauty and harmony that can be achieved through the classical principles of scale, proportion, material and decorative detail, but he was also a progressive who realized that architecture was not a static entity. Lyle considered architecture an art form that must be open and receptive to new and potentially radical ideas and concepts. He was, then, a progressive traditionalist, embracing change and outside influences and incorporating them into his basic aesthetic.

Lyle's work evolved throughout his career. He embraced new ideas, construction techniques and materials that ensured his work always remained contemporary and relevant. The works he produced over his forty years as an architect have been considered some of the best examples in their genre in Canada. This list includes his early Beaux-Arts classical buildings the Memorial Arch, Kingston; the Bank of Nova Scotia, Ottawa; and Union Station, Toronto, as well as his best-known Canadian School work – Runnymede Library, Toronto; the Bank of Nova Scotia, Halifax; the Modernist designs of the Parkwood Gardens, Oshawa; and his own unexecuted residential design Highfields.

In 1936, Lyle's influence had been evident in the limited competition held by the Royal Canadian Mint for new designs for Canadian coinage. A dozen sculptors, artists and architects were invited to submit designs, and Lyle produced twelve images influenced by his earlier work of indigenous flora and fauna motifs. The mint selected the English artist George Kruger Gray and Canadian sculptor Emmanuel Hahn to create five-cent and twenty-five-cent coins. The final designs they produced were based on a stylized beaver and caribou, similar to Lyle's proposals. Geoffrey Hunt noted in his exhibition catalogue on the architect that Lyle's

> chief contributions to the formation of a 'Canadian School' of architecture lay in his writings, addresses, and the exhibitions of his designs and decorative fixtures. Lyle's espousal of a new spirit of design led others to original Canadian sources for inspiration. His work had always been meant to evoke associations, but later came to express the Canadian heartland through stylized symbols. Lyle's use of a repertoire of natural motifs created a succession of images that were then adopted in our coinage and much later in our flag. These symbols, while politically neutral, became the national emblems which represented the emerging Dominion.[8]

Lyle had abandoned the use of Canadian and regional imagery in his buildings by 1932, yet other architects picked up on these themes. Canadian imagery appears in the design and decorative programs for many of the federal buildings constructed under the Public Works Construction Act during the mid-1930s and early 1940s. Examples of this influence can be seen in the work of architect Charles B. Dolphin, who was commissioned to design the Postal Delivery Building on Lakeshore Boulevard and Bay Street in 1938–46 and the Arthur Meighen Building on St. Clair Avenue in 1950–54, both in Toronto. These buildings use a decorative program that is thoroughly Canadian, with indigenous pictorial scenes and motifs. Many other government structures, including the Dominion Building in Halifax, beside Lyle's Bank of Nova Scotia, used nationalistic and regional imagery, stylized leafs, floral motifs and allegorical figures representing the natural resources and industries of Canada. The federal building (now the City Hall) in Prince Rupert, British Columbia, had a decoration program based on native West Coast motifs and themes, complete with a totem pole. Another structure incorporating totem figures into its decorative program was the Toronto *Globe and Mail* building designed by Mathers & Haldenby in 1938. A pair of carved panels framed the front entrance with large prominent figures and side panels of totem creatures.

The most significant building inspired by Lyle's Canadian decorative program was the Bank of Montreal at King and Bay streets, in Toronto. Started in 1937 by Chapman, Oxley & Facey, the project was brought to a halt at the outbreak of the

7.8, 7.9 Part of the decorative program on the Postal Delivery Building, Lakeshore Boulevard and Bay Street, 1938–46.

war and was not completed until 1948 by the architectural firm of Marani & Morris. The building's sculptural program included six exterior bas-reliefs of scantily clad idealized figures representing the provinces and territories, and six stylized animal panels depicting a skunk, polar bear, walrus and howling wolves.

Another of Lyle's legacies was his contribution to the development of the next generation of Canadian architects who either worked for him or were taught at his privately run ateliers or the University of Toronto. The collegial and co-operative environment of the educational program at the École des Beaux-Arts in Paris had had such a strong impact on the young architect that he embraced the spirit and continued to recreate it through his teaching programs and work environment. Also, the strong bond between students and *patron* continued with some of his former pupils, for whom Lyle remained a mentor throughout their architectural development. The collaborative atmosphere Lyle had nurtured among his students lingered well into their professional careers and the respect that was felt could be seen in the way a number of them paid homage to him after his death. Douglas Kertland, a former student and employee of Lyle's, wrote his obituary in the *Journal* and stated, 'Canada is made poorer by his death.'[9] And A. S. Mathers, in a paper read before the Vitruvian Society and printed in the *Journal*, which summarized his thirty-five years of architectural practice, singled Lyle out for praise. Mathers reminisced that he would

> never forget my friendship with the late John M. Lyle who was not only active in the promotion of architecture and architects, but took a keen interest in and gave his time to furthering the cause of the arts in general...his death was a sad event for his friends and in the profession. He was perhaps the greatest friend that the profession had in the years between the wars. His interest in the younger men was sincere and wholehearted. While he was a member of the best clubs in town and his personal friends were among the great figures of finance and industry, he spent almost every lunch with a group of young architects at the Diet Kitchen.[10]

Another memoir that recognized Lyle's influence and the unique interaction among members of the architectural profession of this period was a private history by the firm of Rounthwaite, Dick & Hadley, founded by F. H. Marani, a former pupil. The account captures the spirit that existed between the wars and then concludes with a fitting and appropriate statement. It notes that the members of the architectural community 'saw a good deal of one another and shared ideas about their profession and its goals. The place where they did this was at a table specially set aside in the Diet Kitchen Tea Room on Bloor Street near Bay. It was presided over each lunch-time by John M. Lyle, a distinguished Beaux Arts graduate who lectured in the department (of Architecture at U of T). The group, of whom were present every day included Eric Haldenby, Roper Gouinlock, Bruce Wright, Ted Yonge, Ferdie Marani, Mackenzie Waters and Martin Baldwin. All were to make a lasting contribution to architecture in Canada.'[11]

Frank Lloyd Wright wrote, '[E]very great architect is – necessarily – a great poet. He must be a great original interpreter of his time, his day, his age.'[12] Lyle, especially in his attempts to give voice to a Canadian and regional consciousness, must be viewed as aspiring to the poetic and an original interpreter of his time. He deserves much credit for being one of the earliest and strongest advocates of the rise of nationalism in the arts during the 1920s and 1930s, which created an environment that made the use of Canadian decorative images acceptable not only in architecture but in other media. In 1931, Lyle reported, '[W]e have adopted as a *parti* the use of new forms, or old forms in new combinations, a new language of ornament based on Canadian forms, having in mind that they all must pass the test of beauty. We believe that the Swedish slogan – 'make beautiful the everyday things of life' – opens up a world of possibilities in collaboration between the skilled designer and the manufacturer; to beautify the world through mass production properly inspired and directed.'[13]

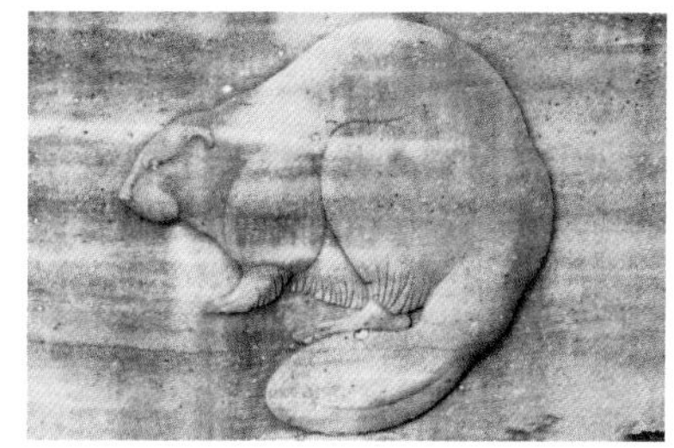

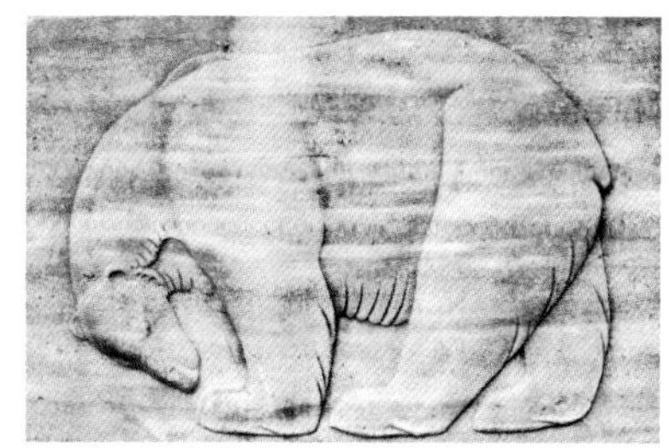

Far left: 7.10, 7.11 Mathers & Haldenby incorporated totem figures into the decorative program for the Toronto Globe and Mail *building in 1938.*

Left and above: 7.12, 7.13, 7.14,7.15, 7.16 Bank of Montreal at King and Bay streets started by Chapman, Oxley & Facey was completed by 1948 by the architectural firm of Marani & Morris, who used a decorative sculpture program that included indigenous animals and stylized provincial motifs.

Appendix

Works and Activities

1872
- Nov. 13, Birth, Connor, Ireland

1878
- Emigrates to Hamilton, Ontario

1878–88
- Central School and Collegiate Institute of Hamilton

1887–91
- Hamilton Art School, wins awards from the Ontario Education Department in categories of Extra Advance Course, Industrial Design; Mechanical Course, Industrial Design; Primary Course, Freehand Drawing, Model Drawing

1891
- Cornell University, Ithaca, New York, attends first semester architectural program, fails fall examinations and returns to Hamilton with jaundice

1891–92
- Yale Art School, New Haven, Connecticut

1892
- Works in New York office of former Hamilton architect Frank Freeman
- Places third in art subjects and fifth in clay modelling, entrance exam for the École des Beaux-Arts, Paris
- Enters atelier Godefroy and Freynet, École des Beaux-Arts, Paris

1893
- Exhibits, World's Columbian Exposition, Chicago, Illinois, student drawings organized by Department of Education of Ontario and Hamilton Art School

1894
- Summer, travels to Ireland
- École des Beaux-Arts, Paris, atelier Paul Blondel

1896
- Sails to New York City
- Works for Howard & Cauldwell as draftsman for two to three weeks (for free) then for brief period with Raymond Almirall before returning to salaried position with Howard & Cauldwell
- Competition entry, places second, New York Public Library, Howard & Cauldwell
- Appointed Chairman of the Dinner Committee, Beaux-Arts Society, New York City

1897
- Losing competition entry, Providence, Rhode Island, Howard & Cauldwell

1898
- Winning competition entry, Newark High School, Newark, New Jersey, Howard & Cauldwell

1899
- Competition entry, places second, New York Yacht Club, New York, Howard & Cauldwell

1900
- Joins firm of Warren & Wetmore

1901
- Joins offices of Carrère & Hastings and works in Buffalo, New York, for six months during building of Pan-American Exposition
- Winning competition entry, two bandstands, Pan-American Exposition, Buffalo, New York
- Returns to New York, freelance designer and draftsman

1902–04
- Establishes own office at 33 Union Square W., New York City (1902–03)
- Competition entry drawings worked on include Brooklyn City Hall, Washington City Hall, Post Office and Custom House, San Francisco (architects unknown)
- Losing competition entry, West Point Military Academy, with architect Charles Haight
- Winning competition entry, President McKinley Memorial, Canton, Ohio, produces drawings for architect Harold Van Buren Magonigle
- Competition entry, places fifth, Soldiers' and Sailors' Monument, Philadelphia, competition entry with architect George Cary of Buffalo
- Losing competition entry, Freeman's Hospital, Washington, D.C., with architect George Cary of Buffalo

1904
- Moves office to 111 Fifth Ave., New York City
- Daniel Burnham of Chicago offers Lyle employment, declined
- Offered partnership with James Brite, works for several months before declining offer

1905
- Moves to Toronto and lives on Bellevue Ave. near College St. and opens office on second floor of 14 Leader Lane
- Hires draftsman R. B. McGiffin
- Hendrie, residence, Aberdeen Ave., Hamilton, Ontario
- Proposal, Caven Memorial Library, Knox College, University of Toronto,

Activities
- Patron, Beaux-Arts Club, Toronto
- Acts as one of three judges in student design competition, Toronto
- Exhibits with Architectural Eighteen Club, Ontario Society of Artists, Toronto, drawings include: Soldiers' and Sailors' Monument, Philadelphia, and some scenes from Holland and Paris

1906
- Sterling Bank, Port Dalhousie, Ontario
- Central Presbyterian Church, Charlton Ave. W., Hamilton, Ontario
- George Robinson, stable and coach house, Beaumont Rd., Toronto
- Dominion Transport Company, stable, Wellington at Windsor streets, Toronto
- Royal Alexandra Theatre, King W., Toronto
- 262 College St., addition, Toronto
- O'Brien's Ladies Tailors Ltd., store alterations and furniture designs, 72 King W., Toronto
- Lt. Colonel Stimson, 60 St. George St., Toronto
- J. J. McCaffery, iron cornice, Bay St. at Adelaide (NE), Toronto
- J. J. McCaffery, alterations, Bay St. at Adelaide (NE), Toronto

Activities
- Exhibits with Ontario Society of Artists, Toronto, student painting 'Twilight, Paris'
- Elected patron, Architectural Studio Club, Toronto
- Architectural League of America, Current Club Work: J. P. Hynes, Toronto chairman, J. C. B. Horwood, J. M. Lyle

1907
- Bank of Nova Scotia, Windsor, Nova Scotia
- Imperial Bank of Canada, Bloor W. and Lansdowne, Toronto
- Conservatory of Music, alterations, College and University, Toronto
- L. Solman, residence alterations, 106 Yonge St., Toronto
- Hobson, residence verandah, Hamilton, Ontario
- F. S. Bachus, residence addition, Homewood Ave., Hamilton, Ontario
- R. A. Lucas, residence, conservatory, Hamilton, Ontario
- Wilcox, residence additions, Hamilton, Ontario

- Church, Cheltenham, Ontario
- Competition entry, places sixth, Department of Justice Buildings, Ottawa

Activities
- Architectural League of America, Toronto Branch, president, J. P. Hynes, vice-president, J. M. Lyle
- Elected vice-president of Toronto Architectural Eighteen Club
- Appointed correspondent by Architectural Eighteen Club of Toronto to communicate with American Institute of Architects
- Exhibits, competition drawings, Department of Justice Buildings, Ottawa
- Relocates, atelier Lyle, Yonge at Yorkville streets, Toronto

c. 1908
- Imperial Bank of Canada, James at Main, Hamilton, Ontario
- Canadian Bank of Commerce, Nelson, B. C.
- Sterling Bank of Canada branches at Toronto, Cornwall, Palmerston, Port Dalhousie, Port Burwell, Watford, Ontario
- George Marks, residence, location unknown
- Alex Garthshore, residence, location unknown
- Losing competition entry, Federal Life Insurance Company's building, Hamilton, Ontario
- Proposal, Lawrence Solman, hotel, Toronto

Activities
- Partnership formed with Herbert E. Moore, associate architect

1908
- Samuel Lyle, residence, Glenfern Ave., Hamilton, Ontario
- John M. Lyle, residence, 19 Avondale Rd., Toronto
- Pickering College, Newmarket, Ontario
- Frank Hobbs, residence, 41 Oriole Rd., Toronto
- W. R. Johnston, fence, 53 Nauton Cres., Toronto
- J. L. Englehart, residence, Petrolia, Ontario (four plans of existing house, signed by Lyle)

Activities
- Marries Isabel Glen Moncrief of Petrolia, Ontario
- Lecture, 'North American Distinctive Style,' League of American Architects convention, Detroit, Michigan

1909
- Hugh Stevens, residence, St. Clair E., Toronto
- George Robinson, residence, 2 Beaumont Rd., Toronto
- Provincial Penitentiary for Ontario, Guelph, Ontario
- Temiskaming and Northern Ontario Railway: Union Station, Cochrane, Ontario; Cobalt Station, Cobalt, Ontario; Matheson Station, Matheson, Ontario
- Hydro-Electric Power Commission, eleven stations in Ontario: Dundas, Guelph, Kitchener, London, Niagara Falls, Preston, St. Marys, St. Thomas, Stratford, Toronto, Woodstock
- Sir William Mulock, residence, sunroom, Jarvis at Wellesley, Toronto
- Sir William Mulock, garage, Jarvis at Wellesley, Toronto
- Conservatory of Music, porch addition, College and University, Toronto
- Dominion Bank, alterations, Queen W. at Dundas, Toronto
- Competition entry, places third, Ontario Government House, Bloor at Jarvis, Toronto

Activities
- Attends RAIC annual meeting, represents Toronto Architectural Society, gives talk on 'Architectural Education'

1910
- J. J. McCaffery Hotel, additions, Bay at Adelaide, Toronto
- Stucco House, location unknown, proposal
- Lt.-Col. J. B. MacLean, residence, Wells Hill Rd., Toronto
- W. R. Johnston, residence, addition, 53 Nanton Cres., Toronto
- G. I. H. Lloyd, residence, alterations, Russell Hill Dr., Toronto
- Imperial Bank, James St. South, Hamilton, Ontario
- Competition entry, places third, Memorial Tower, Northwest Arm, Halifax, Nova Scotia
- Competition entry, places second, Hamilton Public Library, Hamilton, Ontario
- Losing competition entry, Bank of Toronto, Head Office Building, Bay at King, Toronto
- Losing competition entry, Knox College, University of Toronto, Toronto,

Activities
- Partnership dissolved with Herbert E. Moore, associate architect
- Appointed Chairman of Civic Improvement Committee; resigns in November to become organization's architect, Toronto
- Lecture, 'Architecture and Its Relation to Art,' 22nd Annual Meeting of the OAA

1911
- Bank of Ottawa, Broadview at Gerrard, Toronto
- Dominion Bank, Bloor E. at Sherbourne, Toronto
- Dominion Bank, Bloor W. at Dovercourt, Toronto
- Report of Civic Improvement Committee, Toronto
- Metropolitan Bank, Petrolia, Ontario
- Dominion Bank, Queen E. at Lee, Toronto
- Dominion Bank, St. Clair W. at Vaughan, Toronto
- Interior decorations, Armouries on University Ave., Toronto, for ball given by RCYC in honour of Duke and Duchess of Connaught
- Conservatory of Music, cloakroom addition, College and University, Toronto
- R. W. King, residence, 10 Walmer Rd., Toronto
- George Moncrieff, , residence, alterations, Pine Hill Rd., Toronto
- D. Coulson, garage, Baldwin St., Toronto
- Convert store to bank, Broadview at Elliot, Toronto
- Convert store to bank, Wilton (Dundas) at Parliament, Toronto
- Proposal, Town Plan for Iroquois Falls, Ontario,
- Proposal, Bloor-Danforth Viaduct and Bridge from Sherbourne St. to Castle Frank Cres., Toronto

1912
- Engineers' Club of Toronto, Victoria Ave., Toronto
- Dominion Bank, St. Clair Ave. W. at Dufferin, Toronto
- Toronto Stock Exchange, Bay St., Toronto
- Bank of Ottawa, Queen E. at Pape, Toronto
- Royal Canadian Yacht Club, addition, Toronto Islands, Toronto
- Mitchell & Son, office, St. Clair W., Toronto
- Hydroelectric Power Commission, factory, River and Dundas, Toronto
- Toronto Conservatory of Music, addition, 4 Ardre St., Toronto
- Sterling Bank, St. Catharines, Ontario

1913
- Union Station, Toronto (Ross & Macdonald, Hugh G. Jones, John M. Lyle associated architect)
- Bank of Ottawa, Danforth at Logan, Toronto
- J. Coulson Residence, 19 Rosedale Rd., Toronto
- MacLean Publishing Company Building, University at Dundas, Toronto
- Sterling Bank, Church St., Toronto
- Wm. Haniand & Son, 400 Eastern Ave., Toronto
- S. F. McKinnon, garage, Avenue Rd., Toronto
- Dominion Bank, garage, Avenue Rd., Toronto
- Losing competition entry, Department and Court Buildings, Ottawa,

Activities
- President, Architectural Club, University of Toronto

1914
- Dominion Bank, Roncesvalles at Howard Park, Toronto
- Dominion Bank, Dundas and McCaul, Toronto
- Dominion Bank, alterations, Queen E. at Sherbourne, Toronto
- Dominion Bank, Danforth at Logan, Toronto
- Conservatory of Music, auditorium and practice rooms, College at University, Toronto

- H. Roberts, residence, sunroom, 301 Huron St., Toronto
- F. L. Coulson, residence, addition, 42 Bedford Ave., Toronto
- Competition entry, Masonic Temple, Toronto,

1915
- Closes 14 Leader Lane office, works from residence 19 Avondale Rd., Toronto
- Receives Secours National Silver Medal for civilian relief work

1916
- Article, 'Status of the Canadian Architect' (*Construction*)

1917
- Canadian Airplanes Limited, Dufferin at Lappin, Toronto
- Dominion Bank, Oshawa, Ontario

Activities
- Exhibits, Garden of the Tuileries, Paris, France (drawing exhibited includes a proposed residence he donated to be constructed in war-ravaged Belgium or France)

1918
- Bank of Toronto, Dundas W. at Ossington, Toronto
- Dominion Bank, Dundas W. & Medland, Toronto

1919
- Bank of Toronto, Meaford, Ontario
- Dominion Bank, 82 Mississauga E. & Peter, Orillia, Ontario
- Bank of Toronto, Christie at St. Clair E., Toronto
- Proposal, Monument, Saint Julien, Belgium
- Proposal, Hotel, Toronto

Activities
- Exhibits, Art Gallery of Toronto
- Awarded medal, Reconnaissance Française by Government of France for building projects in France and Belgium

c. 1920
- George Brown, residence, addition, 186 Beverly St., Toronto

1920
- Bank of Toronto, Cambridge (Preston), Ontario
- Bank of Nova Scotia, St. Andrews, New Brunswick
- Bank of Nova Scotia, Lakeshore Blvd. W., Toronto
- Proposal, Women's Building (Whitney Hall), University College, Toronto

Activities
- Appointed lecturer, Department of Architecture, University of Toronto

1921
- Temple Murrich, residence, 8 Rosedale Rd., Toronto
- Bank of Nova Scotia, alterations, Main St., Petrolia, Ontario
- Winning competition entry, Memorial Arch, Royal Military College, Kingston, Ontario

Activities
- Address, 'Tax Exemption Plan,' RAIC AGM, Toronto

1922
- Bank of Toronto, College at Dovercourt, Toronto
- Bank of Toronto, 687 St. Clair W. & Christie, Toronto
- Dominion Bank, Dupont at Christie, Toronto
- Dominion Bank, Dufferin at Lappin, Toronto
- Dominion Bank, temporary building, Long Branch, Toronto
- Thornton-Smith Building, 340 Yonge St., Toronto
- Losing competition entry, Chicago Tribune Tower, Chicago, Illinois
- Losing competition entry, Clubhouse Argonaut Rowing Club, Centre Island, Toronto

Activities
- Article, 'American Architecture,' from address for Architectural Club, University of Toronto (*Construction*)

c. 1922
- Proposal, W. C. Lee, residence, Cluny Dr., Toronto

1923
- Clarence A. Bogert, residence, 142 Forest Hill Rd., Toronto
- Bank of Nova Scotia, Sparks St., Ottawa
- John Jackson Beck starts as office manager

1924
- Dominion Bank, Runnymede Branch, Dundas W. at Runnymede, Toronto
- Dominion Bank, alterations, Belleville, Ontario
- Dominion Bank, Teddington and Yonge, Toronto
- Dominion Bank, alterations, Sarnia, Ontario
- Sir William Mulock, redecorating of residence, Jarvis St., Toronto
- Dalley Residence, Ancaster, Ontario
- Proposal, Office Building for Burroughs Brothers, Bloor St., Toronto

Activities
- Exhibits, Wembley Exhibition, London, England, works include Royal Alexandra Theatre and Union Station
- Address, 'English Interior Decoration from the Adams to the Tudor Period,' Hamilton Chapter of OAA, Hamilton, Ontario
- Hosts tour of Union Station with twenty Hamilton architects

1925
- Dominion Bank, Main St. North, Huntsville, Ontario
- Dominion Bank, alterations, Napanee, Ontario
- Woodbine Race Course, stands scheme, Queen St. E., Toronto
- Toronto Golf Club, alterations, Toronto
- Dr. King Smith, residence, 15 Highland Ave., Toronto
- J. A. McLeod, residence, 15 Forest Hill Rd., Toronto
- Johnston, residence, Rosedale, Toronto
- Proposal, Apartment building, Bloor and George, Toronto
- Proposal,Wright Hotel, Oshawa, Ontario

Activities
- Selection committee, New York Architectural and Allied Arts Exposition, Grand Central Palace, New York. Organized by RAIC, committee consists of Percy E. Nobbs, John S. Archibald, A. Beaugrand-Champagne, Henry Sproatt and John M. Lyle
- Exhibits, New York Architectural and Allied Arts Exposition, Grand Central Palace, New York (Lyle's works include Bank of Nova Scotia, Ottawa, Thornton-Smith Building and Union Station, Toronto)
- Article, 'Sproatt and Rolph: An Appreciation' (*Journal of the RAIC*)
- Elected associate, Royal Canadian Academy, Montreal (along with fellow architects H. G. Jones, Montreal; Hugh Vallance, Montreal; J. O. Marchand, Montreal; Ernest Cormier, Montreal; A. T. Chapman, Toronto)

1926
- Front door design for house near Rowanwood on Yonge St., Toronto
- Gage Memorial Fountain, Gage Park, Hamilton, Ontario
- W. R. Johnston, residence, alterations, Toronto
- Williamson, residence alterations, Bay and Grosvenor, Toronto
- R. J. Christie, residence, 3 Frybrook Rd., Toronto
- Dominion Bank, Bleury St. at St. Catherine, Montreal
- Proposal, Sigmund Samuel, residence, Forest Hill Rd., Toronto
- Proposal, Hotel, Chateau Simcoe, King and York, Toronto, (with Ross & Macdonald of Montreal)
- Losing competition entry, Ottawa War Memorial, Ottawa, Ontario (won by Vernon Marsh)

Activities
- Address, 'Canadian Architect,' Sproatt and Rolph Memorial Dinner, Hart House, University of Toronto, Toronto
- Awarded Gold Medal of Honour by OAA for most meritorious work exhibited. Works include: Domestic: Honourable Mention for Residence of C. A. Bogert, Toronto; Memorials: first award for Memorial Arch at Royal Military College, Kingston; Commercial Buildings: first award for Thornton-Smith Building, Toronto
- Lecture, 'Architecture,' Women's Art Club, Toronto
- Letter to the Editor ('Correspondence,' *Journal of the RAIC*)

- Article, 'Exhibition of Student Work in the Department of Architecture, University of Toronto' (*Journal of the RAIC*)
- Honoured Guest, special meeting and dinner, Toronto Chapter of OAA, Toronto (Lyle was awarded the Gold Medal)
- Exhibits, Exhibition of Dominion and Colonial Architecture, Royal Institute of British Architects, London, England (Lyle's work includes Thornton-Smith Building, Toronto; Memorial Arch, Royal Military College, Kingston; and the Bank of Nova Scotia, Ottawa)

1927
- Dominion Bank, alterations, Laughton Branch, Davenport at Laughton, Toronto
- Dominion Bank, Lakeshore at Long Branch, Toronto
- Dominion Bank, alterations, St. Clair W. at Dufferin, Toronto
- Dominion Bank, Yonge at Teddington Park, Toronto
- Dominion Bank, alterations, Yonge at Eglinton, Toronto
- Dominion Bank, Lakeshore Boulevard at Long Branch, Toronto
- Dominion Bank, 210 Muskoka South and Royal, Gravenhurst, Ontario
- Toronto Stock Exchange, alterations, Bay St., Toronto
- Woodbine Race Course, paddock and directors' building and members' stand, Queen St. E., Toronto
- Proposal, Canadian Pacific Hotel, Banff, Alberta
- Proposal, Civic Improvement, Toronto
- Proposal, Niagara Boulevard Country Club and Hotel, near Buffalo, New York
- Competition entry, places third, High Level Bridge, Hamilton, Ontario

Activities
- Lecture, 'Canadian Architecture,' Canadian Club, Toronto
- Lecture, 'Canadian Architecture,' Art Gallery of Toronto, Toronto
- Exhibits, Architecture and Applied Arts Exhibit, Art Gallery of Toronto, Toronto
- Article, Architecture and Applied Arts Exhibit, Art Gallery of Toronto, Toronto (*Journal of the RAIC*)
- Elected but declines Vice-Presidence of OAA

1928
- F. W. Cowan, residence, 174 Teddington Park Ave., Toronto
- Bank of Nova Scotia, stationery building, Pearl St., Toronto
- Dominion Bank, Yonge at Cottingham (formerly Marlboro), Toronto
- Dominion Bank, Danforth Ave. at Danforth Rd., Toronto
- Dominion Bank, Davenport at Dovercourt, Toronto
- W. R. Johnston, summer residence, Lake Couchiching, Orillia, Ontario
- Toronto Stock Exchange, alterations, Toronto
- Losing competition entry, Canadian National Exhibition, Automotive Building, Toronto

Activities
- Elected Fellow, Royal Institute of British Architects
- Travels to England and France for ten weeks
- Address, 'Civic Beautification,' Toronto Board of Trade, Toronto
- Article, 'Civic Beautification' (*Journal of the RAIC*)
- Resigns from RAIC's Examination Board
- Address, 'Modern Treatment of Shop Fronts,' Toronto Board of Trade, Toronto

1929
- Bank of Nova Scotia, Eighth Ave. SW, Calgary, Alberta
- Bank of Nova Scotia, Head Office Building, Hollis at Princess, Halifax, Nova Scotia
- Central Canada Savings and Loan Company, Simcoe at Bond, Oshawa, Ontario
- Dominion Bank, Kenilworth at Barton, Hamilton, Ontario
- Dominion Bank, Yonge at Gerrard, Toronto
- Dominion Bank, Yonge at Lawrence W., Toronto
- Runnymede Library, Bloor W. at Glendonwynne, Toronto
- Proposal, Bank of Nova Scotia, general office building, King at Bay, Toronto

Activities
- Address, Royal Architectural Institute of Canada annual meeting, Art Gallery of Toronto
- Elected member, American Civic Association in recognition for promoting architectural improvement in Toronto
- Awarded, Chapter of the OAA's Exhibition of Architecture and Allied Arts at Art Gallery in Toronto; First Award in Details, Commercial, for main entrance doorway, Dominion Bank, Bleury St., Montreal; Honourable Mention in Details, Domestic, for the Governor General's Box, Ontario Jockey Club, Woodbine Park, Toronto; First Award in Memorials for Gage Memorial Fountain, Hamilton, Ontario; Second Award to Arthur H. Eadie, for the Cenotaph, Calgary; Honourable Mention in Financial Institutions for Dominion Bank, Bleury St., Montreal

1930
- Lyle and Eadie travel to New York to see buildings for General Office
- Dominion Bank, alterations, Belleville, Ontario
- Dominion Bank, Davenport Branch, Davenport and Avenue, Toronto
- Dominion Bank, garage, Queen at Augusta, Toronto
- Dominion Bank, Lakeshore and John, Toronto
- John M. Lyle, dining room addition, 19 Avondale, Toronto
- F. W. Cowan, residence, fence and gates, Oshawa, Ontario
- Royal Bank, Oshawa, Ontario

Activities
- Exhibits, RAIC 'Institute Medal Exhibition,' Art Gallery of Toronto, November 1930, works include Runnymede Branch, Toronto Public Library; Dominion Bank, Yonge and Gerrard, Toronto; Bank of Nova Scotia, Calgary, Alberta
- Chair's lecture, 'Modern Architecture,' by Jacques Carlu, Art Gallery of Toronto
- Elected Fellow, Royal Architectural Institute of Canada

1931
- Bank of Nova Scotia, proposal Stationery Building, Adelaide St. W., Toronto
- Col. H. A. Bruce, residence, Bayview Ave., Toronto
- Dominion Bank, Avenue Rd., Toronto
- Dominion Bank, alterations, Oshawa, Ontario
- Whitney Hall, University College, University of Toronto, St. George and Hoskin, Toronto (Mathers & Haldenby, architects, with John M. Lyle, consulting architect)

Activities
- Travels to France, April 7–June 18
- Lecture, 'Canadian Architecture,' at annual dinner of the Building Owners and Managers' Association, Toronto
- Exhibits, Third Biennial Exhibition of Architecture and Allied Arts, Toronto Chapter of OAA, Toronto; First Prize Award, Banks, alterations to Central Canada Loan and Savings Building, Oshawa; Second Prize Award, Domestic Exteriors, Over $75,000, R. J. Christie residence, Toronto; Domestic Interiors, Over $75,000, R. J. Christie residence, Toronto; Honourable Mention, Domestic Exteriors, $25,000 to $30,000, W. R. Johnston, Orillia; Second Award, Architectural Details (Commercial), exterior detail of bronze grille, Bank of Nova Scotia, Calgary; Honourable Mention, entrance detail, Dominion Bank, Toronto; Honourable Mention, bronze door, Dominion Bank, Toronto; Honourable Mention, Semi-Public Buildings, Exteriors, Runnymede Branch Library

1932
- Bank of Nova Scotia, King at Bay, Toronto, delivery of drawings and specifications
- Bank of Nova Scotia, Bank Manager's House, Kingston, Jamaica
- Dominion Bank, enlargement, St. Clair W. at Dufferin, Toronto

- Hamilton High Level Bridge, Hamilton, Ontario
- Teagle & Sons, office building, New St., Toronto
- Woodbine Race Track, alterations to Grandstand, Queen St. W., Toronto

Activities

- Article, 'The Bank of Nova Scotia Building, Halifax' (*Journal of the RAIC*)
- Article, 'Canadian Decorative Forms,' (*Journal of the RAIC*)
- Staff cuts and salary reductions
- Member of Royal Canadian Academy Hanging Committee, Toronto Art Gallery, other members include President E. Wylie Grier, J. William Beatty, Emmanuel Hahn and A. Y. Jackson

1933

- Col. H. A. Bruce, verandah, Bayview Ave., Toronto
- Dalley, garden and finishings, Ancaster, Ontario
- Bank of Nova Scotia, King at Bay, Toronto, revisions
- Dominion Bank, Josephine St., Wingham, Ontario

Activities

- Juror, poster competition for Toronto Chapter Architectural Exhibition (won by A. E. Eadie)
- Elected Officer, Fourth Biennial Exhibition of Architecture and Allied Arts, other officials included Col. R. Y. Eaton, President of the Exhibition Committee; the Governor General; Mackenzie Waters, Chairman Executive of Toronto Chapter, OAA; Hon. Vincent Massey; and John M. Lyle, Convener of Hanging Committee
- Exhibits, Toronto Chapter of OAA, Exhibition of Architecture and Allied Arts; Second Place for own residence in category of Domestic Interiors $12,000 to $25,000; Second Place as consulting architect for Mathers & Haldenby's Whitney Hall, University of Toronto, for category of Institutional Buildings, Exterior; First Place for Bank of Nova Scotia, Halifax; Second Place as consulting architect for Mathers & Haldenby's Whitney Hall, University of Toronto, in category of Architectural Details, General; First Place for Bank of Nova Scotia, Halifax, in category of Monumental Buildings, Interiors; First Place for Approach to Bridge, Hamilton, in category of Miscellaneous
- Elected Member, Royal Canadian Academy of Arts
- Exhibits, Four Annual Exhibition of RAIC, Montreal, Honourable Mention in the category of Public Buildings–Exteriors for High Level Bridge, Hamilton, Ontario

1934

- Col. H. A. Bruce, gate, Bayview Ave., Toronto
- Barclay Bank, alterations, King St. W., Toronto
- Toronto Club, alterations, 107 Wellington St. W., Toronto
- Eaton's, interior alterations, Queen St., Toronto
- Lyle and Eadie travel to New York City and Philadelphia re: Eaton's Queen St. renovations

Activities

- Exhibits, International Architecture, 1924–1934, London, England, exhibits Runnymede Library, Toronto
- Letter to the Editor (*Journal of the RAIC*)
- Lecture, 'Tax Bonus Plan' National Construction Council of Canada, Ottawa
- Juror, Welland War Memorial Competition

1935

- Woodbine Race Track, alterations, Queen St. W., Toronto
- Col. R. S. McLaughlin, Formal Garden, Parkwood, Oshawa, Ontario
- John M. Lyle, proposal, Highfields, Vaughan Township, Ontario
- Proposal, J. Coulson, alteration, 19 Rosedale Rd., Toronto

Activities

- Exhibits, Toronto Chapter of OAA, Exhibition of Architecture and Allied Arts, at Toronto Art Gallery, Toronto, wins first prize, Class D – Domestic Exteriors, and Class D – Domestic Interior categories, for Bank of Nova Scotia, Bank Manager's House, in Kingston, Jamaica
- Elected Member, RAIC's Committee on Scholarship and Price Funds
- Juror, RAIC's Architectural Inter-school Competitions
- Committee member, serves on RAIC committee for various financial proposals for National Construction Council of Canada
- Radio address, 'Street Architecture,' for Toronto Chapter of OAA
- Article, 'The Work of Henri Hébert, RCA' (*Journal of the RAIC*)

1936

- Dominion Bank, Belleville, Ontario

Activities

- Dominion Coin Competition, Royal Canadian Mint, Ottawa, Ontario, designs submitted
- Member of the William Lyon Mackenzie Centennial Committee
- Juror, Eaton's Model Home Competition, Toronto
- Bank of Nova Scotia, King at Bay, Toronto, second revision
- Sir Adam Beck Memorial School, alterations, Toronto

1937

- Woodbine Race Track, bleachers, Queen St. W., Toronto
- Dominion Bank, Durham and Cedar, Sudbury, Ontario
- Dominion Bank, St. Clair Ave., Toronto
- Eaton's, alterations, Albert St. section, Queen St., Toronto
- Ross, residence, alterations and garage, Maple, Ontario
- Col. H. A. Bruce, alterations, Bayview Ave., Toronto
- R. Y. Eaton, residence, alterations to front door, 1 Highland Ave., Toronto
- Eaton's, preparation of working drawings for Eaton's Model Home

Activities

- Hanging Committee, Sixth Biennial Exhibition of Architecture and the Allied Arts, Art Gallery of Toronto, Toronto Chapter of OAA
- Travels to Sweden and France, attends Paris Exhibition
- Convener, RAIC's architectural inter-school competitions
- Article, 'The Paris Exposition of 1937' (*Journal of the RAIC*)

1938

Activities

- Exhibits, Seventh Biennial Exhibition by Toronto Chapter Ontario Society of Architects, Honourable Mention, alterations to T. Eaton Company, Queen St., Toronto
- Co-host with W. L. Somerville for OAA, lecture by Charles D. Maginnis, President of American Institute of Architects

1939

- Bank of Nova Scotia, Charlotte St. Branch, Saint John, New Brunswick

Activities

- Elected vice-president Art Gallery of Toronto
- Exhibits, Seventh Biennial Exhibition of the Toronto Chapter of the Ontario Society of Architects, Art Gallery of Toronto.: Honourable Mention, alterations to T. Eaton Company main store
- Canadian Pavilion, New York World's Fair, New York, competition entry

1940

- Col. R. S. McLaughlin, bedroom alterations, Parkwood, Oshawa, Ontario
- Col. R. S. McLaughlin, art gallery, Parkwood, Oshawa, Ontario
- Col. R. S. McLaughlin, mausoleum, Oshawa, Ontario

1941

- Dominion Bank, alterations, Bloor St. W., Toronto

Activities

- President, Art Gallery of Toronto, Toronto

1943

- John M. Lyle retires and partnership of Beck & Eadie formed

1945

- Nominated for Honorary Degree from University of Toronto
- December 19, John M. Lyle dies

Glossary of Architectural Terms

angle: the intersection of different planes.

architrave: the beam that spans columns; used in classical orders; the lowest section of the entablature, also used to frame doorways and windows.

ashlar: is the dressed stone work of a building or wall, and can be any type of stone.

balustrade: includes the top and sometimes the bottom rail of a railing system.

bellcast: refers to a roof that has a bell-like shape, typical of early Quebec residences.

bombé: a projecting curving shape, resembling the form of a bomb.

bracket: an overhanging member projecting from a wall to support a weight (such as a cornice) that is outside the wall.

brazier: is a bowl container used for holding fire or light, usually on a stand.

cartouche: a curvilinear styled decorative form.

cornice: any overhanging moulded projection that crowns or finishes the part to which it is attached, usually referring to the exterior trim of a structure at the meeting of the roof and wall.

dentil: the repeating small-block shape that is the main decorative feature of a cornice.

Doric: is one of the three orders of the ancient Greek and classical architecture, along with Ionic and Corinthian.

engaged column: a half-column built into the wall, not freestanding.

entablature: in classical architecture, the horizontal member above columns, consisting of three sections: architrave, frieze and cornice.

elevation: an external face of a structure; a scaled architectural drawing of a building facade.

fenestration: arrangement of windows in a building.

festoons: a string or garland of leaves or other fauna, forming a loop or curve between two points.

furring: the preparation of a surface (wall, ceiling, or floor) with building material to create an air space for insulation, wiring or the building's mechanical services.

gable: the triangular end portion of a building created by double-sloping roofs.

keystone: the central, usually embellished, voussoir (stone) of an arch.

lambrequin: an ornamental drapery for the top of the stage's proscenium arch.

lintel: a horizontal member which carries the weight of the wall over doors and windows.

mansard roof: double sloping roof, with the lower portion much steeper than the upper.

mullion: the vertical member of doors and windows which separates adjacent openings and supports.

oriel: a projecting bay (window) from a room.

palladian window: a window that is divided into three parts with a larger centre section that is usually arched and flanked by two smaller side sections. Used in Renaissance architecture and other buildings in a classical revival style.

parapet: section of wall that is entirely at the eaves edge of a roof.

parging: is a thin coat of a material, usually cement, that is applied to a wall in order to create a continuous surface.

pediment: the triangular gable-end above the entablature, also used over windows and doors.

pier: a load-bearing support.

pilaster: mostly a decorative flat column, engaged to the wall with base and capital.

portico: a porch with columns supporting the roof.

quoin: stone of a differing distinctive quality from wall masonry used at the angles.

soffit: the underside area that is formed from the outer edge of the roof to the top of an exterior wall.

spandrel: is the space between two arches or a rectangular enclosure. Also, the section of the wall between the top of a window and the window sill.

stringcourse: is a continuous horizontal band of brick or cut stone in a wall.

voussoirs: are the wedge-shaped stones used in an arch.

Endnotes

Introduction

1. John M. Lyle, 'Address on Architecture,' *JRAIC* 7 (April 1929), p. 135.
2. Notes taken from a telephone conversation between Hilton Wilkes (a friend of John Lyle) and Stephen A. Otto, recorded April 7, 1979. In the possession of Stephen A. Otto, Toronto.
3. John M. Lyle, 'Data on John M. Lyle' (unpublished manuscript), insertion #9, office practice. In the possession of Norah Harris, Victoria, B.C.
4. John M. Lyle, 'Life History Notes, for Mr. S. Mathers,' letter to A. S. Mathers, 1945, collection of Norah Harris, p. 7.
5. 'Toronto Architect Is Signally Honored,' Toronto Star, June 1, 1928, sec. 1. The other Canadian architects bestowed with a fellowship in the Royal Institute of British Architects were C. B. Cleveland, V. D. Horsburgh, John A. Pearson, Ernest R. Rolph and Henry Sproatt.
6. Lyle, 'Data on John M. Lyle,' Isabel-Helpmate, insertion #10, sheet no. 1.
7. Ibid., pp. 49–50.

Chapter 1

1. Jesse Edgar Middleton and Fred Landon, *The Province of Ontario: A History, 1615–1927*, v. 4 (Toronto: Dominion Publishing Company, 1927), pp. 505–7.
2. Nora-Francis Henderson, 'In Feminine Focus, Mrs. Lyle,' unnamed newspaper and date, collection of Norah Harris.
3. John M. Lyle, letter to his mother, Paris, March 26, 1896, Archives of Ontario.
4. John M. Lyle, 'Life History Notes, for Mr. S. Mathers,' letter to A. S. Mathers, 1945, collection of Norah Harris.
5. Percy Nobbs, 'The Delineation of Architecture,' *Canadian Architect and Builder* 17 (February 1904), p. 40.
6. John M. Lyle, letter to his mother, Rijsoord, August 27, 1895, Archives of Ontario.
7. Lyle, 'Life History Notes,' p. 1.
8. John Ireland, 'Hamilton,' *Canadian Architect and Builder* 8 (May 1895), p. 68.
9. Lyle, 'Life History Notes,' p. 3.
10. Ibid., p. 5.
11. J. Omer Marchand, 'Sketching Competitions in the Second Class of the School of Fine Arts, Paris,' *Canadian Architect and Builder* 9 (April 1896), p. 47.
12. Ibid.
13. John M. Lyle, letter to his mother, Paris, March 26, 1896, Archives of Ontario.
14. Richard Chafee et al., *The Architecture of the École des beaux-arts* (New York: Museum of Modern Art, 1977), p. 83.
15. W. S. Maxwell, 'Architectural Education,' *Construction* 1 (April 1908), p. 50.
16. John M. Lyle, letter to his mother, Paris, March 26, 1896, Archives of Ontario.
17. Ibid.
18. Lyle, 'Life History Notes,' p. 3.
19. Lyle, 'Data on John M. Lyle,' p. 24.
20. Ibid.
21. Ibid, p. 26
22. As quoted in Geoffrey Hunt, *John M. Lyle: Toward a Canadian Architecture* (Kingston: Agnes Etherington Art Centre, Queen's University, 1982), p. 19.
23. Lyle, 'Data on John M. Lyle,' pp. 26–27.
24. *Architectural Record* (December 1, 1897), p. 68.
25. Lyle, 'Data on John M. Lyle,' p. 27.
26. Lyle, 'Life History Notes,' p. 24.
27. Ibid.
28. 'Bohemian Artists at Exposition,' *Buffalo Enquirer*, April 5, 1901.
29. 'Band Stand Like a Butterfly,' *Buffalo Enquirer*, April 12, 1901.
30. Ibid.
31. Ibid.
32. Lyle, 'Data on John M. Lyle,' p. 29.
33. Lyle, 'Life History Notes,' p. 5.
34. Ibid., p. 29a.
35. Ibid., pp. 30–31.
36. Ibid.
37. Ibid., p. 34.
38. Ibid.
39. Ibid.

Chapter 2

1. 'A Branch Bank Building,' *Construction* 2 (May 1908), p. 29.
2. John M. Lyle, 'Dominion Bank Architecture,' *Canadian Banker* 45 (April 1938), pp. 305–6.
3. Alan Sullivan, *John A. Pearson, Master Builder* (Toronto: The Yearbook of Canadian Art, compiled by the Arts and Letters Club, 1913), pp. 257–62.
4. Lyle, 'Dominion Bank Architecture,' p. 304.
5. Lyle, 'Data on John M. Lyle,' p. 35.
6. Ibid, p. 36.
7. 'Royal Alexandra Theatre,' *Construction* 1 (November 1907), p. 37.
8. John Lindsay, *Royal Alexandra: The Finest Theatre on the Continent* (Erin: Boston Mills Press, 1986), p. 10.
9. 'Royal Alexandra Theatre,' *Construction*, p. 37.
10. Lyle, 'Data on John M. Lyle,' p. 37.
11. Ibid.
12. Ibid.
13. As quoted in Carole Rifkind, *A Field Guide to American Architecture* (New York, N.Y.: The New American Library, 1980), p. 157.
14. Lyle, 'Data on John M. Lyle,' p. 65.
15. John M. Lyle, letter to George Hope, Hamilton, July 27, 1907. Central Presbyterian Church archives.
16. 'Rebuilding Pickering College,' *The Canadian Friend* (March 1906), p. 6.
17. Lyle, 'Data on John M. Lyle,' p. 62.
18. Archives of Ontario, RG 8-5 B69 J. M. Lyle Correspondence, February 21, 1910.
19. Archives of Ontario, RG8-5 B69 J. M. Lyle Correspondence, January 18, 1910.
20. Contentworks Inc., *Ontario Realty Corporation, Cultural Heritage Report on Correctional Complexes in Ontario, Guelph Correctional Centre N00249*, January 22, 2007, p. 5.
21. Ibid.
22. John M. Lyle, letter to the editor, *Contract Record and Engineering Review* 28 (April 1, 1914), p. 404.
23. Ibid.
24. 'Architects' Competitions,' *Canadian Architect and Builder* 20 (May 1907), p. 70.
25. Lyle, 'Data on John M. Lyle,' pp. 30 1.
26. Ibid., insert #1, sheet 2.
27. W. S. Maxwell, 'Architectural Education,' *Construction* 2 (April 1908), p. 50.
28. 'Artistic Conditions: Traditions and Tendencies of Styles,' *Architectural Record* 46 (January 1919), p. 329.
29. Ibid.
30. Grant Helliwell, 'Suggestions on House Planning,' *Canadian Architect and Builder* 11 (June 1898), p. 106.
31. Ibid.
32. John M. Lyle, 'Domestic Interiors,' *Canadian Homes & Gardens* 11 (October-November 1934), p. 17.
33. Ibid.
34. Ibid., p. 18.
35. John M. Lyle, 'Address by John M. Lyle,' *JRAIC* 6 (April 1929), p. 135.
36. Lyle, 'Data on John M. Lyle,' p. 34.
37. Lyle, 'Data on John M. Lyle,' insertion #6, RCYC Ball, sheet 4.
38. Ibid.
39. John M. Lyle, 'For Civic Improvement,' *The Globe*, February 2, 1905, sec. 1, p. 2.

40. Harold Kalman, *A History of Canadian Architecture* (Toronto: Oxford University Press), p. 651.
41. John A. Ewan, *Report on a Comprehensive Plan for Systematic Civic Improvements in Toronto* (Toronto: Toronto Guild of Civic Art, 1909), unpaginated foreword.
42. *Report of Civic Improvement Committee for the City of Toronto*, (Toronto: City of Toronto, 1911), p. 5.
43. Lyle, 'Life History Notes,' p. 7.
44. *Construction* (July 1911), p. 53.
45. Lyle, 'Life History Notes,' p. 8.
46. Ibid.
47. Ibid, p. 9.
48. Anne M. de Fort-Menares, 'Durability and Parsimony: Railway Station Architecture in Ontario, 1853–1914,' *Society for the Study of Architecture in Canada* 21 (March 1996), p. 30.
49. 'Toronto Union Station,' *Construction* 7 (May 1914), p. 199.
50. Lyle, 'Data on John M. Lyle,' p. 63.
51. Kalman, *A History of Canadian Architecture*, p. 492.
52. Trevor Boddy, 'Regionalism, Nationalism, and Modernism: The Ideology of Decoration in the Work of John M. Lyle,' *Trace: A Canadian Review of Architecture* 1 (January 1981), p. 11.
53. A speech by J. R. W. Ambrose, 'New Union Station – Toronto,' January 7, 1935. Toronto Archives, SC 410, box 1, file 10.
54. 'Toronto Has Grown Like Chicago Did,' *The Toronto Star*, July 9, 1914, sec. 1, p. 1.
55. 'New Bank to be only 3 storeys,' *The Toronto Daily Star*, June 9, 1910, sec. 1, p. 1.
56. Ibid.
57. Editorial, *Construction* 4 (July, 1910), p. 52–3.
58. Editorial, *Construction* 4 (September 1910), p. 41.
59. 'No American Work Wanted,' *The Toronto Star*, April 8, 1911, sec. 1, p. 8.
60. *Toronto Society of Architects, Sixth Exhibition* (Toronto: Toronto Society of Architects, 1912), p. 9.
61. Geoffrey Simmins, *Ontario Association of Architects: A Centennial History, 1889–1989* (Toronto: Ontario Association of Architects, 1989), p. 49.
62. John M. Lyle, 'Architecture and Its Relation to Art,' *Construction* 3 (January 1910), pp. 75–6.
63. 'Beaux Arts Club,' *The Toronto Star*, February 4, 1905, sec. 1, p. 15.
64. 'Toronto Has Beaux Art Society,' *Construction* (1908), p. 80.
65. Ibid.
66. *Torontonensis: The University of Toronto Architectural Club* (Toronto: University of Toronto, 1915), p. 292.
67. Ibid.

Chapter 3

1. *The Globe*, March 1, 1917, sec. 1, p. 10.
2. John M. Lyle, 'Status of the Canadian Architect,' *Construction* 9 (August 1916), p. 271.
3. Ibid.
4. Ibid.
5. Hunt, *John M. Lyle: Toward a Canadian Architecture*, p. 103.
6. *JRAIC* 4 (February 1927), p. 65.
7. 'Recent Architecture of the Bank of Nova Scotia,' *Canadian Banker* 44 (1937), pp. 150–57.
8. John M. Lyle, 'Correspondence,' *JRAIC* 3 (May–June 1926), p. 126.
9. Eric R. Arthur, 'Toronto Chapter, OAA Architectural Exhibition,' *JRAIC* 3 (March-April 1926), p. 56.
10. 'The Chicago Tribune Competition,' *Construction* 16 (February 1923), pp. 61–62.
11. John M. Lyle, 'Memorial to be Built on Historic Site,' *Construction* 12 (April 1919), p. 126.
12. Thomas Laqueur, 'The Past's Past,' *London Review of Books* 18 (September 19, 1996), p. 7.
13. 'Conditions of Competition for the Selection of an Architect for the Proposal Memorial Arch of the Royal Military College Club of Canada' (Kingston: Royal Military College, 1920), Royal Military College archives.
14. Ramsey Traquair, 'Assessors Report, 19 January 1921,' Royal Military College archives.
15. John M. Lyle, letter to Col. H. J. Lamb and Col. W. B. Kingsmill, February 24, 1922, Royal Military College archives.
16. John M. Lyle, letter to Lt.-Col. E. G. Hanson, December 16, 1922, Royal Military College archives.
17. John M. Lyle, letter to Col. Clyde Caldwell, President of the Royal Military College Club, February 15, 1924, Royal Military College archives.
18. Lyle, 'Data on John M. Lyle,' insert #1, sheet 2.
19. Ibid.
20. John M. Lyle, 'Monumental Architecture and Town Planning,' *Construction* 14 (May 1921), p. 137.
21. 'The Thornton-Smith Building, Toronto,' *Construction* 14 (May 1922), p. 151.
22. Eric R. Arthur, 'Toronto Chapter OAA Architectural Exhibition,' p. 52.
23. 'Lyle Awarded Medal,' *The Toronto Star*, January 28, 1926, sec. 1, p. 3.
24. Arthur, 'Toronto Chapter OAA Architectural Exhibition,' p. 50.
25. Ibid.

Chapter 4

1. Arts & Letters Club, comp., *The Yearbook of Canadian Art, 1913: Literature, Architecture, Music, Painting, Sculpture* (Toronto: J. M. Dent & Sons, Limited, 1913), p. 266.
2. Hugh G. Vallance, 'Architecture in Canada,' *Construction* 16 (October 1923), p. 356.
3. John M. Lyle, 'Canadian Architecture,' *JRAIC*, February 1927, p. 65.
4. Lyle, 'Correspondence,' p. 126.
5. Ibid.
6. John M. Lyle, 'Canadian Architecture,' *JRAIC* 3 (February 1927), p. 65.
7. Frederick Griffin, 'Native Architecture Wins Its Spurs,' *The Toronto Star Weekly*, January 8, 1927, magazine sec., part one, p. 1.
8. John M. Lyle, 'Correspondence,' *JRAIC* 2:3, May–June 1926, p. 126.
9. Ibid.
10. Griffin, 'Native Architecture Wins Its Spurs,' p. 1.
11. W. L. Somerville, 'Recent Domestic Architecture in the Province of Ontario,' *JRAIC* 5:6, July 1928, p. 268.
12. 'Notes from the Architects' Show,' *Canadian Homes & Gardens* 10:9, March 1933, p. 20.
13. John M. Lyle, 'Canadian Architecture,' *JRAIC* 4:2, February 1927, pp. 71–72.
14. *Canadian Homes & Gardens* 8:2, February 1931, pp. 22–27.
15. Ibid, p. 22.
16. John M. Lyle, 'Correspondence,' *JRAIC* 3:3, May–June 1926, p. 126
17. W. L. Somerville, 'Is Our Domestic Architecture Mediocre?,' *JRAIC* 9:4, April 1932, p. 103.
18. Eric R. Arthur, 'Toronto Chapter Architectural Exhibition,' *JRAIC* 6:3, March 1929, p. 98.
19. Eric R. Arthur, 'Toronto Chapter Exhibition of Architecture and Allied Arts,' *JRAIC* 6:2, February 1929, p. 109.
20. William White, 'Ernest Hemingway Dateline: Toronto, Betting in Toronto,' *The Toronto Star Weekly*, December 29, 1923 (New York: Scribner's Sons, 1985), p. 436.
21. Letter from John M. Lyle entitled 'Descriptive Notes of Photographs,' Toronto, October 6, 1931, p. 6, John M. Lyle fonds, Archives of Ontario.
22. 'Society at The Woodbine,' *The Toronto Star*, May 20, 1912, p. 8.
23. Lyle, 'Descriptive Notes of Photographs,' pp. 6–7.
24. Ibid., p. 6.
25. Arthur, 'Toronto Chapter Architectural Exhibition,' p. 101.
26. H. M. Ridley, 'Canada's Architecture Movement the Diet Kitchen School and Its Propaganda for the Art,' *Saturday Night*, March 12, 1927.
27. R. B. Wolsey, 'The Ontario Association of Architects,' *JRAIC* 4:4, April 1927, p. 157.
28. Eric R. Arthur, 'Toronto Chapter OAA Architectural Exhibition,' *JRAIC* 4:4, April 1927, p. 149.

29. 'Says Yonge St. Shabby has Mean Shop Fronts,' *The Toronto Star*, January 31, 1927, p. 1.
30. 'Editorial' *JRAIC* 5:8, August 1928, p. 273.

Chapter 5

1. John M. Lyle, 'Address on Architecture,' *JRAIC* 7 (April 1929), p. 135.
2. Ibid.
3. Ibid.
4. Ibid.
5. Percy E. Nobbs, 'Present Tendencies Affecting Architecture in Canada,' *JRAIC* 8 (November 1930), p. 392.
6. Lyle, 'Address on Architecture,' p. 135.
7. Ibid.
8. Jean Chauvin, *Ateliers: Études sur vingt-deux peintres et sculpteurs canadiens* (New York and Montreal: Louis Carrier & Cie, 1928), pp. 28–40; reprinted from 'Ernest Cormier, Architecte, peinture, sculpteur,' *La Revue Populaire* (June 1927), pp. 7–11.
9. Lyle, 'Address on Architecture,' p. 135.
10. Ibid.
11. Ibid.
12. Ibid.
13. Ibid.
14. Walter R. Agard, 'American Architectural Sculpture,' *The American Magazine of Art* 24 (March 1932), pp. 206–12.
15. Lyle, 'Data on John M. Lyle,' p. 6.
16. Trevor Brody, 'Regionalism, Nationalism and Modernism: The Ideology of Decoration in the Work of John M. Lyle,' *Trace: A Canadian Review of Architecture* 1 (January 1981), pp. 12–13.
17. 'Dominion Bank (Yonge and Gerrard Streets Branch) Toronto,' *Construction* 24 (February 1931), p. 50.
18. Ibid., p. 48.
19. 'The Bank of Nova Scotia, Halifax,' *JRAIC* 9 (January 1932), pp. 5–13.
20. J. H. Mitchell, 'The Bank is in New Home,' *Halifax Star*, August 4, 1931, sec. 1, 8.
21. Percy E. Nobbs, 'Recent Architecture in Canada,' *JRAIC* 13 (September 1936), p. 169.
22. 'The Bank of Nova Scotia, Halifax,' p. 13.
23. Nobbs, 'Recent Architecture in Canada,' p. 169.
24. Mitchell, 'The Bank is in New Home,' p. 8.
25. Lyle, 'Data on John M. Lyle,' p. 60.
26. Susan Wagg, et al., *Money Matters: A Critical Look at Bank Architecture* (New York: McGraw Hill in association with Parnassus Foundation and the Museum of Fine Arts, Houston, 1990), p. 221.
27. Alan Gowans, *Looking at Architecture in Canada* (Toronto: Oxford University Press, 1958), p. 188.
28. John M. Lyle, letter, March 17, 1932, Archives of Ontario, John M. Lyle fond.
29. 'Awards in the Competition for a North-Western Entrance to the City of Hamilton', JRAIC, 6:4, April, 1928, p. 132.
30. Ibid., p. 141.
31. Eric R. Arthur, letter to Mr. MacQueenston, May 28, 1928, Toronto (Royal Botanical Gardens Archives, R1996 1, administration, S.G. North West Entrance to Hamilton, S. General, file).
32. *Contract Record & Engineering Review* (September 7, 1932), pp. 1000–08.
33. As quoted in 'High Level Bridge,' *Royal Botanical Gardens Newsletter* (1991–92), p. 15.
34. Percy E. Nobbs, 'Recent Architecture in Canada,' *JRAIC* 13 (September 1936), p. 167.
35. Eric R. Arthur, 'The RAIC Exhibition in Montreal,' *JRAIC* 10 (December 1933), p. 203.
36. John M. Lyle, 'Letter to the Editor,' *JRAIC* 11 (February 1934), p. 31.
37. Philip J. Turner, 'Library Buildings,' *JRAIC* 6 (May 1929), p. 186.
38. John M. Lyle, letter, Runnymede Branch – Toronto Public Library, March 17, 1932, Archives of Ontario, John M. Lyle fond.
39. Margaret Penman, *A Century of Service: Toronto Public Library 1883–1983* (Toronto: Toronto Public Library, 1983), p. 28.
40. *Toronto Public Libraries Annual Reports, 1929, 1930* (Toronto: Toronto Public Library, 1930), p. 6.
41. Eric R. Arthur, et al., 'Architecture in Canada,' *Yearbook of the Arts in Canada* (Toronto: Arts and Letters Club, 1928–29), p. 112.

Chapter 6

1. John M. Lyle, 'Canadian Decorative Forms,' *JRAIC* 9 (March 1932), p. 65.
2. Ibid., p. 70.
3. 'A Plan to Revive the Construction Industry,' *JRAIC* 10 (February 1933), p. 25.
4. Ibid.
5. 'Dominion Government Contemplates Programme of Public Works,' *JRAIC* 10 (December 1933), p. 206.
6. Janet Wright, *Building in the Bureaucracy: The Architecture of the Department of Public Works 1927–1939* (Kingston, Ontario: Queen's University, MA Thesis, 1988), p. 88.
7. Leland M. Roth, *A Concise History of American Architecture* (New York: Harper & Row, 1980), p. 240.
8. John Jackson Beck, *Diary*, October 6, 1933.
9. Willa Cather, letter to W. A. Clarke, September 21, 1940, Archives of Ontario, John M. Lyle fond.
10. Ibid.
11. John M. Lyle, letter to Willa Cather, September 27, 1940, Archives of Ontario, John M. Lyle fond.
12. Ibid.
13. Ibid.
14. 'Housing and Slum Clearance,' *JRAIC* 12 (March 1935), p. 53.
15. John M. Lyle, 'Street Architecture,' *Architecture in Modern Life*, a series of radio broadcasts under the auspices of the University of Toronto and sponsored by Toronto Chapter of the OAA, broadcasted on CRCT, March 7, 1935.
16. 'Awards in Dominion Housing Act Small House Competition,' *JRAIC* 13 (May 1936), p. 89.
17. Ibid.
18. John Vaughan, letter to H. F. Merchandise office, February 13, 1936, Archives of Ontario.
19. R. Y. Eaton, letter to John Vaughan, February 13, 1936, Archives of Ontario.
20. W. L. Somerville, 'Is Our Domestic Architecture Mediocre?' *JRAIC* 9 (April 1932), p. 100.
21. H. Carver, 'Infant Architecture,' *Saturday Night* 52 (November 7, 1936), p. 3.
22. Ernest Cormier, 'New Buildings for the University of Montreal,' *JRAIC* 8 (June 1931), p. 248.
23. *JRAIC* 10 (April 1933), p. 80.
24. John M. Lyle, letter to the editor, *JRAIC* 11 (February 1934), p. 31.
25. Mackenzie Waters, 'Tradition Regency in the Modern Rendering,' *Canadian Homes & Gardens* 12 (October–November 1935), p. 37.
26. Mary-Etta MacPherson, 'The Canadian House of Today,' *Canadian Homes & Gardens* 16 (June 1929), p. 17.

Chapter 7

1. John M. Lyle, *Art Gallery of Toronto, Annual Meeting May 9th, 1942, Report of the President* (Toronto: Art Gallery of Toronto, 1943).
2. John M. Lyle, *Art Gallery of Toronto, Annual Meeting 1944, Report of the President* (Toronto: Art Gallery of Toronto, 1945).
3. A. Y. Jackson, letter to John M. Lyle, February 27, 1942, Art Gallery of Ontario archives.
4. John M. Lyle, letter to W. H. Lovering, Hamilton, January 11, 1943, Hamilton Public Library correspondence file.
5. John M. Lyle, letter to Freda Waldon, Hamilton, January 11, 1943, Hamilton Public Library correspondence file.
6. A. S. Mathers, 'The Bank of Nova Scotia,' *JRAIC* 28 (November 1951), p. 317.
7. Ibid, p. 318.
8. Hunt, p. 60.
9. Douglas Kertland, 'Obituary for John M. Lyle,' *JRAIC* 23 (February 1946), p. 47.

10. A. S. Mathers, 'Thirty Five Years of Practice,' *JRAIC* 22 (December 1955), pp. 462–64.
11. Arnold Edinborough, *The First Fifty Years: A History of Rounthwaite Dick* (unpublished manuscript, Arnold Edinborough Collection, box 17, the William Ready Division of Archives and Research Collections, McMaster University, Hamilton, Ontario, 1969), pp. 6–7.
12. William Harris. 'Publius Vergilius Maro: The Secret Life of a very private Poet' (2005), http://community.middlebury.edu/~harris/Classics/VergilTheSecretLife.html (accessed June 21, 2006).
13. John M. Lyle, 'Canadian Ornament Goes Native,' *American Architect* (December 1931), p. 36.

Select Bibliography

Periodicals

American Architect and Building News
Architectural Magazine and Journal
Architectural Record
Canadian Architect and Builder
Construction
Contract Record
Journal of the RAIC
The Hamilton Spectator
The Globe
The Toronto Daily Star
Toronto Civic Guild Monthly Bulletin
Toronto World

General

American Architect and Building News 61 (9 July 1898), 15, plate #1176.

'The Art School Booms,' *The Hamilton Spectator*, 10 September 1889, sec. 1.

'Architects Chosen for Knox College,' *The Toronto Star*, November 26, 1910, sec. 1, p. 13.

Architectural Record (1 December 1897).

Archives Nationales de France, série AJ52, AJ52 407.

Arthur, Eric R. 'The Early Architecture of the Province of Ontario,' *JRAIC* 4:8, August 1927, pp. 289-301.

'Bachelor of Architecture Course at McGill University,' *Canadian Architect & Builder* 18 (October 1905), p. 158.

'Canadian Aeroplanes Limited, Toronto,' *Construction* 12 (January, 1919), p. 4.

Canadian Architect and Builder 20 (March 1907), p. 47.

'The Caven Memorial Library at Knox College,' *The Toronto Daily Star*, May 1, 1905, sec. 1, p. 1.

Construction 12 (February 1919), 60–1.

Construction 14 (March 1921), p. 93.

Eaton, Flora McCrae. *Memory's Wall*, (Toronto: 1956), pp. 145–7.

Fleury, Bill. Conversation (worked in Lyle's office) recorded May 14, 1981. In the possession of Stephen A. Otto, Toronto.

Globe and Mail, February 13, 1938.

'Govt. Takes Curtis Plant?,' *The Toronto Star*, 16 November 1916, sec. 1, p. 19.

Haggart, Ron. 'Are they going to give us a New Station or Not? The Politics of Union Station,' *The Open Gate, Toronto Union Station*, Richard Bébout et al. (Toronto: Peter Martin Associates Limited, 1972).

Hamilton, Robert D., Megan J. Hobson, Sharon L. Vattay, *A Catalogue of the John M. Lyle Collection of Architectural Books* (Hamilton: Heritage Hamilton Foundation, 1994).

Higgens, Delwyn. *Art Deco, Marketing and the T. Eaton Company Department Stores: 1918–1930* (York University, Master Thesis, 1991).

Holt, H. S. Report of the Federal Plan Commission on a General Plan for the Cities of Ottawa and Hull, 1915, Ottawa, 1916, pp. 110–11.

Hutchinson, A. C. 'Architectural Training,' *Canadian Architect and Builder*, 4 (November 1891).

Hunter, Robert. *Theatre Architecture in Canada: a study of pre-1920 Canadian theatres*, (Ottawa: Produced by Environment Canada, Parks, for the Historic Sites and Monuments Board of Canada, 1985).

First and Second Annual Reports of the Hydro-Electric Power Commission, of the Province of Ontario (Toronto: L.K. Cameron, 1910), p. 210

'For King and Country,' *Construction* 8 (December, 1915).

Kuwabara, Bruce. 'The Architecture of John M. Lyle' (lecture, Art Gallery of Hamilton, Hamilton, Ontario, October 21, 1999).

Lemon, James. 'Plans for Early Toronto, Lost in Management,' *Urban History Review* 18 (June 1989), p. 14.

Lyle, John M. Letter to the Council of Applied Science, University of Toronto, December 2, 1910, Archives of Ontario.

Maxwell, W. S. 'Architectural Education,' *Construction* 1 (April 1908).

Meeks, Carrol L. V. *The Railroad Station, An Architectural History*, (New York: Dover Publications, 1995).

Middleton and Landon, *The Province of Ontario*, p. 507.

National Executive Committee minute books in the possession of the Canadian Institute of International Affairs, Richmond Street, Toronto.

Niedringhaus, Lee I. 'The Panic of 1893,' *Financial History* 61 (winter 1998), pp. 16–19.

O'Neil, Mora. *A Partial History of the Royal Alexandra Theatre, Toronto, Canada 1907–1939*, 3 vols. (Ph. D. diss., Louisiana State University, 1976).

'New Church at Cheltenham,' *The Presbyterian* (February 27, 1908), p. 264.

'Notes – Concluded,' *JRAIC*, 6:4, April, p. xxviii

Saddlemeyer, Ann. *Early Stages: Theatre in Ontario 1800–1914*, (Toronto: University of Toronto Press, 1990).

'Railway Architects,' *The Toronto Star*, August 4, 1906, sec. 1, p. 7.

'Partnership Dissolved,' *Toronto Star*, 12 January 1910, sec. 1, p. 9.

'Proposed Club House for Argonaut Rowing Club, Toronto,' *Construction* 15 (May 1922), 139–46.

Province of Ontario, The Ontario Reformatory, Guelph, Ontario, Canada (Toronto: Province of Ontario, c. 1930), unpaginated.

'Second Day's Session,' *Construction* 14 (October, 1921), p. 314.

The Toronto Star, 19 March 1920, sec. 1, p. 12.

Tracquair, Ramsay. 'The Old Architecture of the Province of Quebec,' *JRAIC* 2:1, January-February 1925, pp. 25–30.

'Toronto Architect Is Signally Honored,' *The Toronto Star*, June 1, 1928, sec. 1.

White, Karen R. *Emerging Modernism in Canadian Architecture: John M. Lyle's Drawings for 'Highfields' and their Context in the Development of the Idea of the Modern House in Canada, 1935–1936* (University of York, Toronto, Master Thesis, 1995).

Picture Credits

All contemporary photograph by Glenn McArthur except for 5.2, 5.3, 5.4, 5.5, 5.6, 5.7, 5.8, 5.9, which were produced by Adina Currie, Calgary, Alberta.

Abbreviations for frequently cited sources are: Archives of Ontario, (AO); Bank of Montreal Archives (BOMA); Buffalo and Erie County Historical Society Research Library (BECH); Canadian Centre for Architecture, Montreal (CCA); CIBC Archives (CIBC); City of Ottawa Archives (COA); City of Toronto Archives (CTA); Fred Dalley, Toronto (FD); Norah Harris, Victoria, B.C. (NH); McCord Museum of Canadian History, New York Yacht Club (NYYC); Notman Photographic Archives (MCCM); National Gallery of Canada (NGC); Royal Botanical Gardens, Hamilton (RBC); Royal Military College Archives (RMCA); Ontario Jockey Club (OJC); TD Bank Financial Group Archives (TDBA); Toronto Reference Library, Baldwin Room (TRL); Toronto Star (TS); University of Toronto, Archives (UTA); University of Toronto, Fisher Rare Book Library (UTFRBL).

Any errors or omissions are unintended and regretted.

Preface

i.2 NH

Introduction

ii.1 AO, c33-4-0-4, AO 5549; ii.2 CCA, ARCH6056; ii.3 NH; ii.4 AO, c33-4-0-2, AO 5550

Chapter 1

1.1 AO, c33-4-0-9-2, 5539; 1.2 AO, c33-4-0-5, 5548; 1.3 AO, c33-4-0-4, 5549: 1.4 AO, c33-4-0-7, 5546; 1.5 NH; 1.6 NH; 1.7 NH; 1.8 AO, c33-2-0-0-1; 1.9 AO, c33-3-0-8, 5552; 1.10 AO, c33-3-0-7-1, 5554; 1.11 AO, c33-3-0-7-1, 5553; 1.12 AO, c33-3-0-1, 5555; 1.14 TRL, *American Architect and Building News*, 61:15, 9 July 1898, plate 1176; 1.15 TRL, *American Architectural Review*, v.4, journal 7, 1 November, 1897, plate XLIV; 1.16 TRL, *American Architectural Review*, v.4, journal 7, 1 November, 1897, plate LII; 1.17 TRL, *American Architectural Review*, v.4, journal 7, 1 November, 1897, plate lii; 1.19 NYYC; 1.20 AO, c33-3-0-6; 1.21 BECH; 1.21 BECH

Chapter 2

2.2 TRL; 2.3 MCCM, MP-0000.766.5; 2.4 BOMA; 2.5 BOMA; 2.6 TDBA; 2.7 CIBC, # 214.001; 2.8 TDBA; 2.9 TDBA; 2.10 CIBC, #123.001; 2.11 TDBA; 2.12 Library of Congress' National Photo Company Collection; 2.12 AO, c33-1-0-32-1; 2.25 TRL, *Contract Record*, 18, Feb. 1914, p. 211; 2.26 CCA, DR1986:0446; 2.27 TRL, *Construction*, May 1911, p. 56; 2.28 CCA, DR1986:0457; 2.29 CCA, DR1986:0453; 2.30 CCA, DR1986:0452) 2.31 CCA, DR1986:0459; 2.34 CCA, DR1986 :0456; 2.36 CCA, DR1986:0464; 2.38 AO, c33-1-0-28-1; 2.39, 2.40 TRL, *Construction*, June 1909, p. 87; 2.42 TRL, *Construction*, November, 1911, p. 66; 2.43 TRL, *Canadian Architect and Builder*, v19, n2, p2; 2.44 TS, 30 December 1911, p5; 2.45 TRL, *Construction*, July 1911, p. 51; 2.46 CTA, series 372 ss 10 item 49 and 50; 2.47, 2.48, 2.49 TS, 27 December 1910; 2.50 CTA, series 372 ss 10 item 189; 2.51 CTA, series 372 ss 10 item 63; 2.52 CTA, series 372 ss 10 item 187; 2.53 CTA, series 372 ss 10 item 882; 2.54 TRL, *Construction*, September, 1910, p. 51; 2.56 MCCM, MP-0000.1415.7; 2.58 MCCM; 2.59 OCA; 2.60 TPL, acc: S 28-2, repro: T 32908; 2.67 TRL, *Construction*, September, 1910, p. 50; 2.68 TRL, *Construction*, September, 1910, p. 52; 2.69 TRL, *Construction*, September, 1910, p. 54: 2.70 TDBA, 77-265-3; 2.71 UTA, *Torontonensis*, Box 5, 1914, p. 259; 2.72 UTA, *Torontonensis*, Box 5, 1915 p. 293

Chapter 3

Title page Memorial Arch, drawing detail of keystone, Royal Military College, Kingston, Ontario AO, c33-1-0-26-9; 3.1 NGC, Acc # 3562; 3.2 TRL, *Construction*, 12:1 January 1919, p. 2-10; 3.3 AO, c33-1-0-5-1; 3.4 AO, c33-1-0-2-1; 3.5 TDA, # 77-797-5; 3.6 AO, c33-1-0-3-2; 3.7 AO, c33-1-0-3-3; 3.11 AO, c33-1-0-7-1; 3.12 CCA, DR1986:0450; 3.15, 3.16, 3.17 TRL, *Construction*, 1923, 16:2, p. 61-2; 3.18 UTA; 3.19 CCA, DR1986 :0455; 3.27, 3.28 RMCA; 3.29 AO, c33-1-0-33-1

Chapter 4

Title page The Dominion Bank, 1401 Bleury and St. Catherine Street West, Montreal, Quebec TDBA, #4245, reference # 77-345-9; 4.2 COA; 4.4 CCA, DR1985-0451; 4.5 UTFRBL, JRAIC, 4:2, February 1927, 71-2.; 4.7 CCA DR1986 :0449; 4.8 CCA DR1986 :0450; 4.9 UTA; 4.10, 4.11, 4.12, 4.13, 4.14 FD; 4.15 UTFRBL, JRAIC, 9:4, April 1932, 103; 4.17 AO, c33-1-0-9-3; 4.22 TDA, #4256, reference # 77-345-9; 4.23 TDA, #4256, reference # 77-345-13; 4.24 TDA, #4245, reference # 77-345-9; 4.25 AO, c33-1-0-29-5; 4.26 AO, c33-1-0-29-1; 4.27 AO, c33-1-0-29-8; 4.28 OJC; 4.30 AO, c33-1-0-20-1

Chapter 5

Title page AO, c33-1-0-4-7; 5.2, 5.3, 5.4, 5.5, 5.6, 5.7, 5.8, 5.9 Adina Currie, Calgary, Alberta; 5.10 TDA, # 77-314-05; 5.11 AO, c33-1-0-19-1; 5.13 AO, c33-1-0-4-12; 5.16 UTFRBL, *J RA IC*, March, 1931, p. 85; 5.18 NH; 5.24 AO, c33-1-0-24-3; 5.26 RBG; 5.27 AO, c33-1-0-23-1; 5.28 RBG; 5.29 RBG; 5.30 AO, c33-1-0-23-3; 5.32 TRL, TPR #10

Chapter 6

Title page AO, T. Eaton Company fonds, Reference Code: 10019241; 6.1 NH; 6.2, 6.3, 6.4 NH; 6.5 TRL, *J RA IC*, 1931, April, pg 135; 6.7 NH; 6.8 TRL, *J RA IC*, v. 13-14, May 1937, p. 88; 6.9 TRL, *J RA IC*, v. 13-14, August 1936, p. 152; 6.10 TRL, *J RA IC*, v. 13-14, July 1936, p. 128; 6.11 TRL, *J RA IC*, v. 13-14, July 1936, p. 132; 6.12 AO, T. Eaton Company fonds, Reference Code: 10019240; 6.14 CCA, ARCH250416; 6.15 CCA, ARCH6056; 6.16, 6.17, 6.18, 6.19, 6.20, 6.21 AO, c33-3-0-4, the reference number is for all 6 drawings; 6.25 AO, T. Eaton Company fonds, Reference Code: F 229-308-0-517.7; 6.26 AO, T. Eaton Company fonds, Reference Code: F 229-308-0-520-2; 6.27 AO, T. Eaton Company fonds, Reference Code: 10019243; 6.28 AO, T. Eaton Company fonds, Reference Code: 10019241; 6.30 The R.S. McLaughlin Estate Parkwood National Historic Site

Chapter 7

7.1 AO, B411552, C 315-3 album E-318; 7.2 AO, c33-2-0-0-3; 7.3 AO, c33-4-0-1; 7.5, 7.6, 7.7, AO, B411552, C 315-3 album E-318; 7.12, 7.13 BOMA

Index

Colophon

In designing this book I tried to base most of my design choices on those that Lyle himself had encountered. For example, in using a sans serif typeface (Gill Sans) there were two factors that I took into account. First, in the late 1920s, when Lyle was on the design committee charged with revamping the look of the *Journal of the RAIC*, he chose a sans serif font for headlines and a serif font for the body text. Secondly, the use of Gill Sans was also an attempt on my part to use a font that would represent some of the issues that Lyle struggled with in finding a way to merge the elements of the modern movement into a traditional personal aesthetic. In designing Gill Sans in 1927-30, type designer Eric Gill much like Lyle, also grappled with finding ways to incorporate the tenets of the modern movement into a design that was based on traditional humanist features. In the usage of colour for the chapter page spreads in the publication, I also tried to mirror Lyle's palette choices for the interior design program of his buildings. Starting with the colour scheme used in period publications, Lyle's colour schemes changed to reflect current trends and the shift toward the modern movement with the use of brighter pastel tones.

Book Design: Glenn McArthur
Photographs by Glenn McArthur, unless noted in photo credits.

Coach House Books
401 Huron Street on bpNichol Lane
Toronto, ON M5S 2G5

416 979 2217
800 367 6360

mail@chbooks.com
www.chbooks.com